the only
REAL
ESTATE
INVESTING
book you'll ever need

THOMAS E. CORONATO AND HELEN CORONATO

BUSINESS

Avon, Massachusetts

Published by
Adams Media, an F+W Publications Company
57 Littlefield Street, Avon, MA 02322. U.S.A.
www.adamsmedia.com

ISBN-13: 978-1-59869-477-2
ISBN-10: 1-59869-477-4

Printed in the United States of America.

J I H G F E D C B A

Library of Congress Cataloging-in-Publication Data
is available from the publisher.

This publication is designed to provide accurate and authoritative information with
regard to the subject matter covered. It is sold with the understanding that the publisher
is not engaged in rendering legal, accounting, or other professional advice. If legal advice
or other expert assistance is required, the services of a competent professional person
should be sought.
—From a *Declaration of Principles* jointly adopted by a Committee of the
American Bar Association and a Committee of Publishers and Associations

Many of the designations used by manufacturers and sellers to distinguish their product
are claimed as trademarks. Where those designations appear in this book and Adams
Media was aware of a trademark claim, the designations have been printed with initial
capital letters.

This book is available at quantity discounts for bulk purchases.
For information, please call 1-800-289-0963.

contents

acknowledgments

This book was made possible because of our colleagues, friends, and family, and we would like to take time to acknowledge them. First and foremost, to our agent Jacky Sach, who remains a constant source of wisdom and insight, thank you.

We would like to thank several people who have helped us achieve our portfolio goals. To Carl Selitto who has extended himself professionally and personally to make this and so many other ventures possible. For Team Succasunna and Team East Stroudsburg who make doing business such a pleasure; and with utmost gratitude to Deborah Hanley and Maura Mowbray for their behind-the-scenes commitment to excellence. Special thanks to colleagues and clients at Wells Fargo Home Mortgage, all of whom have shared in making this book achievable.

Members of our personal financial team, Mark Sessanta, Alex Fleischer, and Bruce Speier, who have worked diligently to help us realize our portfolio potential. Bob and Rose Ann Olson of RJ Olson Log Homes, Olson Realty, and Devil's Tower Inn for their entrepreneurial spirit and commitment to helping a community grow and prosper; Wayne Wilson for his legal expertise; Tom and Twylia Waugh and our friends in Hulett, Wyoming, who have helped turn our investments into favorite addresses. Special thanks to Shawn Baldwin and Elite Construction for building homes, not houses.

When we needed to find just the right reader-friendly explanations, we knew exactly who to turn to. Thanks to Gerry Manger and the staff of Wyndemere Real Estate Company, Inc., for their encouragement and knowledge; Gail Masson Romano and Ravi Romano for their enthusiastic participation in this book; Rich Rondi, Joe Mackey, Robert Forder, John Ryan, Tom LaPella, Brenda Hildabrandt, Brian Natale, Ben Fargeon, Todd Sacchiero, and John Stache, who all made time in their demanding schedules for our questions and supported this book along the way. Thank you very much.

Time to complete this project was made possible by Karen and Joni Templin, Kira and Anya Campbell, and Amanda Woods; thank you for your time, energy, and enthusiasm. For Kim Bohn, who has been there since the beginning, Wendy DeSarno, who got on board right away, and my friends in the Holistic Moms Network, thank you so much.

For Mike and Kathy Coronato, who are the best cheering team anyone could ever ask for, and for Bob and Dean Coronato, who continue to be inspiring and inspired, thank you. This book is dedicated with love to our children, our most precious investments.

note to readers

The information contained in this book is not intended as a substitute for personal financial advice, nor should any substantial financial decisions be based on the content of this book. Check with your personal financial advisor and financial team before making any substantial decisions involving money. We do not make any recommendations or endorsements as to any investment, advisor, or other service but are sharing the real-estate investment strategies that have worked for us over the years. Consider your own financial risk behavior, financial portfolio, and family concerns, and consult your legal advisor before making any final decisions. You should not rely on material in this book to make or refrain from making any decision or any action. We are providing you only with suggestions. It is up to you to seek personal financial and legal advice when evaluating your choices in real estate investing.

introduction

It seems as if everywhere you look, be it the evening news, popular magazines, or cocktail parties, everyone is talking about real estate. Likely you have recognized that the conversation participants can often be divided into two camps: those who believe that real-estate investing is a fad that warrants no consideration, and die-hard enthusiasts who are convinced that this is the opportunity they have been waiting for. Our intention is to shed some much-needed light on the middle ground between these two extremes.

Real-estate investing can be an exciting and profitable means of building a solid financial future, but like all successful financial ventures that have stood the test of time, there are no shortcuts, gimmicks, or quick-buy products to turn you into an overnight real-estate sensation. What we intend to offer is a hands-on reference guide for designing a real-estate investing plan that relies on a well-comprised financial team to help you see your investing intentions to profitable fruition.

We recommend you read through the book in its entirety to get a big-picture idea of what real-estate investing really means, then use the chapters section by section to organize your plan of action and take the steps necessary to set yourself up for success. For your convenience, here is an overview of what to expect:

Chapter One: Commitment Issues. We introduce real-estate investing by talking about some of the myths and methods of this financial venture, outline a business plan for organizing your investment vision, and help you assess where you are in beginning your new real-estate investing business.

Chapter Two: Assembling Your Team. We strongly encourage you to treat real-estate investing as a business whose success depends largely on an experienced and educated team of supportive professionals. In this section we name names, focusing on the qualities and advantages of each individual's area of expertise, and suggest interview questions for selecting the right team members.

Chapter Three: Financing Your Investment. Financing your real-estate purchases is a lengthy and detailed process that deserves your full attention. It is not something that you should figure out as you go along. Here we will help you organize the financial paperwork necessary to get started, outline the process of applying for a mortgage, and provide a brief overview of the loan programs and practices that are most commonly used by investors.

Chapter Four: Acquiring Real Estate. Building a relationship with your local Realtor is an excellent way to gain knowledge and insight into your target area. In this section we'll suggest ways of becoming an investing expert, discuss the different rental properties available and how best to measure the pros and cons of each with a critical eye, and cover the importance of evaluating the real-estate market so that you can continue to invest wisely despite the ebb and flow of local trends.

Chapter Five: Renter Relationships. This section covers critical information for the beginning investor as it answers many questions you may have about the legalities of landlording. Topics covered here include the Fair Housing laws, finding and keeping reliable tenants, negotiating contracts and rent, and how to protect yourself from expensive problems.

Chapter Six: Paperwork: Leases and Record-Keeping. Many new real-estate investors are caught off guard by the amount of paperwork required to protect their assets, keep their portfolio plan on track, and prepare their taxes. We will make suggestions about what to include in your rental agreements, recommend ways to help you keep track of necessary paperwork, and help you set yourself up for tax advantages.

Chapter Seven: Expanding Your Empire. There is no finish line when it comes to financial success, so here we talk about ways and means of evaluating your progress and continuing to build a more profitable portfolio. In this last section we make recommendations for establishing and maintaining a limited liability company, suggest methods for increasing your chances of profitable success, and close with advice on updating your business plan's vision.

Throughout this book we have done our best to provide you with the most even-handed information about real-estate investing based on our personal experience. We have employed a user-friendly format in an effort to address concerns and questions many beginners have about real-estate investing. What we came up with was a detailed, step-by-step plan accompanied by functional advice. We hope that this book encourages you to explore your own real-estate investing opportunities and begin what will be a positive and profitable investment portfolio.

chapter one **commitment issues**

Why is everyone talking about investing in real estate?

Real-estate investing has become a hot topic. No longer limited to those in financial circles, property ownership and management is being embraced by people from all walks of life. What is it about real-estate investing that makes you want to consider it?

Recent developments in real estate have made it a media darling. All-time-high sales prices, interest rates at an historic low, and unprecedented value increases made real estate the investment du jour for quite a while. However, recently a slight dip in the economy precipitated a negative campaign in the press, which declared real estate a dangerous and often disastrous financial pursuit. Between these two extremes lies the truth.

Many people have friends, neighbors, or colleagues who made a ton of money in real estate, but for every story of riches there is also a story of ruin. This is par for the course. There will always be the next must-have product; in fact, all the recent talk about investing may have been what has prompted you to seek out this book. But instead of warning that you are too late, or worse, that this is a fast way to make a quick buck, we hope to encourage you to take a serious look at the opportunities available and the commitment necessary to become a savvy and successful real-estate investor. Based on that, you can make an informed decision about whether to proceed with this endeavor.

Is real-estate investing a passing trend?

It seems that everywhere you look—be it the morning paper or the evening news—naysayers are predicting a housing market crash. National headlines warn against declining real-estate prices, conjuring up catchy headlines such as "Real Estate Bubble About to Burst." Critics of real estate constantly refer to the stock market's Black Monday as proof that a crash is inevitable, comparing stocks to property rentals and warning that what goes up must come down. But is this really accurate?

The short answer is no, it's not. First of all, the stock market operates on a worldwide economy. Stock-market investors must consider global finances, while real-estate investors need only concern themselves with their local economy. The sale price of a three-bedroom villa situated along the Pacific Coast Highway in California has little, if any, influence over the two-bedroom ranch for sale in Portland, Maine. Concerning yourself with rental prices in Beijing when you have a summer rental in the Hamptons isn't necessary. The educated real-estate investor is well versed in the ebb and flow of his immediate area of interest and doesn't become distracted by what's going on across the country. Statistics from such resources as the U.S. Bureau of Labor Statistics record a steady increase in home prices over the past fifty years. Even the basic buy-and-hold real-estate plan obviously has merit. While hot markets garner a great deal of media coverage, they are by no means an accurate indication of national real-estate trends because local economies dictate neighborhood sale and rental prices. Instead of looking at national trends, it makes more sense to become an expert in your particular location.

Furthermore, comparing a stock-market crash to a real-estate crash is nothing more than media propaganda. It makes for good headlines but isn't an accurate picture. A crash happens quickly and usually without warning. A stock-market dive on one afternoon has nothing to do with a real-estate market correcting itself after an unusually profitable boom. Have you ever heard of listing a house one day at $500,000 and having to reduce it to $250,000 the next day? Of course not. While particular markets may readjust, there are several predictors that a smart investor has access to, preventing any sudden or shocking surprises. Besides, it is only the flash-in-the-pan investor who looks to get rich quick. A real-estate investor committed to building wealth knows it's possible to make money in any housing market.

Finally, unlike stocks, real estate is based on supply and demand and fulfills a basic need: We all require a place to live. When we acknowledge that real estate is a necessity, it becomes clear that it cannot also be a fad.

What are the myths of real-estate investing?

Most myths of real estate are based on the idea that goals and fortune should be accumulated and enjoyed more quickly than in other areas of investment. But real-estate investing is a business, and like any other business it takes time and perseverance to grow and prosper. The following six myths reflect this:

"Real-estate investing doesn't really work."
Translation: *"I'm not sure where to start and I don't know who to ask."*

In recent years, many new investors flooded the housing market, lured by tales of overnight fortunes. Some subscribed to online courses chock-full of "secrets" or attended one-day seminars to learn "everything there is to know." Others made phone calls to Realtors, demanding to be shown some investment properties. These approaches lack focus, education, and commitment; therefore, they do not bring success. There are no secrets in real-estate investing. Successful investing takes a well-orchestrated plan navigated by an experienced team dedicated to meeting short- and long-term goals. If you are committed to doing the necessary work, real-estate investing can work for you.

"I've never been good at business. Some just have the magic touch."
Translation: *"I'm afraid of trying something new. I don't want to appear foolish."*

Every expert was once a novice. Every millionaire had his first deal. There is no such thing as a magic touch, but there is education, effort, and experience. Many avoid success because they're afraid to ask for help. While being the new kid is often frightening and disheartening, you can target the right people to talk to, prepare your questions, and set yourself up for success, making the process more manageable and less intimidating.

"Investing in real estate is too risky."
Translation: *"I don't know who can help me minimize my risk and maximize my profit."*

Investing is only as risky as the investor. One of the major reasons we focus on the need to build a personalized investment team is to limit your risk. No deal, no transaction, and no taxes should be handled without calling your team into play. In order to be a successful investor, one who maximizes profits while limiting losses, you must have accredited experts guiding your portfolio. Such guidance will reduce your risk and keep your business on track. We can help you design an investment team to fit your needs.

"This is going to take too much time."
Translation: *"I have a hard time budgeting my time."*

We completely empathize with this problem. Time management is one of the hardest strategies to master. In addition to writing this book, our responsibilities include raising our toddler, planning for our second child, writing two monthly columns, a full-time job for one of us as a mortgage consultant, and hosting a monthly talk show. In addition, we have purchased an out-of-state family restaurant, manage multiple rental properties, and continue to network and develop our financial portfolio. We have had to make some tough decisions about our time. We don't watch much television. We don't take long vacations. We don't get to have dinner together every night. We make a great many sacrifices regarding leisure time, creature comforts, and holiday spending. For us to be successful investors, we had to take a look at what commitments were obligations and what activities were negotiable. You may have to make some tough choices also.

"I don't want to be bothered fixing things."
Translation: *"I'm afraid I won't know what to do."*

We have heard so many capable individuals scoff at landlording because they don't want to fix a clogged toilet at 3 AM. Surprisingly, we don't know anyone who has ever had to do this, including us. Furthermore, as renters for several years, neither of us had ever had to call our landlord at 3 AM for a maintenance issue. This myth strikes an emotional chord, as no one wants to be asked to do something that they can't do. But the chances of this ever actually coming up are slim, especially when, as we will discuss in Chapter Five, being proactive with repairs and upgrades can keep your property low maintenance. In addition, you can always hire a property manager to call on if an emergency situation arises. Don't let this myth prevent you from making additional money and benefiting from tax advantages.

"I don't know where to start."
Translation: *"I'm feeling overwhelmed about taking on this new business venture."*

Perhaps your credit is a mess, and you just don't have the time to deal with it. Maybe everyone you know lives paycheck to paycheck, and you're not sure who could lead you in the right direction. Whatever the reason, it no longer has to hold you back. By purchasing this book, you have taken the first step toward building a fruitful real-estate investing portfolio. There are reliable resources, reputable organizations, and numerous facilities available for new investors. We can help you put up a door so opportunity will knock. And if it doesn't, we'll help you crawl through a window.

Am I too young to start this?

We never thought we would say it, but it's true: If we knew then what we know now, we would have done things differently. As a young couple starting out, we rented a house until we could save enough to buy our first home. Using real-estate investing as a way to make home ownership a reality faster was not a method we considered with any seriousness. While we cannot change the past and can only look toward the future, there are things we can suggest for those entrepreneurs who may be fortunate enough to begin building assets at a young age.

Renting is a common first step when you begin living on your own. You are probably starting a new career, paying off school loans, and just beginning to come into your own. You probably assume that you do not have the financial means or credit history to even begin looking at homes, and the thought of actually owning a house may be emotionally overwhelming. But there are some things about buying a home at any age that should be considered before you sell yourself short and continue renting when you could own.

First, much of the same advice that we would give to an "older" real-estate investor, we would give to you. It is important to have a handle on your credit history, make timely payments on all recurring debt such as credit cards, and remedy any credit problems as soon as possible. You should organize a financial team, talk with an experienced and reputable mortgage consultant, and take things one step at a time.

Very few people are able to buy their dream home as their first home. If you are convinced that you must be able to afford a four-bedroom, center-hall colonial before looking for a first home, you may miss out on opportunities along the way. For instance, consider purchasing a multiunit property where you can rent out one or more of the units. You get a place to live and income to help defer mortgage costs. Instead of paying someone else's mortgage, other tenants help to pay your mortgage. Once you discuss the financial advantages and disadvantages of buying a home, you will need to think about how much you can handle emotionally. Being a landlord has its fair share of responsibilities. Are you prepared to screen clients, learn about the Fair Housing laws, perform maintenance repairs, and collect rents? Since this is probably your first experience with any type of homeownership, do you have a network of people on whom you can rely for advice and insight? If you are up to it financially and emotionally, pursuing real-estate investing sooner rather than later may be advantageous for you. If now is not yet the right time, use this book as a means of preparing yourself for a potentially lucrative business when the time is right.

Am I too old to start this?

The most important asset any of us will ever have is time. The more time you have to invest in the market, the more opportunities you will have for gaining knowledge, experience, and profit. Buying a property, holding on to it for twenty years, and selling it at a huge profit is not the only way to succeed in real-estate investing. In fact, it can be one of the least profitable as you could miss many deals in the interim. With age comes wisdom, humility, and self control. The longer you've been around, the more apt you are to appreciate that hard work pays off, an emotional frenzy can be detrimental to business, and luck does not qualify as a business plan. You appreciate that time is of the essence, and you are willing to see a task through. On the flip side, if you are worried because you have not taken the necessary steps to secure a financially sound retirement, we caution you against thinking that real estate is a get-rich-quick plan. Yes, there are stories of flipped properties that have brought in a lot of money in a short period of time, but as we will discuss, these examples are the exception, not the rule. Making money investing in real estate takes a well-developed business plan, the assistance of a competent team of professionals, and perseverance. In order to maximize your profit potential, it is critical to enlist the services of a financial advisor who is familiar with your goals and strategy. There is no such thing as coming too late to the real-estate party. There is always money to be made. Working with a professional who can help you make the most out of your time is critical for every investor, regardless of age, and especially important so you can maximize your future profits. Discuss your monetary concerns and goals with a financial advisor who can help you determine if pursuing real-estate investing is the most advantageous approach for your financial future.

What does a real-estate investor look like?

A real-estate investor can look like a banker, a lawyer, a construction worker, or a mother. There is no one-size-fits-all description of an investor, which means there is room for everyone. This is a business where it's best to dress the part you're playing. As we move through the questions, we will help you determine which particular housing market you want to target. A clear, focused goal will help ensure your success, as a specialized niche can be more profitable than a random approach. Real-estate investing is a business, and to do well in business you must know your clients.

For instance, Tom is a new construction specialist and spends a great deal of time with contractors. Wearing a three-piece suit to a construction site would not put others at ease, so he opts for jeans. He spends Saturday afternoons meeting with clients at new sites, where his more relaxed look makes others more comfortable. He has found that new homeowners are wary of anyone who looks like a banker, so he forgoes formal attire in favor of casual comfort. His expertise in new construction and renovations has led us to several rental properties in one of Wyoming's flourishing communities, where again a formal suit would not be well received. Fitting in with this cowboy community's standard—trading in Levis for Wranglers—is more beneficial than showing off in fancy clothes. However, if you are looking to do business on Manhattan's Upper West Side, it would behoove you to dress according to the standards of those who live and work there. When you want to make a good impression, be sure to know what kind of impression you should be making.

It is also imperative to sound like a professional investor. Once you have determined your target area, practice your pitch. All your networking, research, and seminars will be for naught if you cannot effectively communicate your intentions. Saying, "I'm in real estate," is a vague and unproductive conversation starter. Who knows when you'll find yourself face to face with a golden opportunity? When you do, you want to articulate confidence and knowledge. When asked what we do, we reply, "We are real-estate investors with rental properties in three states. We target properties in vacation communities, where we have recently expanded our residential portfolio to include two commercial ventures, a high-profile family restaurant, and a partnership in an international hotel chain. We are currently researching shore communities and look forward to purchasing a multifamily unit within the next year." Our answer invites questions, furthers conversation, and often ends with the other person mentioning, "I have someone you might be interested in talking to." When you make educated and interesting comments, other investors will be drawn to you. By looking and sounding the part, you increase your chances of success.

How do I determine my financial literacy?

A business background is not necessary, but treating your real-estate venture as a business is. In any industry, there is an established body of basic knowledge, including methods of operation, common jargon, and professional standards. While a four-year business degree may give you a nice overview of what to expect in regards to general business conduct, do not feel that a lack of formal education puts you at a disadvantage. It is possible to learn the ins and outs of real estate through continuing education classes, reliable resources, and experience. But before you sign up for the community college's next summer session, gauge your personal strengths and weaknesses, then determine how to best proceed. Before even focusing on real estate, make sure your personal finances are in line.

Start with your household. Do you keep a balanced monthly checkbook? Do you pay your bills on time? Do you follow a budget? Do you and your partner have an open and honest dialogue about family finances? As a real-estate investor you are, essentially, a business owner. You are responsible for the profit and losses of your properties. If you always defer the bill-paying responsibilities to your partner, it is time to start taking a more active role in your personal finances.

If there are discrepancies in the household finances, your business will fall victim to the same problems. Don't try to convince yourself that you'll manage money better in business than you do in your personal life. You could end up with bigger problems. Before you consider taking on further financial responsibilities, make sure your household is running smoothly. If this is a challenging area for you, consider a personal organizing tool such as QuickBooks.

Now consider your present occupation and your past employment history. Have you held a management position? Can you delegate responsibility? Do you set goals and meet them in a timely fashion? If you have no experience being your own boss, you will struggle as an entrepreneur. There are many distractions along the road to success. If you do not have the motivation and self-discipline to follow through on your tasks, solicit help when necessary, and set your own work hours, you will not be able to manage your real-estate ventures. If this is a challenging area for you, consider working with a mentor or life coach who can help you manage your time and determine how to eliminate unnecessary distractions.

Even if you have a business degree, take an honest look at your personal finances. Pursuing a new business venture may not be advantageous if you are suffering from financial hardship and struggling with personal management issues. Take time to honestly assess your standing and proceed with caution.

How can I become more financially literate?

Having determined the state of your personal finances and having begun to take the necessary steps to remedy any issues, you can now turn your sights toward measuring your current financial skills in regard to business. Can you read a financial report? Do you understand a profit-and-loss statement? Have you ever examined a cash-flow statement? If you have had no exposure to these documents, take a finance class as soon as possible. Local colleges often offer basic economic classes where a trained professional will walk you through each of these tools. Learning how to measure assets, liabilities, income, spending, and profit will benefit your business plan.

In addition to taking a finance class and working to tighten up your household finances, you should increase your exposure to financial media. We strongly suggest subscribing to reliable business periodicals such as *Money, Entrepreneur*, and *BusinessWeek*. The articles in these magazines are concise, clear, and focused. They are not heavily laden with jargon. Instead, they strike a conversational tone, offering user-friendly tips and strategies that reflect current market developments. You can read these helpful articles as your schedule allows. We would suggest committing to one article per day. A magazine rack in the bathroom can help make this an achievable goal.

These publications also offer free e-mail newsletters and have excellent Web sites with archived articles. If online reading and research fits your lifestyle better, register for these services. But make a commitment to read the content. Signing up for several e-letters and deleting the deliveries as soon as they're received is a waste of time. Choose one, at most two, online resources, and meet your weekly reading requirement.

If you are a book enthusiast, take advantage of the material available for browsing at Amazon.com. While researching financial books, take time to scan the table of contents of bestsellers and read excerpts from titles that sound interesting. Whose approach reflects your own values? Whose suggestions make the most sense for your financial situation? There is a slew of advice available, and it's neither necessary nor possible to read it all. Choosing one or two reference guides can help you narrow your focus.

Always remember, your new real-estate career is not a hobby but a professional venture. Surround yourself with materials that will increase your knowledge base and keep you interested in the subject matter.

Can I be a successful real-estate investor?

While there are no guarantees that you will become a successful real-estate entrepreneur, many successful business owners share similar characteristics with one another. In preparing your financial portfolio, do not neglect to assess your character. An honest inventory of your personal strengths and weaknesses is just as critical to your success as a desirable credit score. Consider the following profiles:

■ profile one...

I can ask for help.

I enjoy responsibility.

I manage my time well.

I do not rely on luck.

I believe hard work pays off.

I have a positive attitude.

I like learning new things.

I know success takes sacrifice.

I am honest.

■ profile two...

I prefer to figure it out on my own.

I prefer being given directions.

I prefer following a prescribed schedule.

I rely on luck.

I look for shortcuts when possible.

I have a positive attitude when things work.

I like being considered an expert.

I look forward to weekends and vacation.

I try to be honest.

There are subtle, though important, differences in each of these characteristics. While there is bound to be crossover—we look forward to vacations too—the first personality profile seems more apt to take charge, take risks, and take responsibility, all necessary elements of entrepreneurship. What often separates employees from employers is the willingness to step outside one's comfort zone. Of course, we will offer you our tried and true experience and give financial advice that has served us well. But there is no one-size-fits-all plan for making money in real estate. If there were, everyone would follow it. After all is said and done, it is up to the individual business owner to achieve his own success.

Consider the quality resources profile one will bring to the business table. Asking for help gives you the opportunity to learn from other investors' mistakes, helps you bounce new ideas off of experienced businesspeople, and provides an excellent networking opening. Taking responsibility for one's actions and being self-motivated are critical factors in self-employment. No one is going to check up on you to make sure you are becoming wealthy. Luck is helpful, but it's not a business plan. Hard work, coupled with sacrifice and a positive attitude, even in the face of adversity, will serve you well, especially as you stumble through the basics. Finally, either you are conducting your operation with honesty or you're not. If you're not, you won't be in business very long.

If you found yourself nodding in agreement as you read profile two, you may be more comfortable and successful trusting your investments to a competent financial advisor who can offer sound advice and manage your money. The rewards of real-estate investing are great because the sacrifices are great. A candid self-inventory can help you determine if you are up to the challenge.

Should I do this full time?

Before you give up the comfort and security of a regular paycheck in hopes of cashing in on real-estate investing, consider the following questions:

- Why are you interested in quitting your present job?
- Are you annoyed that your boss has discontinued casual Fridays?
- Are you under the impression that working for yourself would be a lot easier?

There are highs and lows in every job. Do not make the mistake of walking away from a secure source of income because you're being asked to rise to a new challenge—be it a demanding boss or a new project. Being self-employed has numerous benefits, but it takes years before you will reap the rewards. In the beginning of any new business, be prepared to scrimp, save, and sacrifice. Instead of compounding your stress by working solely for commission, we suggest transitioning slowly from your position of employee to entrepreneur. If you are interested in pursuing real-estate investing full time, set yourself up for success.

Before walking away from a steady income, consider how you will meet your current living expenses. Take a hard look at restructuring your household finances. If you are a dual-income household, immediately readjust your expenses so they can be covered by one income. You may find out that your dual income covered a large home and numerous vacations, but your new budget makes such pleasures unattainable. Are you willing to downsize your home, give up travel, and rein in excessive spending? Practice living by these new rules for a while, and then decide if you and your family are willing to make the necessary sacrifices required to build a new career.

As real-estate investing does not guarantee a profit or paycheck, you should have a minimum of one year's expenses saved. You can do this by readjusting your household budget and saving one partner's entire paycheck. This reserve will provide a safety net as you build your new business.

Seasoned veterans may make it look easy, but these investors are committed to building wealth over the long haul. If you are hoping to get rich quick, keep your job and stick with buying lotto tickets. If you are committed to building a lucrative real-estate business, take the steps necessary to ensure your family's security before launching your new career.

Are there big beginner mistakes I should avoid?

The biggest mistake any beginner can make is trying to skip steps. Today, with all the recent real-estate investing hype, many novices convince themselves that they've heard all they need to hear and they're ready to get started. They're not. Instead of speaking with an experienced mortgage representative, polishing one's credit score, and discussing loan options, the beginner investor fears missing a *once-in-a-lifetime-chance*. The dangers are grave. For starters, sift through the advice being advertised on infomercials. Take no heed of the late-night promises that claim a small fortune can be made without any cost to you. While we will discuss numerous financial options available to investors, including some loan programs that require little or no down payment, these mortgages have specific criteria that must be met to qualify. In addition, once you get into your new property there are many costs associated with finding renters, employing property managers, setting up limited liability companies, and further building your portfolio. Do not fool yourself into thinking that these late-night promotions are a substitute for personalized, professional financial guidance.

A common mistake many beginner investors also make involves chasing down "secrets." Instead of organizing a financial team, reading up on market happenings, or investigating and researching neighborhoods, anxious beginners pay self-proclaimed experts for their bravado. We have seen many aspiring landlords rush off to seminar after seminar, intent on finding real-estate investing secrets. These poor souls are convinced that these secrets will save them time and money, expedite their real-estate goals, and make them rich. While there are reputable seminars available, endorsed by Realtor associations and national banks, no financial expert worth your time and money is going to promise super easy money-making secrets—because there are no such secrets to reveal. Reputable speakers will focus on business plans, calculated decisions, and hard work. Get-rich-quick gurus are getting rich by selling you their tailor-made products, which amount to little more than well-packaged clichés.

As a beginner, you are starting at the bottom of the ladder. In order to efficiently and safely climb this ladder, you have to take it one step at a time. Trying to skip steps is a waste of your time and money. Remember, every millionaire investor was once a beginner.

How do I know I'm financially ready to invest in real estate?

Before you start canvassing the neighborhood for your first real-estate purchase, take inventory of your financial situation. Do you have a reliable income? Does your spending deplete your income, or have you managed to consistently save money? An excellent mantra for building wealth is live simply and invest wisely. Living below your means and thoroughly investigating financial opportunities can provide you with economic security. If you are already struggling to make ends meet, do not count on real estate as a saving grace. The money management problems you have in your personal life will be compounded, not solved, by starting a new business.

Consider, too, how taking on an additional expense will affect your current financial status. Unfortunately, many people get into real estate with the idea that they'll pay a minimum for their property then charge a premium rent. While such opportunities do exist, more often than not the beginner investor ends up covering his mortgage payment and only making a minimal profit. If you have a vacancy or if your property is taking longer to sell than expected, will you be able to carry the additional expense and maintain your current standard of living? If you have no cash reserves, even a brief setback could be financially disastrous.

Now is also a good time to determine your investing preferences. Do you intend to purchase raw land and wait until inflation boosts its resale value? Do you intend to fix up neglected homes and cash in on your work? Are you intent on buying new construction? Each of these approaches requires different up-front costs, financing, and time frames to maximize profit and limit liability. Matching your investing objectives to your financial profile will help you make the most of your money.

Therefore, this is not a question you should answer in isolation. As a beginner real-estate investor, chances are you do not know all the loan programs available, the tax ramifications involved, or how a new real-estate purchase will affect your overall financial portfolio. For these reasons, it is imperative to enlist the help of experienced financial professionals. Your financial advisor and your mortgage representative can walk you through the programs you qualify for and help you determine if now is the best time to take on a new project.

How do I know I'm emotionally ready to invest in real estate?

When making financial deals, people often neglect to evaluate their emotional well-being. Many assume that real estate is a numbers game, and therefore they concentrate on credit scores, interest rates, and rental agreements. While these monetary factors are important, one's emotional health is no less critical to a successful investing career.

Before you even begin to scan the classifieds for potential properties, take a look around your current home. Are rooms neat and tidy? Can you find what you are looking for? Is your living space warm and inviting? If you come home to a space littered with dirty dishes, unopened mail, and overflowing ashtrays, you may want to put a new financial venture on hold. Successful real-estate investors are organized, orderly, and optimistic or they don't last very long. Take this opportunity to clear away the clutter in your home and make room for success. Adding another responsibility onto an already burdened life will not prove prosperous.

Next, take time to have an honest conversation with yourself and your significant other about your feelings toward money. Do you count every penny and obsess over every purchase? Do you spend frivolously then panic when the bills arrive? Are you gravely afraid that you will never have enough money to feel secure? There are no guarantees in real-estate investing. If you're going to lose sleep at night worrying over vacant apartments and rising interest rates, you may want to consider other investing alternatives. If you are hoping that a few hot buy-and-flip deals will finally bring you the money you deserve, we warn you that such fortunes are hardly ever made. Wealth is most realistically built by following a solid business plan, not by rushing head-first into so-called hot deals.

Finally, have you jumped into other money-making opportunities, convinced that you were onto a sure thing, only to lose your shirt? Is real-estate investing your latest obsession in a long line of frenzied financial plans? We have seen people hastily move from one project to the next only to find themselves burnt out, disappointed, and with less financial security than before. To be an investor, you must invest not only your money but also your time and energy. You cannot take the time for your investments to mature and develop if you are hopping from scheme to scheme. If real estate is your investment du jour, you should expect the same shallow level of success you have previously experienced.

A solid appreciation of your emotional well-being is an excellent predictor of your financial future. If you see there are areas that need improvement, we encourage you to address these fields before opening your checkbook. Being emotionally ready to invest is just as important as being financially ready.

How do I get started?

There are three steps to starting a new financial venture: education, organization, and action. Most people do not follow this order. Anxious to get started, impatient with a process, and convinced that it's better to learn as they go, many trigger-happy investors start with action, barely touch on organization, and usually burn out before approaching education. The exciting battle cry, "Get in the game before it's too late," is dangerous and disastrous. Experts in every field of business will tell you that before you start the game you have to read the instructions. The same holds true in real-estate investing.

The sage wisdom, "If you think education is expensive, try ignorance," should not be dismissed. By picking up this book, you have started your real-estate career. Throughout your purchasing process, when interviewing your financial team, and whenever dealing with tenant issues, you should refer to a reliable real-estate reference book. We also encourage you to seek out Realtor networks and reputable online sites (see Appendix D) to benefit from the advice of professionals in the field. If you have the time and means to attend a real-estate investing seminar, look for programs endorsed by national banks or Realtor organizations. You should expect to pay a reasonable, not exorbitant, amount of money for your investing education. Well-written books and recommended networking forums are excellent beginning tools when starting your investing career.

As you learn about this field and begin to determine which course of action best suits your needs, you'll want to organize your focus before taking action.

What often separates the sideline spectator from a leading industry player is a comprehensive business plan. A business plan is an action plan that details and defines your goals, timeline, and mission. While there is no set format, all worthy plans share certain characteristics. See the next two questions for a user-friendly example that you can modify to meet your needs.

Having begun your education (it will continue throughout your career) and completed your business plan, you are ready to take action. By no means are we suggesting you are ready to make a purchase, but you are ready to contact the financial professionals who will make your first purchase possible. In Chapter Two we will go into detail about the experts you'll want on your financial team. Having the best people in place before you open your checkbook will save you money, time, and energy. When you find the right deal, you will have the right people ready to make it happen. If you follow these three steps in the suggested order, you'll be on a successful path to real-estate investing.

Is there a formula I should follow?

We cannot stress it often enough: Real-estate investing is a business. As such, it deserves a well-thought-out business plan. When your financial team is in place, they will help you organize your goals into manageable financial tasks. Right now, we want to focus on a bare-bones business plan, a simple three-step formula for helping you organize your ideas and intentions.

1. **Keep it simple.** Define your business. As an entrepreneur, it is imperative to succinctly describe your business. Real-estate investing offers many avenues of revenue to pursue. Narrowing your focus will help you organize your efforts. Consider these questions:

   - What do you plan to do?
   - Where do you plan to do it?
   - Who is your target customer?
   - How will you match the competition?

2. **Keep it focused.** Target your customer. Tenants are customers, and without them your vacant property costs you money. Instead of hoping

that someone—anyone—will eventually rent from you, determine what need you can meet, then meet it better than the competition. Having a clearly determined tenant base can increase your asking price and decrease your turnover.

- Who are my target customers?
- What needs are not being met?
- What would be on my customer's wish list?
- What is a deal breaker for my customers?
- Which type of property would best suit these customers?
- Why do I want to serve these customers?
- How will I most effectively keep my properties rented?

3. **Keep it realistic.** Define your goals. As an entrepreneur, you are a business owner. You set the standards; you are responsible for meeting the goals. As this is a new venture, give more consideration to the short-term goals; experience and education will help determine realistic and productive long-term goals.

Short-term goals
- What do you want to accomplish in six months?
- What do you want to accomplish in one year?
- Which needs will your business serve?
- Will you require staff?
- How will you find reliable customers?
- How will you service your customers?
- How will you match the competition?

Long-term goals
- What do you want to accomplish in two to five years?
- Which needs will your business serve?
- What will be your area of expertise?
- How big do you want your business to grow?

The old business adage remains true: When you fail to plan, you plan to fail. The "I'll just learn as I go" approach is costly and ineffective. While talking about your investing idea probably feels much more natural than actually writing a detailed business plan, taking such a tangible step is evidence of your commitment to this endeavor and will help put you on the road to real-estate success.

Can you walk me through a sample business plan?

As an entrepreneur, it is your responsibility to effectively manage your real-estate investments. This begins with a comprehensive business plan. Consider the following example of a bare-bones business plan as you begin to manage your new business venture.

1. **Keep it simple.** This is your mission statement, your opportunity to clearly explain what your business is. These one to two sentences define what you do and how you do it.

    > **Example:** As a real-estate investor, I plan to purchase [unfurnished][single unit][rental]properties in the [Xyz]area, where I will target [long term/lease]tenants, offering [washer/dryer]incentives.

2. **Keep it focused.** This is your action plan. When you ask yourself what your primary focus is, "real-estate investing" may seem like the obvious answer, but it is too broad and not effective. You need to answer the *who, what, where, why,* and *how* questions.

    > **Example:** Xyz is a stylish suburb largely populated with college graduates who commute to the city. The area's rental properties do not offer washers and dryers, and the town Laundromat is expensive and poorly maintained. I will furnish my properties with washers, dryers, irons, and ironing boards. I will also install sensor lights at the entrance for added safety. Meeting the needs of this growing tenant pool will help ensure low turnover and limited vacancies.

3. **Keep it realistic.** This is your reality check. Your goals, profits, and losses should be spelled out and measured, with plans to review them in a timely fashion and readjust them as needed.

> **Example:** Within six months to a year, I will be prepared to purchase my first single-unit rental property in Xyz suburb, where I will serve the commuter community. As I live in my target area, I will not yet require staff. I will advertise my property in the local paper, online, and with neighborhood flyers, then conduct interviews to cover credit checks, emphasize lease standards, and review maintenance agreements, including a twenty-four-hour response time to tenant issues. I will supply an onsite washer and dryer and offer a modest rental deduction for early payment.

> **Example:** Long term, I want to be a leading landlord for commuters in the Xyz area. I plan to purchase additional rental properties with the intention of staffing a property manager when I have four units leased.

Keep in mind, a business plan is not written once then regarded as an unchanging law. It is a living, breathing tool that should be modified as your real-estate portfolio grows. It is a checkpoint to measure your progress and a reminder of what you are working toward.

Who can help me put this plan into action?

The United States Small Business Administration cites poor management as the number-one reason new businesses fail within the first three years. As a real-estate investor, you are essentially a self-employed small-business owner. How you manage yourself and your business team will determine your financial success. Now that you have completed a bare-bones business plan, it is time to talk about the staff who will help bring this plan to fruition.

No real-estate transaction is completed in isolation. Between finding the property, acquiring the purchasing finance, closing the deal, renting the residence, filing the taxes, maintaining the property, and building your portfolio, you will be working with dozens of professionals. We will go into detail about the role of each major player in Chapter Two; for now, here is an overview of your team players:

Financial advisor. A financial advisor's role is to look at all of your assets and liabilities, suggest programs for protecting your financial well-being, and help you determine the next financial step to take.

Realtor. Establishing a working relationship with a local Realtor will keep you informed about market changes and give you an inside track on upcoming properties. A Realtor acts as your eyes and ears in the field.

Mortgage representative. An experienced loan officer is a critical member of your real-estate investing team. There are several investor-friendly programs that an experienced mortgage consultant can help you qualify for, expanding your buying potential.

Tax accountant. Real-estate tax laws should be deciphered by a well-trained, experienced expert who can help you take advantage of every deduction and avoid overpaying. Tax laws are constantly changing, and you will need a professional to keep you informed.

A business plan that remains locked away in your personal computer will do you little good. Your business plan is a tool used to discuss your intentions, ideas, and goals. In order to turn these ideas into profit, you should solicit the help of these four professionals. Your team will be instrumental in helping you chart your course, offering tangible tools for achieving your goals, providing benchmarks to measure success, and helping you restrategize, should you miss the mark. An unbiased appraisal of your business plan is critical before attempting to take action.

Why can't I do this all on my own?

Why would you want to? Not assembling a financial team makes as much sense as trying to perform surgery on yourself—you might get lucky, but you'll probably make a big mess and hurt yourself. Many expensive mistakes could be avoided if more investors would take the time to enlist the help of finance experts instead of assuming that they will be able to do it themselves. We have seen many homes sit on the market while lonely lawn signs declare their availability. In a booming market that is more forgiving of investor mistakes, doing it all yourself might work, but we're interested in making money in every kind of market. Realtors have access to media and Internet sites, and, most importantly, they make their living selling houses. Why treat something like a hobby when you can hire someone to treat it as a job? We work with professionals who make a living in their area of expertise.

Even if you come to the table with a strong background in money-management skills, have previously purchased real estate, or do your own taxes, you probably do not have enough experience to consider yourself an expert. And that's whose advice you want to have at your fingertips: an expert's. Perhaps you feel intimidated by experts. We'll help you prepare interview questions and a business plan so you feel better equipped to ask for what you want. Remember, experts become so because they perform the same activity over and over again. As a beginner, you have not had their experience, nor do you need to get that experience before becoming an investor. It's not necessary to become an expert in every aspect of real estate to achieve success, but it does help to work with the best in the business.

Of all the assets you will ever possess, time is by far the most important. You must protect your time like a prized possession, not waste it chasing down pointless leads or pursuing hype. Having a team of experts at the ready will greatly benefit you in this respect. Take the time now to collect your experts, so that when an opportunity presents itself you have reputable counsel and trusted advice at the ready.

Who is qualified to give investment advice?

On the one hand, you want to solicit counsel from an unbiased, reputable source who has received some formal education and conducts business under a professional code of ethics. Licensed mortgage representatives, financial advisors, and tax accountants make a living dealing in economics and are held accountable to serve their clients to the best of their ability by their individual corporations or licensing boards. On the other hand, financial advice is personal advice. As such, you want to know as much about the person giving you the advice as possible. Trusted family friends, parents, and colleagues have all been cited as an investor's main influence for making investment decisions. So the question becomes whose advice should you solicit, a professional or someone with whom you have personal a relationship?

While a quality professional opinion is worth its weight in gold, there is no denying that money is very personal. Investors not only make their decisions based on how the numbers look but how the numbers feel. Ideally, you should work with financial professionals with whom you have a good personal rapport. Being new to real-estate investing, you probably don't have several professional advisors at your fingertips with whom to forge a strong working relationship. But chances are you do have a few trusted friends whose investing portfolio has caught your attention. Perhaps there is a neighbor or family member who speaks confidently and comfortably about where his money goes and why he is pleased with his decisions. Asking this person for a financial referral can give you the added confidence you need to seek professional advice. Even if your investing methods vary somewhat, enlisting the help of an expert who has already served a friend well is an excellent starting point.

If you have friends or family members who renounce financial experts entirely, explaining that they've always figured things out for themselves, we encourage you to probe this reaction a bit further. It has been our experience that everyone has asked a professional a few questions along the line. Some people are just wary of saying they have financial advisors, concerned perhaps that such an indulgence would seem pretentious. Don't be discouraged. As the conversation continues you will most likely find out the name of the neighborhood bank manager who always has a few minutes to chat or the name of the loan officer who has seen the family through two new home purchases and a refinance. Referrals come in all shapes and sizes. Be on the lookout for a style that sounds as if it could match yours and you'll find the qualified advice you are looking for.

Is there financial advice I should be wary of?

There is a slew of financial advice to be wary of. One of the ugliest and most unregulated terms to rear its head in recent years is *consultant*. It seems as if everyone wants to hang a shingle outside their living-room window, call themselves an authority, and charge you a fee for their self-proclaimed expertise. So how do you best navigate through the plethora of consultants without drowning?

When seeking counsel, keep in mind that if it sounds too good to be true, it is. This is especially true when it comes to bad credit. We have seen tons of advertisements claiming that you can be a homeowner with no money down, even if you have terrible credit. But when you read the fine print, you'll see that these loans carry exorbitant fees and origination costs. If you have bad credit, you are a risk to the bank and will have to pay more for the privilege of borrowing money. A better approach is to work with a reputable mortgage consultant to repair your credit so your fees and rates remain manageable. Many national mortgage lenders can refer you to their corporate credit rehabilitation division, where, at no additional cost, experts can help you repair your credit. In finance, you do not get something for nothing. Anyone who claims you can is misleading and incorrect.

Consultants who claim to offer hot tips for a fee are probably getting rich by collecting fees, not working the real-estate market. Hot-tip specialists prey on beginners who are hoping to skip steps. Instead of paying their dues, these novices pay for flashy, though shallow, advice.

Hot tips are usually riddled with problems. Zoning changes may be on the horizon, making it impossible to benefit from the brand-new housing development the consultant is urging you to invest in. No matter how enticing a prospect may seem, always have a knowledgeable, objective member of your financial team review the proposed paperwork. If you're being pressured to sign on the line before having your investment team evaluate the deal, walk away. Only amateurs and unscrupulous characters rely on pressure to close a deal.

Probably the most misleading term currently thrown about is *no risk*. In investing, be it real estate, stocks, or collectibles, there is always risk. A commitment to continuing education, a comprehensive business plan, and a well-chosen financial team are all guards against unnecessary risk, but nothing can eliminate risk entirely.

As you pursue your investment career, you will become more and more able to distinguish bogus counsel from reputable guidance and better able to decide which information will suit your needs.

When will I know it's the right deal?

The right deal will come along more often than you think. There is no shortage of real-estate opportunities. In fact, we have turned down more prospects than we have ever pursued. Before we move forward with a new project, we check our financial status, our emotional well-being, and run the scenario past our investment team. For us to decide we have found the next right deal, all systems must say go.

Financially speaking, we never want to get in over our heads. With several properties on our plate, it's important that we focus on quality investments, not become distracted by the pursuit of quantity accumulation. While spouting off how many pieces of property you own may sound impressive at a cocktail party, it is far more productive to work a prudent inventory into steady, positive cash flow. Regardless of how good a deal seems, you must always ask yourself how an additional financial burden, such as if your property becomes vacant, will affect your household budget. If your son needs braces, the family car is due for an upgrade, and you'll be traveling for your niece's wedding, now may not be the best time to take on another financial commitment. Even if you qualify for excellent loan programs that will get you into a property for very little money down, be cautious not to overextend yourself. If now is not the right time financially, then it's not the right deal.

As we mentioned, neglecting your emotional well-being can be as detrimental as straining your finances. For instance, we have never purchased a new property during the holiday season. Why? We have too many family obligations. We want to make money whenever we can, but we know that trying to launch a new project between Thanksgiving dinner and Christmas morning would be exhausting and unproductive. If you are trying to get a deal off the ground when your calendar is packed with personal obligations, you may be setting yourself up for disaster. If now is not the right time emotionally, then it's not the right deal.

Finally, we never make major financial decisions without enlisting the counsel of our team members—in particular our financial advisor. We, too, have become overly excited about a potential project and have needed our advisor to remind us of our long-term goals, our short-term commitment, and how this deal may or may not fit in with our agenda. Having an unbiased, knowledgeable professional to bounce ideas off of has saved us from many headaches. Patience is a virtue. If you don't have the time or the desire to talk to your team because the deal is too good to be true, then it is. Don't worry that your advisors will squelch your enthusiasm. On the contrary, they will keep your energy focused and prevent your enthusiasm from waning. If your team doesn't agree that it is the right deal, then it's not the right deal.

Checking your financial and emotional status then getting the backing of your team will help you make the best decision and take advantage of the right deals.

Is it true you need money to make money?

Yes and no. You certainly want to have adequate funds on hand to cover your down payment, incidental expenses, and the carrying costs of a property should it sit dormant. It has been our experience that things always cost more than you anticipate. A property that needs minor repairs ends up requiring a roof replacement. A new townhouse in an up-and-coming neighborhood sits vacant. A market shift makes it more difficult to sell a fairly priced building. For reasons such as these, we recommend having cash reserves available. This is not pessimistic but a reality of homeownership. Being prepared is the way of the responsible investor.

But if you're afraid you'll never have enough disposable income to begin investing, take heart. The amount of cash you need to have will vary according to your credit score. The better your score, the less risk you are to the bank and the more loan programs you will qualify for, be it low-money-down mortgages, home-equity lines of credit, or refinances. In today's financial world, good credit is almost important as cash on hand. A knowledgeable mortgage consultant can help you evaluate the best programs to meet your needs.

Cash is not the only asset that businesspeople depend on. Perhaps you are looking to partner with someone who will provide financial backing while you contribute your time and energy to finding properties, researching town ordinances, or marketing rehabilitated projects. In partnerships like limited liability companies, which we'll discuss in Chapter Seven, it is possible to exchange services for a share in the venture and subsequent profits. We will detail the importance of a well-constructed LLC contract, reviewed by a knowledgeable attorney. Talented craftsmen, motivated businesspeople, and savvy salespeople are always in demand. Don't discount your abilities, as their value can be your greatest marketable asset.

While it is true that you want to have money on hand as you accumulate investment opportunities, you also want to build a strong credit score and mine additional profitable resources. There is more than one way to make a valuable contribution to your financial future.

What is earned income?

Earned income is the payment you receive for performing a predetermined service. It is the paycheck employees work for. When you stop performing a service, your income ends. This is the way most workers make their money. This is the hardest way to build wealth, as you have to work harder and longer to earn more money, and you receive the fewest tax breaks. For those of us who depend on jobs to finance our standard of living, we know how important it is to make our earned income work for us. Earned-income recipients can be broken down into three kinds of people.

1. **Spenders.** These people spend their paycheck in its entirety, rationalizing, "I earned it, it's mine." Such spenders are an advertiser's dream. They love the latest and greatest inventions, take great joy in acquiring things, and often fund their pleasure pursuits with credit cards at a high rate of interest. Their money works once, when it is exchanged for consumer goods. Spenders usually do not believe they have financial options, and many will be in dire straits as they approach retirement.

2. **Safe savers.** These earned-income recipients appreciate that their money can do more for them than merely purchase creature comforts. Savers usually want to know where their money is at all times, and they often place their trust in a 401(k) or 403(b) account, stocks, bonds, and other regulated systems. Choosing savings is a relatively reliable way to ensure a modest return on your investment; remember, there is no such thing as risk free. Savers are on the right financial track. Their money is working more than one time, and they are planning for their financial future.

3. **Investors.** The last group of earned-income recipients want their money to work as hard for them as they have worked to earn it, so they invest in projects that will generate cash flow. These workers appreciate that earned

income is a vehicle to acquire money-making assets. This ambitious financial plan carries the most risk but can also yield the greatest reward.

While almost everyone has a source of earned income, what people choose to do with their earnings can vary dramatically.

What is portfolio income?

Portfolio income refers to the money made on paper assets. Paper assets include mutual funds, stocks, bonds, pensions, and automatic savings plans. With portfolio income, your original earned income continues to work for you. Instead of exchanging your money for consumer goods, you invest it in the stock market or savings plans; in essence, you receive monetary compensation, interest, or profit sharing for loaning your money to different organizations. As we just mentioned, this is a preferred investing plan for most people. These plans are considered safer, as they yield pretty consistent returns. They're also easy to maintain. Whether you choose to manage your own paper portfolio, made increasingly popular through online services, or enlist the expertise of a qualified broker, you can take comfort in itemized updates and timely statements regarding your finances.

What is passive income?

Passive income is money earned on investments that do not require your physical labor. You collect an income without having to perform a job. A prime example of a passive-income activity is a rental property. You have taken your earned income, your paycheck, and invested it in real estate, which you rent for a profit. While maintaining a rental property requires your time and energy, your properties make you money without you physically having to be there. Turning earned income into passive income uses your money's greatest potential.

As a real-estate investor, you move away from looking for a great job to build earned income and instead look for a great opportunity. Again, we are not encouraging you to quit your job; rather, we suggest using your job's income as a means to cultivate money-making assets. Your earned income can continue to generate revenue, and you can benefit from tax advantages.

While everyone enjoys luxury, self-motivation and self-restraint make it possible to turn short-term sacrifices into long-term goals. Investors are most interested in finding ways to turn their income into cash-flow-generating opportunities and capitalize on the advantages of building passive income. This book will focus on helping you build a real-estate investing portfolio that will maximize your potential passive income.

What are assets and liabilities?

An *asset* is something of value that you own. Current assets, commonly referred to as liquid assets, are resources that can quickly (within one year) be turned into cash. Generally speaking, current assets are broken into five categories:

1. Cash: As the intention of liquid assets is to have access to cash, cash itself is your most current asset as it is readily available. Checking and savings accounts are included as cash since you can directly access them.

2. Short-term securities: These are investments held for a limited amount of time then sold with the intention of realizing modest gains.

3. Inventory: This is the fair-market value of business supplies.

4. Prepaid expenses: These are company operating expenses, like insurance or workers' compensation, which are paid before being needed.

5. Receivables: This refers to money due and expected for a rendered service.

Noncurrent assets are your long-term investments and are not intended for use in the immediate future; they are not cash ready. Bonds, pensions, and stocks are noncurrent assets. Fixed assets refer to the necessary expenses needed to maintain a successful business, such as office computers. Finally, intangible assets include copyrights, patents, and trademarks. As investors, we want our money to achieve its greatest potential. Individuals interested in building wealth see money as a vehicle for assets and assets as a vehicle for wealth. For all financially savvy investors, a combination of short- and long-term assets can be structured to generate cash flow and provide security.

Liabilities are what you owe. They are your financial obligations. Liabilities are broken into two categories:

1. Current liabilities: These are expenses that must be paid off in a short period of time, usually less than one year. Examples include payroll wages, taxes, and operating expenses (like paying off those office computers).

2. Long-term liabilities: These are mortgages or pensions, which are not expected to be satisfied within one year.

In business, it is virtually impossible to avoid liabilities altogether, nor would you want to. How could you get a business off the ground without loans? How could you realize your real-estate buying potential without a mortgage? Taking on manageable debt gives you the opportunity to build your assets. As you build your assets and pay down or limit your liability, you increase your equity. *Equity* is the difference between your assets and liabilities; it is your net worth. The goal of business is to build your net worth, through profit-making assets, while limiting your liabilities.

How can I build profitable assets while limiting liabilities?

As we just stated, avoiding liabilities is not the goal, but limiting debt is. One of the best ways to limit liability is to have a clear understanding of your short- and long-term goals, then make timely, well-guided decisions with the assistance of your financial team. All of us have fallen victim to delusions of grandeur. Thinking that a precarious deal will be worth the risk in the long run, we overextend ourselves, compromise our objectives, and get off track. Instead of moving our portfolio forward, the goal of each new project, we end up taking two steps back. Consulting with your team of experts can help you keep your eye on the prize and avoid distractions.

To further complicate matters, consider that a project can be both an asset and a liability at the same time. For instance, if you purchase a property that needs considerable repair before it can be rented, you will have to budget for the renovations and the cost of carrying a vacancy. This could end up being a considerable amount of money. While improvements and inflation will help you build home equity, and a nicer unit may bring in a more attractive rent, you must develop an action plan for meeting the short-term costs instead of merely holding your breath in anticipation of a big payday down the road. Be realistic about your financial and emotional abilities. If you do not have the means to see a renovation property through, pursue other opportunities lest you risk losing your initial financial investment and having to abandon the property before you can benefit from its improvements.

It is important to remember that until a property is making you money, it is costing you money. You must give each new project its due consideration, weigh the risks and benefits, take stock of your capabilities, then activate your team. Such a plan will help you limit your financial exposure and begin to build a more profitable portfolio.

How safe is this type of investing?

Investing is as safe as the investor, just as driving is as safe as the driver or spending is as safe as the spender. Before you purchase a car, you determine what your automobile needs are. Do you drive across country or across town? Are you looking for a sporty style, or would a family sedan better suit your needs? You probably ask friends and neighbors for their input, check the manufacturer's safety records, consider gas mileage, and take a few models out for a test drive. Having weighed your options, you purchase the car of your choice, take advantage of the safety features, and respect the rules of the road. You keep your insurance, registration, and maintenance current. Now imagine buying a car without considering your needs, without soliciting recommendations, and without taking a test drive—obviously, a foolish idea. Unfortunately, when it comes to investing, people often jump in the first vehicle that catches their eye instead of researching the best project for their needs.

Before you begin canvassing the neighborhood for available properties, you must have a clear understanding of what your investment goals are. Are you looking to finance your children's college education? Are you concerned about being forced into early retirement and want to supplement your paycheck now? Have you just come into some cash and are looking to expand your portfolio? Decide what you want and what you need your money to do for you. What works for others may not work for you. Be clear about your intentions, timetable, and comfort level prior to pursuing this line of investing, and you will be a much more successful financier.

To repeat, investing is as safe as the investor, which is why we have begun this book by emphasizing how important it is to create an effective, focused business plan; organize a personable, professional financial team; and sift through the litany of expert advice available. No one can guarantee your absolute financial safety—it is not possible. But committing to a realistic, reasonable business venture, grounded in reliable education and slow and steady experience, can help you limit risk while capitalizing on opportunities.

Am I guaranteed a profit?

If real-estate profits were guaranteed, we'd be too busy counting our cash to write this book. When it comes to investing, there is always going to be some risk. Despite taking all the necessary precautions, carefully weighing every decision, and moving forward with the support of your financial team, there is still no guarantee that you will make money.

Those looking for guarantees often cite the buy-and-hold plan: Buy property now, preferably undeveloped land, hold it for twenty years, then cash in on inflation. Proponents of this approach subscribe to the common wisdom about land: "They're not making any more of it!" Since there is only so much developable land available, it stands to reason that buying what you can now will have beneficial repercussions down the line. While there is validity to this idea—land is a precious resource—there are several variables that prevent such an investment from being guaranteed. While future economic inflation is likely, a resource's future worth cannot be assumed. Let's say you purchase a three-acre parcel of land in a residential area with the intention of selling it twenty years from now at a premium, courtesy of inflation. But five years from now the town's zoning changes, and new homes must be built on ten-acre lots. Your guaranteed plan has been interrupted, and you will have to apply for zoning exceptions, a long and tedious process, if you want to keep your lot marketable. Your "guaranteed" plan has hit an expensive and time-consuming snag. Consider, too, that the buy-and-hold plan relies heavily on supply and demand. It is very difficult to predict an area's future needs. A once-charming residential area could easily become overdeveloped, with crowded schools and inadequate natural resources. While you could probably still sell your property, will you be able to guarantee a huge financial payday? Not likely.

Real-estate investing warranties don't yet exist, but by following a structured investing plan, you and your team will have created a valuable resource to monitor your activity, giving you opportunities to tweak your action plan accordingly. If you purchase land and there are zoning or demographic changes, call your team into play and discuss possible plan B strategies, reassess your plan, and get back on track. Realistically, no single deal is going to make you wealthy, but no single deal has to crush you either.

Will this make me rich?

It's up to you. The only thing that will make you rich is hard work. Most people struggle with making a plan, setting goals, sticking to a budget, obtaining an education, and making sacrifices. They want to be comfortable, watch television, eat out, and look nice. There is absolutely nothing wrong with wanting that. It's a lovely life, but it probably won't make you rich. The questions then become, "What am I willing to do to become rich?" and "Why do I want to be rich?"

Self-control and emotional maturity are critical aspects of building wealth. Those who live by the seat of their pants, saying, "You can't take it with you!" as they accumulate additional credit-card debt, are most likely headed for financial ruin. Rationalizing that you deserve a vacation, deserve a new car, or deserve a new wardrobe calls into question your emotional well-being and maturity. Prizes and treats seem like childish rewards for your hard work. Don't you really deserve excellent health care as you age, an active retirement, and a peaceful night's sleep? Chances are you're going to be around a lot longer than you think, and things are not going to get less expensive. If you are only interested in instant gratification and have limited self-control, work with a sound financial advisor who can tell you how much you can afford to spend on your luxuries while helping you set up sensible provisions for your future.

If you want to work toward becoming rich in real estate, you have to take care of your physical, mental, and emotional responsibilities. This takes hard work. Money is not made in isolation. You have to do the necessary legwork: Make contacts, pass out business cards, ask questions, get involved, and get excited. You must balance your work, family, leisure, and business obligations. You have to see a project through, keep going when the going gets tough, and keep yourself motivated. You have to learn to make deals with your head, not your heart. You have to make that first solid deal despite your fear of the unknown, learn to avoid selling hastily or hoarding unnecessarily, and find the faith to trust your instincts. Meeting these responsibilities head on will help set you up for financial success.

Being rich is a lofty aspiration that takes commitment, dedication, and hard work. Being rich will not solve all your problems, but it can provide a comfortable lifestyle and a secure future. The choice is yours.

Will this make me poor?

In any new business venture, it is a lot easier to lose money than it is to make money. A common pitfall when entering a new industry involves misdirection of start-up funds and energy. It can be extremely exciting to purchase innovative business materials, sign up for continuing education classes, and have a new calendar filled with potential goals. There is no denying the pleasure you feel when detailing your latest potential investment project to friends and family. Everyone likes to look good and sound smart. However, this should not take the place of developing a portfolio.

Whenever we are asked this question, we make a comparison to joining a gym.

Expensive gym memberships don't help you get in shape; consistently going to the gym and following a fitness routine gets you in shape. New workout clothes don't help you lose weight; working out does. The same is true in investing. Subscribing to a dozen trade magazines will not make you smarter; reading them will. Keeping business cards in your pocket will not help you make contacts; handing them out will. While we encourage you to invest in marketing devices, your money will be wasted if you do not actually use your tools. It is possible to go broke trying to look the part. Proper planning and execution can help you make financially sound decisions at the start of this venture and throughout your real-estate career.

We have seen many would-be investors burn themselves out before even starting because they wasted all their enthusiasm in the start-up phase. In real-estate investing, slow and steady wins the race. Anyone can have a great attitude for fifteen minutes. Successful business entrepreneurs appreciate the value of self-motivation and know it is imperative to keep a positive outlook despite the market's ebb and flow, a bad deal, or a financial setback. Those who find themselves in financial difficulties are quick to hop on the bandwagon and quick to jump off when the road gets bumpy. Emotionally driven investors buy too high, sell too soon, get discouraged, and then give up entirely.

Poor planning, poor attitude, poor execution—if you start poor, you end poor. Treat yourself and your investing venture as precious commodities, and you will be more likely to prosper.

How long will this take?

It takes as much time as you have, and the more time you have, the better. With time comes experience, an irreplaceable asset in real-estate investing. Experience helps give you the confidence, self-control, and insight necessary to take advantage of viable opportunities and recognize when you're in danger of wasting your time. The more exposure you have to different scenarios, the better equipped you become to handle the next issue that presents itself. You'll become less and less emotionally attached to your projects, making it possible to fine-tune your business plan, resolve tenant issues, and walk away from a questionable deal. In addition, the longer you are in the real-estate market, the more wealth-building opportunities you'll be privy to. Not only will you be able to take advantage of appreciation, equity, and inflation, but you'll build a reliable supply of contacts, an excellent resource for collaboration, idea exchange, and motivation. Instead of starting from ground zero each time, you'll know contractors, property managers, movers, and players who can help you close a deal more efficiently.

Real-estate investing is not recommended for the impatient businessperson. There are too many variables. We have known deals to be pushed back for months due to circumstances that were out of our control. While we prefer to have our transactions completed in a timely fashion—who wouldn't—permits, mortgage approvals, tenants, and weather have all stalled our plans. Instead of saying, "We want to have x completed by x date," we now know the importance of managing our money and building a flexible budget. We have never gone into a deal thinking this will be the last one. Instead, we view each new acquisition as a catalyst for the next project.

The time you spend in the real-estate market is more important than trying to time the market. Successful investors know that it's possible to make money in any market whether the economic advantage lies with buyers or sellers. Instead of waiting for the next boom, develop an economic strategy that makes financial sense in any economy. Real-estate investing is an equal opportunity money maker. The more time, experience, and energy you contribute to your business, the more success you are likely to enjoy.

Scenario: I don't have a financial advisor or other key team players. Will these professionals be willing to work with a beginner and take me seriously?

Professionals will take you as seriously as you take yourself. We have been approached by so-called investors who are fired up and ready to make a deal but have no plan of action other than, "Show me a property I can make money on." It is difficult to take this kind of request seriously. One of the first requirements of any new businessperson is to treat an expert's time and energy with respect. Walking into a specialist's office expecting—or worse, demanding—to have a money-making real-estate portfolio ready and waiting is a waste of everyone's time. Come to the table able to articulate your business intentions, action plan, and portfolio goals, and you'll have a much more productive meeting.

As you are the entrepreneur, you get to choose your team players. When making appointments with referrals and recommendations, take time to prepare for the occasion. Before arriving, ask what paperwork, if any, you should have on hand. As we suggested, completing a bare-bones business plan is an excellent way to organize your thoughts and keep the conversation focused. Be up front about your investing experience, or lack thereof, and have a list of questions you would like answered. Most of all, throughout your appointment check your comfort level. Is this professional helping to put you at ease? Is he answering your questions coherently? Are you encouraged to talk, or do you feel intimidated? While you may be tempted to focus exclusively on an expert's credentials, don't overlook the importance of choosing a good personal match.

Each expert can be considered a most valuable tool, but if you avoid using a tool, it becomes worthless.

Financial professionals make their livings by servicing their clients. They need you as much as you need them. When we first began coordinating our team, we worried that our meager savings and lean business plan didn't warrant a professional's time. However, we found people who were not only willing to work with us, they were excited to help us get our plans off the ground. We were eager to work, had no bad habits, and welcomed suggestions and new ideas. Today we work with several members of our original team, and it has been a personal and professional pleasure to grow with these experts. Choose a specialist whose qualifications are complemented by a hospitable demeanor and you'll be paired with a professional who can help facilitate your transition from beginner to seasoned veteran. 🏠

How can I better educate myself about real-estate investing?

Treat your real-estate education as you would any other formal education, and surround yourself with the best experts in your area. When we applied to college, we sought out the best and brightest faculty for our intended professions. Do the same now. Enroll in reputable seminars, as you would college classes, having considered the course's material, requirements, and intention. Invest in course books like this one, and choose subject matter in line with your level of comprehension. Reading an advanced finance journal instead of a beginner's manual is a waste of time if you don't understand it. You will learn as you go.

As we mentioned earlier, there is no national real-estate market, so researching national trends or statistics is not necessary. Instead, become an expert in your area of interest. Become intimately acquainted with your target neighborhoods. Contact the local chamber of commerce or town library and ask for the latest demographic census. Who lives in your area? Are there families, college graduates, transients? What is the median income? How are the schools? Are merchants moving in or out of the area? When formulating your business plan and deciding what needs you can best fulfill, this information will help you stay focused.

The Internet is an excellent resource for learning about the housing prices in your area. The Realtor Multiple Listing Service at *www.mls.com* provides links to every state in the country, with information about area schools, neighborhood housing sales, and informative articles. Your team Realtor will have additional resources, including the number of days a property has been on the market and the difference between the asking price and the selling price. Partner your enthusiasm and energy with a Realtor's professional insight and you can further increase your knowledge base.

Most cities have real-estate investing clubs, organized professionals who meet to share strategies, ideas, and experiences. A good place to start is the National Real Estate Investors Association at *www.nationalreia.com*. Often groups will invite you to attend one meeting without charge, giving you the chance to get a feel for the club's dynamic. Are you interested in an organization that emphasizes rehabbing homes, landlord strategies, or multiunit properties? Do you want a group facilitated by a long-time, take-charge veteran, or do you prefer a lighter exchange among all experience levels? Connecting with a group you feel comfortable with is much better than choosing a club in which you feel intimidated. Take your time deciding which organization best suits your needs, then commit yourself to networking with your area's professionals. Approaching your real-estate career as a student looking to achieve a valuable education is an excellent tactic and one that will help you achieve success.

Scenario: I have a demanding career and limited free time to set up a team, make a plan, and investigate the market. Luckily, I have a hot tip on a sure thing. Shouldn't I take this opportunity and learn as I go?

This idea has disaster written all over it. We would never advise anyone to learn as they go, especially when it is painfully obvious that you are about to be taken advantage of. Even if there was such a thing as a sure thing—which there is not—hoping to hit the real-estate jackpot without industry education, a credible financial team, or a well-developed business plan is a fool's approach, and a fool and his money are soon parted. While it may sound much more exciting to get tipped off, the truth is you are more likely to get ripped off. Earlier we explained why a hot tip cannot be counted on: hidden issues, unreliable resources, paper-thin promises. We don't put a lot of stock in magic touches or divine financial intervention. Instead we encourage a solid business plan, reviewed and endorsed by a credible financial team who can help you design an action plan to meet your investing goals.

As you have a demanding career, we don't advise quitting your job to take on a new venture. Instead, try to figure out how to balance your obligations and manage your time so you can make informed decisions about real-estate investing, limiting your financial vulnerability and preparing you for a solid deal.

How much time you want to dedicate to learning about real-estate investing is up to you, but learning power is earning power. There is no benefit to skipping steps. To be a successful real-estate investor, you must invest your time, energy, and enthusiasm. Real estate is a business, and as the business owner it is your responsibility to manage yourself and your decisions. If you feel you really don't have the time to do this, consider turning off the TV, unplugging the phone, waking up one hour earlier, or passing on a party invitation. The time is there if you are willing to look for it. If you are not, we advise you to seek the counsel of a financial advisor who can best manage your investment portfolio for you. There is no such thing as something for nothing. If you insist on pursuing shortcuts, you will suffer the consequences. 🏠

I am committed to seeing this investment opportunity through. How can I best devise realistic goals and benchmarks to make sure I am on the right path?

The key word in your question is *realistic*. To remain realistic, you must have the unbiased opinions of seasoned professionals. One of two things usually happens when newcomers design a business plan: They either overshoot reasonable goals, creating scenarios that no one could achieve, or they sell themselves short and miss out on earning potential. Both are bad business scenarios.

Overzealous entrepreneurs who make grand, impractical plans have probably fallen short of the mark in several areas of their life. The person whose real-estate goal is to own ten properties in two years has most likely started a diet with the idea of losing ten pounds in two weeks or has begun a new job with the intention of running the company in two months. Instant-fame-and-fortune fanatics thrive on media coverage portraying overnight success stories, wishing that they too could just be in the right place at the right time. We started in the right place at the right time and we just celebrated our first overnight success—it took almost five years.

What sensationalized news stories tend to overlook is the struggle, sacrifice, and commitment it takes to make money "instantly." Lucrative rental properties may garner a great deal of attention, but what about the investments that are just breaking even? What about the projects that never got off the ground? Being at the right place at the right time usually happens because you have studied where and when that right place and right time are. You can achieve great financial success in real estate, and we hope you do. But instead of trying to become an industry superstar, why not make reasonable demands on your time and money?

The other side of the overly ambitious investor is the investor who focuses on failure. Afraid to say out loud what he really wants, he low-balls his goals to avoid disappointment. This person probably has a history of deflecting compliments, downplaying his contributions, and gravitating toward the background. It is much easier to keep your expectations low and act surprised at your success than to announce your plans and risk making mistakes. Let us assure you, everyone fears failure. It is intimidating when your friends and family know you are taking on a new project, especially one that does not guarantee you success. Confidence comes after a little experience, but experiences don't happen without a little confidence. Draw on the strength of your team and make a plan that is bold, not brazen. You do not have to rival the real-estate success of Donald Trump to consider yourself a worthy entrepreneur, but be careful not to sell yourself short and risk avoiding your full potential.

Working with a financial team will help you design an action plan that balances your undisciplined dreams with attainable goals. We are not always the best judge of our talents and abilities. Having experienced, unbiased professionals by your side is critical to your success.

Chapter Two assembling your team

What are the benefits to assembling a team?

There are personal, social, and educational benefits to assembling a professional financial team. As a new real-estate investor, you may feel overwhelmed at the prospect of organizing a business team, especially if you have never had to take the lead in such an endeavor. But a project that exposes your financial security and challenges your comfort level should not begin without one. Having knowledgeable experts in your corner will afford you several important advantages.

To begin with, there is comfort in numbers. Instead of feeling isolated and adopting a fear-driven, me-versus-the-world attitude, you can surround yourself with helpful team members who have a genuine vested interest in your success. While real estate can be a competitive industry, it does not have to be a lonely one. You will enjoy a much more rewarding business if you satisfy your personal needs. Being able to draw on the experience of experts will help build your confidence as you begin investing. Having trusted advisors who offer valuable feedback to your ideas is a critical advantage when beginning a new business. It is a common truth that when we enjoy what we do, we are more likely to continue doing it. Team camaraderie is an important staple of the long-term investment plan and one that we have greatly benefited from.

We have mentioned, and will continue to emphasize, the importance of networking, which is really another term for socializing. Investing is not done in isolation. Networking is a significant part of business success. If you feel awkward about handing out your business cards or introducing yourself to prospective colleagues, you are at a disadvantage. Having a financial team can help you build your social network. You will get to know your Realtor, then his colleagues, then his associates, their clients, and so on. With each new expert you add to your team, you add all of his or her clients and connections. You can build an industry network exponentially by tapping into your team's resources.

Finally, the educational advantages of working with a financial team are unsurpassed. When starting a new business venture, keep in mind that there is an entire unwritten world of professional standards and practices. Real estate is no different. While we encourage you to commit yourself to a formal education, there is no book yet written on real-estate investing street smarts. Commonsense practices are a tremendous indicator of potential success. Take advantage of your team's time in the field, and increase your interpersonal industry skills. There is no denying that team building is a time-consuming endeavor, but with all the advantages it yields, it is well worth your energies.

Who are the right people for my team?

The right people for your team will share your enthusiasm and see your real-estate investing business as a collaborative effort. Their individual expertise will move you closer to your portfolio goals. Your team members should be experienced, educated, and energetic. To enhance your success, choose professionals whose business styles complement your own. Are you looking for constant direction and feedback, or do you prefer a lighter touch? Do you need one-on-one interaction, or are you comfortable with phone and e-mail correspondence? Do you want to be associated with major financial houses, or will you opt for smaller local businesses? Determine which methods of operation you prefer, then seek out the following individuals:

> *Financial advisor.* Your financial advisor will help you devise a business plan that has measurable goals. You'll want to work with someone who discloses her own business plan and is personally invested in the real-estate market. It is very important that your styles match, as your advisor will

be a constant contact throughout your portfolio's life. Choosing someone whose technique parallels your own will increase your likelihood of using this expert, thus increasing your chances for financial success.

Mortgage representative. Your mortgage representative helps you finance your investments. He knows the programs that will best suit your needs and what it takes to qualify for each. Choose a lender who is also a realty owner and is familiar with loans for second homes and investment properties.

Realtor. Your real-estate agent can offer an inside market perspective, keeping you up on neighborhood trends and industry changes. She is your eyes and ears on the street. Choose a licensed Realtor who owns multiple investment properties and works full time in the business.

Tax accountant. Your tax accountant's job is to help save you the most money. Tax law is long, complex, and ever changing. Choose an attorney who is an investor, has several real-estate investors as clients, and keeps current with tax law modifications.

These four professionals comprise your starting team. As your business grows, so will your network, but these specialists will always be needed. Throughout this chapter, we will go into further detail about each person's contributing expertise and discuss interview strategies that will help you choose your financial team members.

Can I trust a professional recommendation from a business associate?

Business associates and other industry professionals can be a valuable source of referrals. The benefit of soliciting a professional referral is that people in the business tend to know people in the business—and not just by name but by character. A professional's reputation is worth his or her weight in gold. Those with successful productivity are coveted, sought after, and enjoy repeat business On the other hand, news of unscrupulous actions, shady dealings, or delinquent projects often spreads like wild fire, tarnishing a person's career. Having an industry insider referral can point you in the right direction, giving you a solid footing from which to begin.

The ultimate goal of your portfolio is to make money. Your team members profit when you do, so they are going to want to see you make solid deals, generate cash flow, and limit risk. Because your team members rely on one another, they will want to recommend the professionals they know can get the job done. For example, a Realtor will want to recommend a closing agent—a title company or an attorney—who can expedite a contract through attorney review and get the negotiators to closing. That's also what you want. A Realtor is not going to recommend an attorney who drags his feet or exacerbates an already stressful situation. Professional recommendations can and should build upon one another. Start with one professional whose style and standards match your own, seek out the person he recommends for your next need, add him to your team, then seek out his referral. In this way you can use educated, professional opinions to build a compatible team.

While this is a relatively safe method of team building, we stress the need to conduct a thorough interview, regardless of how strong the recommendation is. Before accepting a referral, ask your current professional for a detailed history of his or her working relationship with the person you're about to interview. While most professionals are just that, there is no denying that unscrupulous characters infiltrate every industry. By conducting your own thorough interview, you'll be able to personally assess a referral's professional standards and personal integrity.

A colleague's recommendation is only a suggestion; it is not law. Do not feel pressured to stay with someone if your styles clash or your expectations are not met. What works for one person may not necessarily work for you. Consider each recommendation a starting point, then proceed.

Can I trust a professional recommendation from friends and family?

If you opt to solicit advice and referrals from friends and family, you'll have the security of knowing that these people have your best interests at heart. Because your relationship extends past the boardroom, friends and family are unlikely to make a haphazard recommendation lest they be held responsible for putting you in harm's way. Who wants to sit across from a resentful relative at Thanksgiving dinner? Wanting to see you succeed, they offer the names of trusted professionals whose expertise has been personally beneficial. You'll be able to ask pertinent questions and benefit from uncensored firsthand accounts. Also, most people love to share an anecdote or two to illustrate their relationship, giving you a glimpse of that expert's demeanor.

This is a good method of building a team, as long as you remember to complete a through interview. You may find that a recommended financial advisor has never serviced someone with your high level of assets or a recommended mortgage broker doesn't know how to rehab your difficult credit history. You should never be someone's biggest, smallest, or most challenging client. Make appointments with several personal referrals to find a comfortable middle ground with professionals who are experienced with your portfolio goals.

You'll probably end up with a team assembled from both professional and personal recommendations. Think of referrals as an introductory handshake, and take the time to get to know the whole person.

Is it important to like the players on my investment team?

Of course you want to like the players on your team, but you're not looking for a new best friend or golf buddy. You want a personable, qualified specialist who will help you make money. You should like the people on your team because they are driven to accomplish your business objectives, have a goal-oriented action plan, and do what they say they will with genuine interest and energy. Your financial team, like your doctor or mechanic, serves a very specific purpose. While it is beneficial to have an agreeable relationship with people to whom you trust your health, safety, and finances, you do not need to make weekend plans together.

When interviewing prospective team members, keep the conversation focused on business. Instead of asking, "What would your best friend say about you?" ask, "What would your clients say about you?" The first question assumes an emotional response, while the second solicits a professional answer. While there is probably overlap between the two, you are interested in keeping the relationship professional and should frame your conversation from that perspective. We have all made the mistake of wanting to like and be liked by everyone, but this is impossible. It is perfectly reasonable to disagree with a specialist's approach or his methods of operation. Even if you are talking to the nicest guy you ever met, do not sign on with someone whose business practices do not complement your own.

Mixing friends and finance is a challenge best avoided. While it may seem like a good idea to hire your cousin to do your taxes or ask your best friend to show you rental properties, many times these relationships end up suffering. You are better off keeping your personal life personal and building a separate business network.

Liking your team can be an important part of your business success. Just remember to keep a balanced view of these new relationships.

What if I make a bad first impression?

No one likes to be a beginner because it makes you feel vulnerable. But as you begin this new business venture, it is important to remember that your goal is not to be impressive. Your objective is to put together an experienced team that can help you reach your financial goals.

Financial experts are made, not born. Even top executives were once new kids on the block. Instead of worrying that you will say the wrong thing or ask a ridiculous question, be more concerned with the trouble that arises when beginners avoid seeking counsel and try to do things on their own. No one we know of has ever lost a huge opportunity because she asked too many questions or tried to learn more, but we often hear stories of investors who could have avoided disaster if they had been more willing to ask for help.

When seeking out experts for your financial team, be up front about your level of experience and knowledge. Working with someone who caters to new investors can make a marked difference in your success. If a particular professional is only interested in working with well-established investors, he will be much less likely to coach you through the initial steps of assembling a real-estate portfolio. That could waste your time, money, and energy.

There is no need to apologize for your beginner status either. Instead of saying, "I'm sorry, I don't understand," or even worse, "I'm an idiot, sorry," keep your comments positive and avoid insulting yourself. A simple, "I'm not familiar with that approach/term/product" is a professional way to ask for clarification. Besides, if anyone reacts to one of your questions with, "I can't believe you don't know this!" he isn't a person you want to be working with. Better to know that up front.

We have all put our foot in our mouth at one time or another, but do not let an occasional misstep frighten you into a full retreat. Ask the questions that need to be asked, and get the answers you need to make your real-estate investing portfolio as successful as possible.

Should my financial team be associated with each other?

If you follow through on professional referrals there is a good chance that members of your team will have had previous working relationships with one another. Business associates who have a positive history of working together will enjoy the opportunity to continue their relationship. Knowing how another team player works, what hours they keep, and their preferred mode of correspondence can help to move deals along more smoothly. However, it is not necessary for success.

More important is your team's commitment to a common purpose. Having completed a business plan and mapped out an action plan with measurable goals, you want to be affiliated with professionals who will get you to your objective. Building a successful portfolio is a collaborative effort, and your team is only as strong as your weakest player. For this reason, we suggest that you use the following recommendations to weed out the less-than-desirable affiliates and set yourself up for success.

First, decide which professional standards are the most important to you. Questions to ask include:

- What is your idea of good customer service?
- Do you expect to have twenty-four-hour access to your advisors?
- Do you prefer to work by e-mail?
- Do you want your team members to initiate contact?

Make a list of everything you expect from an advisory team. Be honest and thorough. Having a clear idea of your expectations will help you to consistently seek out the same type of businessperson. If you want to be able to reach a member of your team through e-mail, stick with professionals who have a strong Web awareness. They'll probably be more accessible and more likely to answer a question or two quickly and efficiently online. If half of your team uses e-mail and the other half doesn't, your communication process can suffer. Choose professionals with similar styles and you'll build a more cohesive team.

Next, contact current clients of your referrals. Ask for feedback about their experience working with a particular expert and compare the answers. An important question to ask is, "How much of Ms. X's advice have you used, and what was the outcome?" If you want to work with specialists who make frequent financial recommendations, be sure to find out about their track record for success. You may discover that a potential member of your team is reluctant to give his opinion. If you work with this person, you may feel let down or dissatisfied.

Finally, ask each potential team member to tell you his or her business philosophy. It could be a company philosophy that he or she subscribes to, or maybe it's a personal mantra. There is a huge difference between "The customer is always right" and "Trust the experts." Similar belief systems will go a long way in ensuring that your team sees things from the same perspective. Professional associates who conduct similar financial practices are more likely to work well together, helping your investment venture move forward smoothly.

What paperwork should I have on hand before assembling my team?

Each team member will have his or her own list of the paperwork requirements necessary to begin your new file. You can expect to be given a precise checklist of items and a timetable by which to submit documents. But as it is the savvy investor's intention to always work most efficiently, you can gather standard financial information and begin organizing your own file.

For starters, you should have a completed business plan at the ready. This useful tool will help you articulate your financial intentions, give your new team members insight into your motivations, exhibit your level of commitment, and make you feel more like a structured, prepared professional. Face-to-face interviews can be intimidating. When working solely from memory, newcomers can easily veer off course during the conversation, forgetting key points they wanted to make or agreeing to an action plan that conflicts with their own interests. Having a reference guide will help keep you on task.

Next, locate your tax forms for the past two years, your W-2 forms, and have several paycheck stubs on hand. Verifying your income is a necessary step in assessing your earning power. There is a big difference between what we say we make and how much income we actually have to work with. Having these documents, as well as recent bank statements and any periodically issued financial reports, will save you time down the road.

Request copies of your credit report from the three national credit agencies—TransUnion, Experian, and Equifax. Familiarizing yourself with your credit standing will provide an opportunity to remedy any mistakes or credit slip ups.

Many people new to real-estate investing greatly underestimate the importance of good credit. They choose to ignore any problems, hoping for the best, or underestimate their buying power, unaware of their solid credit standing. We don't recommend either approach. An honest and accurate account of your credit history is necessary for financial success.

What can I expect to find on my credit report?

Each of the three national credit agencies gathers information from different businesses and categorizes it into six major parts. Here is a general overview of a typical credit report:

- Personal information. Such things as your name, past and present addresses, date of birth, and past and present employers. The information here does not affect your credit score, nor does the report record data that has no bearing on your credit, such as race, religion, sex, or marital status.
- Summary. Your credit history at a glance. It will list all of your accounts, both active and inactive, and the dates on which they were opened. It lists your credit cards, credit card limits, payment patterns, balances, and delinquent activity. Here you will also find matters of public record, such as tax liens or delinquent child-support payments. Finally, an inquiry section tracks who has requested to view your credit score whenever you have applied for a new line of credit.
- Account history. Detailed information about your account activities, including information on home mortgages, car loans, and credit cards. You'll find the latest information regarding late payments, resolved delinquencies, and the names of those responsible for each account.

- Public information. Account of legal matters and/or actions that directly affect your credit. It includes such things as bankruptcies and garnished wages.
- Inquiries. Records businesses, such as mortgage lenders and creditors, who have checked your credit history as part of their application process. We'll discuss these inquiries and their repercussions later. We encourage you to check your own report, as according to credit reporting agency TransUnion, checking your own credit report is considered a "soft inquiry" and therefore does not harm your credit.
- Creditor contact. A list of all businesses with which you hold credit and all the businesses that have made inquiries about your credit for application purposes. You may find a phone number, address, or both.

It is a good idea to obtain your credit report from each of the three credit agencies to compare their information and check for mistakes. You can expect minor numerical differences on each report as processing times vary; while a resolved account may be satisfied on one statement, it could still be listed as overdue by another agency. Remember, educated consumers make the best customers. Take the time to obtain your credit reports and review their contents.

Where can I get a copy of my credit report?

According to federal law, you are entitled to a free, yearly credit report from each of the three reporting agencies. You may obtain an online copy of each of your three reports by logging onto a site such as *www.annualcreditreport.com*. Take this opportunity as well to check for misinformation or inaccuracies. If a problem arises, there are several available tools to help you begin to remedy any problems. Each site will direct you on how to print, save, and review your report. This free credit report service will not assign you a credit score. We will discuss obtaining a credit score later.

If you have already taken advantage of this service in the last year and would like to view your report again, a good place to start is each of the three agencies' user-friendly Web sites. In addition to obtaining your credit report, you can read relevant articles that deal with common credit problems, get advice on possible solutions, and benefit from frequently asked questions. The following agencies charge a nominal fee for additional products that are available for purchase. However, you may want to hold off on these sites' products until you speak with your financial representatives as many advisors offer such things as credit-repair services at no cost.

Equifax is a credit-reporting company that has been in business for more than one hundred years and can be accessed at *www.equifax* *.com.* It features a three-in-one option that allows you to view all three credit reports simultaneously, making it easier to compare information. You can choose to view your report online or receive a hard copy by mail or fax. There are credit-monitoring products for sale and several helpful articles about home buying.

Experian is a credit-reporting agency that promotes consumer education as an excellent means by which to protect and manage personal or business finances. This site (*www.experian.com*) outlines a sample credit report, which makes an excellent tutorial for finance report novices. They also offer several free strategies for repairing damaged credit.

TransUnion is a credit reporting agency whose site is geared toward credit basics. This site (*www.transunion.com*) features excellent articles on a myriad of credit topics, written to keep consumers informed and educated about their financial decisions. There is even a question-and-answer section with the site's credit expert that tackles everyday concerns in a conversational tone.

Even if you obtain your credit reports courtesy of the federal government, we highly recommend visiting all three of these sites. Each has something to offer, from reliable advice to budgeting tools, making them a superb addition to your education plan.

How important will my credit score be?

Your credit score is determined by a mathematical model conceived and designed by the Fair Isaac Corporation. This company developed a means by which a single number could be assigned to a person's entire credit history. This number, commonly called a FICO score, gives creditors a common denominator to assess a borrower's likelihood of repaying his loans. The company considers one's credit history and borrowing patterns in comparison with thousands of other consumer patterns, then attempts to predict a borrower's likely future credit behavior. A high FICO score is attained by someone who pays back her loans promptly, while a low credit score is usually the result of late payments, default, collections, bankruptcies, or a combination of these discrepancies joined with high credit-card balances. The lower your credit score number, the higher your risk to the bank.

A FICO score can be purchased from any of the three independent credit agencies or when you check your yearly annual credit report at the central source site. While there is no harm in obtaining your credit score, and many people are interested to know how they measure up, this service can be provided by your mortgage representative free of charge. He will then help you determine the meaning of your score.

While there is no question that a high credit score is ideal, a lower score does not disqualify you from real-estate investing opportunities. An educated mortgage representative can help determine the best course of action for you. In addition, he can offer counsel and facilities to help fix credit issues, further broadening your buying potential. Those investors with high credit scores will want to explore their options as well. Instead of going a more conventional route, your lender may be able to suggest more exotic programs that are available to you because of your exceptional credit standing.

As you begin organizing your own credit profile, concentrate on the accuracy of your credit report instead of focusing on the credit score. In this preliminary stage it is wise to get all your ducks in a row, then work with a seasoned professional to determine the necessary next steps.

Should I improve my credit score before I begin assembling my team?

If you have chosen to find out your credit score and you see that there is room for improvement, you can begin to make progress while you reach out to your financial team. There are several advantages to this proactive approach.

For starters, it is never too early to begin working toward a solution. If your problems are due to poor budgeting skills, you need to make some necessary changes immediately. Improving your credit score doesn't just mean cleaning up the issues that appear on your report, it means addressing the underlining causes. Paying back your creditors is essential, but unless you deal with your spending and saving habits you are likely to repeat the same mistakes. For instance, a financial advisor who appreciates your budgeting struggles can better design a program to suit your needs and make reasonable suggestions to keep you on track. If you withhold this information, chances are you'll get in over your head again.

As you begin to organize your financial team, you'll benefit from your specialists' experience and be able to draw on their network of colleagues. Instead of having to search out credit-repair organizations or track down necessary customer service contacts, your financial team can save you time and energy by pointing you in the right direction. Many financial experts are affiliated with reputable consumer credit organizations or offer in-house credit counseling to help you get back on track. Instead of opening up the yellow pages and looking for help, you can take advantage of a referral and begin the process of remedying your credit problems.

Finally, as we previously mentioned, until you are working with experienced professionals, you don't really know what a "problem" credit score is. Instead of trying to make everything seem perfect before beginning your venture, trust that most financial professionals have probably had clients with your circumstances before. Seasoned veterans have helped sort through all kinds of complicated credit issues, and your circumstances may not be as difficult as you anticipate. Most professionals want to help a serious investor turn her financial standing around, since they hope to make a new client for life. Remember, there is no such thing as a perfect client. If you wait until you're one, you'll be waiting forever.

You may be tempted to fix all of your problems by yourself, convinced that doing so may make you more appealing to specialists. However, you'll risk missing many financial opportunities. Start the process, but solicit assistance to move that process along.

Why do I need a financial planner?

Many people are reluctant to seek help from a financial advisor, assuming that they'll save money going it alone or convinced that their portfolio doesn't warrant such professional assistance. Yet a financial planner is an integral part of a successful investment team. If you had enough time and resources, you could probably act as your own advisor, but it would take years to familiarize yourself with the ins and outs of an increasingly complicated economic market. Instead of trying to master another career, hire a dedicated professional who continuously studies the market, analyzes available tools, and builds networks.

An experienced, reputable advisor has worked through a variety of economic scenarios and can devise a cohesive strategy that evolves with the ebb and flow of the financial market. Your advisor will remain objective when circumstances threaten your emotional well-being, cautioning you against knee-jerk decision making and reminding you of your long-term goals. His role is similar to a quarterback's: He is part of the team but also helps to direct the next action. With so many different pieces needing to fit together for a real-estate deal to happen, it is essential to have someone who can complete the puzzle.

When you are beginning a new venture, it is very easy to procrastinate. How often have we opted to start a new project next weekend only to find that we've made no progress a month later? Procrastination becomes even more of a problem when we add in the stresses of career, family, and community obligations. Or perhaps you are a perfectionist. Instead of putting things off, you are stuck in the beginning steps, reworking business plans and checking credit scores over and over. A financial advisor can keep projects moving along by reminding you to send in requested paperwork, encouraging you to take the next step, and monitoring your progress along the way. She is able to evaluate your portfolio strengths and weaknesses, filter through all the available advice, and then add balance where necessary.

While you will pay for these services, this is a necessary expense that can increase your long-term assets. At the very least, you will have a qualified sounding board available for counsel. A third-party opinion can help protect two of your most precious resources: time and energy. Your financial advisor can help you boost your earnings, increase your savings, and limit your liability in an organized and timely fashion. No professional investor should deny himself this advantage.

How can I prepare for my interview with a financial advisor?

While almost everyone has experience being interviewed, not everyone has had the opportunity or responsibility to facilitate an interview. Now that the tables are turned, so to speak, you want to realize the significance of this first meeting. With so many professionals to choose from, you have your pick of the litter. Don't underestimate how important your business is. Present yourself as a premier business owner because you are, and conduct your interview accordingly.

You may want to prepare by thinking back to past jobs you have applied for and recalling key points about your own interview. When did you feel at ease? Was there an incident that made you become defensive? Which questions really struck a chord with you? At what point did you realize this was the job you really wanted? Jot down significant details from your own experience and incorporate them into this interview. You are not only interested in this advisor's financial philosophy, but you are trying to get a feel for his or her personality. Concentrate on open-ended questions that give the interviewee a chance to share an anecdote, providing insight into her character. She may talk about a successful business relationship she's had for years or recall a challenging problem she was able to solve.

Remember how you have prepared for interviews? You should expect the same level of professional courtesy at your initial meeting. When possible, meet your advisor at his office and take inventory of your surroundings. Is the space clean, tidy, and warm? Are the phones being answered promptly? Is there a buzz of activity among the staff? Walking into a messy, cold office that lacks energy is a bad sign. If your advisor insists on meeting you at your home, agree on a specific time and check for promptness. As this is a business appointment, he should dress appropriately; this is a business call, not a social outing. A house call is more casual than a formal meeting in an office, but it is not a license for leisure.

Keep track of how easy or difficult it was to set up an initial meeting. Were your calls returned promptly? Did your potential advisor offer alternate dates if there was a conflict? While you want to work with someone who is busy, not someone who is sitting by the phone waiting for it to ring, you don't want to be lost in the shuffle either. Did he call back within twenty-four hours? If it has been a week since you heard from this advisor, you'll probably want to find someone else. These initial contact calls are a good indication of the level of service you can expect once you are a client.

You are about to launch a successful real-estate investing business and deserve to work with professionals who are energetic and enthusiastic about an opportunity to work with you. Anything less is a disservice to you and your business.

What interview questions should I ask my financial planner?

Your financial advisor is a critical member of your investment team and his input will help to direct your overall financial picture, so do not approach your initial meeting haphazardly. Well-planned interview questions can help you get a sense of an advisor's professional philosophy, his preferred investment styles, and his personality.

If your potential advisor seems to be avoiding questions or is constantly checking her watch, she is not the right person for you. Once you are comfortably situated for your interview, take out your written list of questions and make notes as you go along. Let the conversation move in a natural direction, but have a written list to keep you on track and ensure that you cover the points important to you. Consider the following suggestions as you begin following up on referrals.

How long have you been in the business? We recommend working with someone who has at least five years' experience as a full-time, accredited financial advisor. While there is no licensing board for advisors, there are common credentials listed on business cards and letterhead that must be earned, such as certified financial planner (CFP) or master of business administration (MBA).

How many clients do you presently have? Assuming for a moment that we are dealing with a metropolitan area and this individual is making a full-time career as a financial advisor, you should expect to hear that he services between 100 and 150 clients. Less populated areas could mean less clients. You may also want to ask how many clients he expects to have five or ten years from now and about his plans to accommodate this growing business.

Can you guarantee that your advice will make me money? There are absolutely no guarantees in investing, and no financial advisor should make you this promise. Instead, she should comment about her approach to giving advice, her ideas about balancing risk and security, and share some of her success stories.

What do your other clients' portfolios look like? You want to hear that this advisor has worked with real-estate investors before. He can talk about similar concerns many clients share and how he addresses them, as well as unique situations that have broadened his perspective.

Can you offer me any hot tips? An experienced financial advisor should immediately caution you against following any hot tips and instead explain why his methods of investing can help you build a solid portfolio.

How much money will you make off of me? You are entitled to know up front how your advisor will be compensated for working with you. Later in this chapter we will address the various fee structures commonly used.

Where is your money? This may seem like a bold question, but it is absolutely appropriate. As a new real-estate investor, you want to work with someone who has her own successful investment properties and is forthcoming about her portfolio. If this advisor shies away from the question, she may not be the right person for your team.

Are there questions my potential financial advisor should ask me?

A financial advisor is your big-picture team member. He is interested in all aspects of your financial well-being. While each individual has his own area of expertise, all advisors should inquire about your present financial circumstances, including earned income, assets, and liabilities; your retirement plans, including health care and cost of living expenses; and estate planning, including leaving your family, friends, and charities an inheritance. In order to assess your overall financial picture, your potential advisor will probably ask questions about these topics, make suggestions about the types of services he can offer, and explain why he thinks he will be an asset to your team.

Expect to answer questions about your present household income, savings accounts, pensions, and investments. Perhaps you have a list of accounts and retirement plans; perhaps you keep your money stashed in the bread box. Either way, the important thing is to fully disclose your current financial status so your advisor can make educated suggestions. He will then ask about your other team members, specifically tax accountants or tax attorneys, since a tax plan that saves you money and protects your assets will be an essential part of your portfolio. And of course, he will want to know about your present investment portfolio, whether you've worked with another financial advisor, and what you hope to gain from hiring a financial advisor now.

After assessing your current holdings, she'll probably ask about your retirement plans, including when you plan to retire, if funds will be needed for your parents' care, and your plans for taking care of your children. Keeping in mind your anticipated years in the work force, your advisor will ask you about the level of risk you are comfortable with, what kind of return you are expecting, and any big plans you would like to see come to fruition.

Having discussed where you are with your finances and where you'd like to go with your portfolio, she will offer suggestions about your circumstances. She should explain her ideas using plain language, and she should pause several times to make sure you are comfortable with the conversation and give you time to ask any follow-up questions.

While there is no scripted series of questions a financial advisor must ask, this is a good overview of what to expect. As this is your initial meeting, don't worry about having all the right answers. Concern yourself instead with your level of comfort throughout the appointment, and congratulate yourself on seeing through an important action step in your business plan.

Which financial advisors work best with beginner investors?

Whether you are a new investor or a seasoned pro, the qualities you look for in a financial advisor—integrity, enthusiasm, professionalism, education—will be the same. Everyone is looking for the right financial advisor, and everyone's needs are different. As a new investor, we encourage you to trust your instincts and concentrate on who can serve you best.

Large companies such as Charles Schwab or Fidelity are a good place to start. These reputable corporations have the means to cater to an inexperienced investor, with services that cover everything from tax returns to estate planning. This is a safe bet for novices who will need coaching and advice every step of the way, as such companies provide a reasonable level of security. Of course, security comes at a price, but having an accredited advisor who's affiliated with a high-profile organization may provide the level of comfort you require.

An alternative to these financial houses is seeking an independent financial advisor. We work with Mark Sessanta of Independent Planning Group and have found his approach to meet our needs. We were interested in collaborating with someone who could cater to our ambitious business plan. We found that working with an independent agent gave us more options, more flexibility, and a better sense of control. In addition, Mark is personable, professional, and a successful real-estate investor. After comparing individual planners and financial institutions, we chose what was best for us. We encourage you to do the same.

Finally, we want to caution against discount financial advisors, many of whom are found online. As a beginner investor, it is very easy to be penny-wise, pound-foolish. Not wanting to spend money on high commission fees, you may be tempted to trust Internet sites that offer discounted financial services. While we are advocates of using the Internet as a learning and networking tool and encourage you to take advantage of your financial advisor's company Web site, we recommend that you seek out a reputable, full-service financial advisor. Being new to real-estate investing, you are bound to have many questions and concerns. Especially during tense moments, you will probably be dissatisfied logging onto an impersonal site. You want your personal advisor to answer the phone. You'll want to talk to someone who knows your history, knows your goals, and can offer a reasonable solution. Your business is too important to trust to an anonymous link.

Successful finance gurus build a team that continuously works toward a common goal. Take your cues from those who have gone before you, and establish relationships that will develop in conjunction with your business.

How are financial advisors paid?

When interviewing your potential financial advisor, it's important to know how you will be billed and what you can expect for your money. The three most common payment structures are asset-based fees, hourly rate fees, and flat-fee rates. Additionally, there are commission fees earned for selling financial products, which you may or may not be responsible for paying. You should consider your assets, portfolio, and needs when deciding which commission structure will work best for you.

A fee based on assets is a payment structure based on all the assets you own or on the specific assets your advisor manages for you. It is an increasingly common billing structure among independent financial advisors. This is a good option for those who have more complex portfolios or a great deal of money, as your advisor will want to increase your net worth using the assets you have. Since you have resources to work with, he can offer programs that may increase your cash flow and save you money. Also, as an independent advisor is not locked into using specific products, he can cherry pick the options that will most appropriately complement your needs.

An hourly rate fee is exactly what it sounds like. As with a psychologist, lawyer, or other professional, you pay for the time you use. If you have limited resources and are just looking for a good once-over and occasional spot checks of your portfolio's progress, or if you have a solid financial background and are more interested in a sounding board than in a manager, this may be a good option. Keep in mind that these advisors for hire may not have the same level of commitment to your success as they will not reap the benefits of your developing portfolio. Nor will they lose money if their advice doesn't work out. For these reasons, you may want to conduct several interviews and call on these advisors' current clients to ensure that you are working with someone who has your best interests in mind.

A flat-fee rate features a one-time workup of your entire portfolio, with several suggestions for increasing your profitability and saving you money. This approach tends to be heavy on bells and whistles and light on substance. While a bound, color-coded report of your assets may look nice, we caution novices against this approach for two reasons. First, it is very expensive, costing upwards of a thousand dollars. Second, there is little consideration given to feedback or collaboration. You receive the professional's opinion, not his guidance.

As far as product commissions are concerned, ask how much money your advisor will make if you choose from among his recommended products. There is nothing wrong with an advisor recommending a product his financial house features, commonly seen with paper investments like stocks and bonds. However, keep in mind that these products are intended to make the company money, the selling agent money, and the investor money—in that order. You want the best product for your needs, not the featured product of the month.

Sometimes advisors may combine payment structures, making it difficult to determine exactly how much you will be paying. Ask questions regarding their compensation and insist that the agreed-upon structure be detailed in writing. Financial advisors are well worth the money when you are working with a professional who caters to your portfolio's needs.

Is there a common financial formula all advisors use?

All financial advisors should have a system for your money that will work under any condition in any economy. This means your financial business plan will work while you live and work, if you become disabled or die, or if the nation's economy falters or collapses. While this may seem like a lofty aspiration for your financial plan, it makes perfect sense. Your advisor should be skilled in considering how your portfolio will respond to sudden changes so that you do not have to worry that your quality of life will be jeopardized. When we speak of your life, we consider three phases.

1. **The accumulation stage.** This is the time when you build wealth. Your goal during this stage is to generate positive cash flow through assets. It is usually the time when you are working full time, raising a family, and acquiring creature comforts like a big house and nice cars.

2. **Retirement.** This is the time when you draw money off your accumulated assets, work less, if at all, and reap the benefits of your labor.

3. **Estate planning.** This involves any inheritances you wish to bestow and the transfer of assets to others, usually family or charities.

When working with your financial advisor, be sure you are planning for all three phases at the same time because one has everything to do with the other two.

In order for this three-stage plan to work, the focus of your financial strategy should be on wealth-building vehicles. For us, those vehicles are income properties. This is why it is imperative to understand your advisor's motivation and areas of expertise. Any formula your financial advisor recommends should include a plan of action to help ensure your financial health during each stage of your life, in all circumstances.

What are my options when choosing a mortgage broker?

As a real-estate investor, you are planning to devote a great deal of time, energy, and money to the housing market. Your mortgage consultant will be instrumental in making each transaction as smooth as possible. Because you are dedicated to this endeavor, you want to build a relationship with someone who has access to numerous investment programs, can speak knowledgeably about the pros and cons of each, and can share her own investing experience with you. While you may already be a homeowner, an investment property is an entirely different animal. Your team's mortgage consultant can help you navigate through these uncharted waters.

When choosing a consultant, you'll have to decide between going with a mortgage broker or a direct lender. For the most part, this decision will be based on your preference. Do you want to work with a smaller firm or have the backing of a large corporation? If a problem arises, do you want to know the owners by name, or are you more comfortable knowing there is a customer service department? Consider the following options.

A *direct lender* is usually a large company that originates, funds, and services the loan you choose from the organization's inventory. Their consultants are well trained in their products and reserve specific programs for their clients. An independent mortgage broker may not have access to these options. Direct lenders can service their clients' transactions nationwide, making this a relationship you can count on regardless of job transfers or when purchasing out-of-state properties. As they specialize in mortgages and have direct access to underwriters—the people who check documentation and approve loans—you may experience a faster turnaround time. They take customer service extremely seriously and adhere to a strict code of ethics. Direct lenders can be mortgage bankers who originate and service their loans then pass them on to such investors as Fannie Mae or Freddie Mac, or banks that offer a varied range of services, including mortgages.

A *mortgage broker* is a state-licensed individual paid to find you the mortgage that best fits your needs. A broker can service a client only in the state where she maintains licensing. As she is an independent agent, she has access to many different lenders and all their different programs. As she must package a loan for immediate sale, she will require more paperwork as she must meet stricter guidelines. She is the middle person who finds the right loan, processes your information to obtain the loan, then sells it to the chosen lender. There is a fee for finding you the mortgage, called a broker's fee. It may or may not include the cost of producing the mortgage, called an origination fee. In addition, a broker may charge whatever fee she sees fit for processing your loan, meaning you will most likely pay substantially higher closing costs.

We recommend using a direct lender over a mortgage broker for several reasons. First, while a broker may have access to many different companies and their varied loan programs, she may not know the particular details of each. If your needs are specific—and whose aren't?—you'll want someone who knows the ins and outs of your loan options.

Second, direct lenders are publicly traded companies with high profiles. Having a human resources department that wants to avoid negative press is a huge help if a problem arises. Finally, and most important for the new investor who is managing his or her money carefully, direct buying never costs more. Whether you choose to go with a direct lender or a mortgage broker, find a consultant who is experienced with investment properties, serves clients who are investors, and has a solid background in the mortgage industry.

Which lenders work best with beginner investors?

Whether you choose to work with an independent mortgage broker or a direct lender is a matter of preference. There are pros and cons to working with either, and as you interview the referrals you've acquired, you'll be able to determine which qualifications are most important to you. While deciding between independent representatives and corporate agents, you'll also be looking for a lender who can best serve a new investor. This profile can further help you choose the right team member.

Let's say that you have decided that working with a direct lender is the best choice for you. You appreciate their commitment to customer service and the company loyalty displayed by the employees. But as you still have multiple choices among different banks, it's time to narrow your requirements even more.

A beginner real-estate investor will probably not know all the mortgage programs available. You may assume that there are home loans and investor loans when in fact there are many different types of investment property loans, with various requirements for each. It is imperative that you work with a lender who does a majority of his business with investors. It is not enough to know which programs exist. Your consultant should have firsthand experience in matching the right program to the right investor, originating the loan, and managing its development. In other words, the consultant you choose to use is more important than the company.

While individual companies will have slightly different programs, we recommend concentrating on the individual, as his experience can influence your financial future. If you are working with someone who is wary of nontraditional loans or uncomfortable dealing with new scenarios, you may be encouraged to choose a program that best suits the advisor's comfort level, regardless of your portfolio's profile.

Which interview questions should I ask my mortgage consultant?

Ideally, you are looking for a lender for life, someone who will always give you the best deal, keep you informed of market trends, and alert you to refinancing opportunities. It is possible, and sometimes necessary, to change lenders down the line, but a well-structured interview can help you establish a strong, meaningful relationship with an ideal mortgage representative from the start.

First, assess your interviewee's experience and credentials.

- How long have you been a mortgage consultant?
- What is your area of expertise?
- How long have you been with this company?
- What made you choose this company?
- How many loans do you originate a year?

Next, ask about the types of programs this advisor favors and what real-estate activities his clients are involved in.

- What programs do you offer that no one else does?
- Which programs do you most often recommend?
- What types of programs are your clients in?
- Which programs have you chosen for your own investments?

Finally, ask about his business relationships and his professional style.

- How many clients have you done repeat business with?
- Which real-estate offices do you have relationships with?
- Which builders do you have relationships with?
- How often can I expect to talk to you?
- What is your preferred method of communication?
- Can you walk me through the loan process?
- Who should I contact if I have a loan question or problem?
- How will you service my loan after we close?

We recommend interviewing at least three mortgage representatives. As you can see from these questions, you want to focus on the lender's qualifications and abilities, not on the current interest rate. You want to work with someone who appreciates that you are looking for the best package, not just a low fee. While rates and fees are important, they are not the only criteria by which you should commit to a lender. Investigate the names of the referrals you've been given, and look for the mortgage consultant who can best provide you with the service you need at a price you can manage.

Are there questions my potential mortgage consultant should ask?

A mortgage consultant will ask you a series of preliminary questions to get an idea of your finances. While he will need copies of your financial statements to process a loan, these questions can help him assess your real-estate goals, giving him a basis on which to make program suggestions. When answering, be as honest and accurate as possible. As we discussed in a previous question, having your own finance file to draw on can move this interview along nicely, providing you with a greater sense of confidence when discussing your options.

Your consultant will collect your personal information, including your social security number. This is necessary to run your credit. While you should have already gone through your credit history in an effort to remedy discrepancies and check accuracies, your consultant will pull your credit for himself and note your credit score. He will ask about your current employment, how long you have been at this job, and inquire about the dependability of your current income.

After this, your consultant will ask about your assets, including bank accounts, savings plans, and retirement plans. He'll want to know about your total monthly payment obligations, such as rent, alimony, or car payments. He'll ask if your obligations are met in a timely fashion. Next he'll ask if you have had bankruptcies or foreclosures in the past seven years. The answers will not turn your advisor off. They will merely help him determine which loans you will be eligible for and the amount of documentation they will require.

Finally, it will be time to talk about your real-estate goals. Your advisor will want to know which types of properties you are interested in purchasing, what you intend to use the property for, and how long you plan to keep it. This is a good time for him to bring up the benefits of property shopping with preapproval and prequalification letters. As these questions are used to assess your portfolio goals, he will most likely ask about the rest of your financial team, specifically your financial advisor and tax accountant. This information will help him get a feel for your intentions, timeline, and business plan.

There is no script that each mortgage representative is required to follow, but these are some of the questions you can anticipate having to answer. As you answer each, check to see how you are feeling. Is the consultant helping to put you at ease, or are you growing increasingly uncomfortable? Is he engaged in the conversation or merely running down a checklist? Does he take time to consider your answers, or do you feel rushed? Even though you are the person being interviewed, this is another opportunity to consider whether you have been paired with the right potential team member.

Will my credit be affected by consulting different mortgage consultants?

Many people neglect to shop around for different mortgage consultants, afraid that too many inquiries could have a negative effect on their credit score. Often this idea is the result of scare tactics used by unscrupulous consultants who want to prevent you from looking at the competition. There are several important reasons why you should compare consultants and should not fret over ruining your credit.

To begin with, you are not going to have two dozen advisors checking your credit. Having decided between a broker and a direct lender, weeding through your referrals and narrowing down your search through comprehensive interviews, you will probably be left with two or three potential advisors. With your permission, these lenders will run your credit. These inquiries are considered *soft hits* and have little, if any, bearing on your credit score. *Hard hits*, which do affect your credit, occur when collection agencies inquire about your credit status. Hard hits and soft hits are not the same thing.

The reason your credit score changes with hard hits is to protect creditors. Let's say a bank loans you $100,000 for a home, based on your credit score. Then you purchase two brand new cars. You have just changed your credit score because you now have hard hits, which lower your score. How will you afford the home mortgage and make payments on two brand new cars?

Having loan officers run your credit and suggest their ideal programs for you is safe, savvy, and highly recommended. If you follow through on this, you may have to supply a mortgage inquiry letter when you are applying for your chosen loan. Again, this is to protect your lender from fraud: for example, if someone were to apply for three separate loans with three different banks, gain approval for all three loans, then accept the money and disappear. The inquiry letter merely states that you were comparison shopping, not attempting to solicit multiple loans on the same property.

Bank sites will be stringent about their loan requirements and may provide you with a different number than the three major credit reporting agencies (TransUnion, Experian, and Equifax). Since it is the bank that is at risk for lending you the money, it makes sense that its requirements and standards would be the most rigorous.

How do I choose the right real-estate agent?

Not all real-estate agents are Realtors. *Realtor* is a registered trademark, designating that an agent has successfully completed a licensing program and belongs to a monitored trade organization, the National Association of Realtors. A Realtor is obligated to abide by a regulated code of ethics, pays fees to keep his license current, and often participates in continuing education and accelerated accreditation programs. We strongly recommend working with someone who has made such a commitment to his profession.

Realtors have access to publicly restricted information on the Multiple Listing Service, which showcases available properties and details such things as tax information and the number of days the home has been on the market. It is a comprehensive tool that can expedite your search, saving you time and money. Once you have established the criteria that your new property should possess, your Realtor can check for new listings, preview potential properties, and later negotiate the asking price and facilitate completion of the transaction.

There will be no lack of available Realtors in your area, as it is a booming profession. But even with the registered trademark accompanying their name, not all Realtors are created equal. We suggest targeting reputable real-estate offices with a strong neighborhood presence, user-friendly Web site, and comprehensive marketing program. Check out their Web sites and see which types of homes they list. Look to see which additional tools are available for clients, such as school statistics, links to area attractions, and awards and accommodations earned by the staff. Does their inventory reflect a nice mix of residential properties, commercial properties, and land? Who are the most sought-after agents? This is an excellent way to familiarize yourself with a company before contacting their office.

Ask friends and neighbors who are investors which Realtors they recommend. Again, we stress the importance of working with professionals who are experienced in real-estate investing. Because you are purchasing an investment property, your time frame, wish list, and target area will be different than if you were looking for your next home. You want to work with someone who appreciates these differences and is interested in helping you find the right properties for your portfolio.

The right real-estate agent can make a world of difference in your investing career. Match your referrals with a well-established office of experienced Realtors and you'll be ready to begin interviewing prospective team members.

Which interview questions should I ask a real-estate agent?

As your money is your investment portfolio's lifeline, do not even consider a part-time agent. While being a weekend Realtor may provide a nice supplementary income for some or a way to get out of the house, we are only interested in working with professionals who are building a career in this field.

Everyone is a successful agent when the market is hot; we want you to find someone who has maintained her livelihood through different economies. The following questions will help you find that agent.

How long have you been a Realtor? You want to check her credentials, making sure she is licensed. You want to know how long she has been in the market. If your area has been booming, you want to see if she has a professional history or is merely a flash in the pan.

How many investment transactions have you done? While some may argue that buying real estate is the same regardless of the property's intention, we disagree. You are not merely looking for one great deal but are interested in building a business, so you want to work with someone who is committed to your being her client for life.

How many income properties do you own or have you owned in the past? If an agent does not own investment properties, the interview is over. Working with an agent who hasn't owned income properties makes as much sense as buying stocks from a broker who hasn't actually owned any stocks.

How will we communicate? You can decide on your preferred method of contact and how often you want to speak to your agent, then see if your styles match up. Be up front about your level of expectation. If you want to have all new neighborhood listings e-mailed to you once a week, say so. Different people want different things from their agents, so be clear about what you want.

What is your marketing plan? Although you are purchasing now and do not need marketing plans, you will want this information for when you are ready to sell. You want to know what the company offers as far as advertising. What promotional methods are used by this individual? All the successful agents we know have spent money on marketing. In addition, you want to work with someone whose ideas sound fresh and exciting.

What percentages of your listings are sold, and how long does it take? This question will give you insight into the agent's market awareness. You are checking to see if her properties are priced right. In a steady market, a home should sell in between six and eight months.

What was your most challenging transaction? Every agent has one: the client they couldn't please, the attorney review that took forever. An anecdote about a difficult deal and how this agent pulled it off is a nice chance to learn about her personality and work ethic.

These questions are a good way to gauge whether you are involved with someone who has the level of professionalism, experience, and energy you want.

Are there questions my potential Realtor should ask me?

A successful Realtor wants to work with a serious buyer. It is very frustrating to have a new investor walk into a business office with no plan but plenty of demands. To set yourself apart from the masses, draw on your bare-bones business plan when considering the following questions:

Have you been preapproved? Your answer, of course, will be "Yes, and here it is." You have already interviewed and chosen a mortgage representative who has used your credit history to offer you a preapproval in writing. A good Realtor wants to work with someone who knows his purchasing power. This saves everyone considerable time and energy.

What is your timetable? As this is an investment property, you should be more interested in making the right deal, not a fast deal. Refer to your business plan, reviewed with your financial advisor, and be clear about your intentions.

Which types of properties are you interested in looking at? Since you have discussed your buying power and loan options with your mortgage consultant, you are equipped to answer: commercial, multifamily, single family, or vacation property.

Do you plan to sell your own home? Perhaps you'll need to downsize to make this investment commitment, or you may be looking to live in one of your own multifamily units. A savvy Realtor is going to want to be your agent for life, available to sell you a new property and list your current home if and when the opportunity presents itself.

Which neighborhoods are you interested in looking at? As you know your comfort zone and are working to become an expert in your target area, you can answer this question, exhibiting your commitment to this endeavor. This will also help to establish the parameters within which your agent will be researching.

What is your availability? As you are not quitting your primary job and will have to make accommodations to see this venture through, be specific about when you are available. "Any time" is vague and untrue. Be committed to making the best use out of both your time and your agent's time.

Not only do you want to find an agent who meets your needs, you want that agent to be excited about working with you. Realtors are far more likely to go the extra mile when they know it is worth going for. Take your business seriously, and your Realtor can help you achieve even greater success.

How can I find a reliable Realtor out of state?

As you begin to focus more on your business you will approach vacations, travel, and family outings with an investor's eye. Instead of merely enjoying the view, you will be more prone to ask how much a view like that costs. While driving through new neighborhoods you will zero in on For Sale and For Rent signs. Taking inventory of new locations can provide unexpected opportunities if you know how to tap into them. This is why you may need an out-of-state Realtor.

Apply the same set of standards when looking for a real-estate agent no matter where you are. You want to work with a licensed Realtor who has personal and professional experience in cash-flow properties, has a compatible communication schedule, and has a full-time career in real estate. Ideally, you will not look for your out-of-state Realtor; your team Realtor will orchestrate that relationship. Many large real-estate companies have relocation departments to refer clients to Realtors in other states. Besides saving you time, this allows you to continue working in an environment you are already familiar with.

If you're interested in hiring an out-of-state Realtor to handle properties designed for tenants who are relocating, add questions like these when conducting your preliminary interviews:

Are you a Certified Relocation Professional? This designation is awarded to individuals who successfully pass a certifying exam issued by the Employee Relocation Council. This exam covers the Realtor's knowledge of things such as tax ramifications, corporate policies, and common family moving issues. While you may not be relocating, purchasing out-of-area properties will have many of the same stress producers as a long-distance move. If your Realtor does not have this designation, ask what kind of training or instruction she has received in working with out-of-state clients. You want to work with someone who can make these transactions as smooth as possible.

How many relocation transactions have you completed? Many people inquire about purchasing properties, but not everyone is a serious buyer. It is prudent, therefore, to ask about closed deals, as opposed to uncompleted relocation transactions.

Do you own any out-of-area properties? You may not always find someone who has purchased real estate long distance. If you do, consider it another reason this Realtor may be able to serve your needs.

In addition, consider these tips. Since you will not be familiar with the area's nuances, it is imperative that you work with a hometown Realtor. While you may see property signs sponsored by familiar corporate names, be sure to find out where these agents live and do business. If the closest corporate office is one hundred miles away, you may not receive the specialized service you require. If, on the other hand, there are several familiar real-estate offices, you should get a feel for them online, then contact the two or three that seem most promising and conduct your interview before making a choice.

Should I opt for a real-estate attorney?

Not all states require that you use a real-estate attorney. Your mortgage representative will be able to tell you if an attorney is necessary for closing or if a title specialist is appropriate. Regardless of the law, we recommend that you add this important individual to your team.

While most attorneys have a general knowledge about real-estate law, you want a specialist who dedicates at least half of his time to handling real estate.

There are numerous state laws and regulations pertaining to buying, selling, renting, leasing, and building real estate. You want to work with someone who is up-to-date on current legislation and can help you navigate through the dense verbiage of contracts. An experienced attorney with at least three to five years' experience is an ally who looks out for your best interests, warning you against that too-good-to-be-true opportunity.

Seek out potential attorneys using your personal and professional referrals, then hone in on their real-estate investment expertise. Since you want to build a relationship with your attorney, be sure he has a history of working with investors. There is a big difference between servicing one client for one transaction and one client for several transactions. Ask for the contact information for his current clients so that you can get a firsthand account of his business practices. You want to work with someone who is a calming voice of reason during a sometimes stressful event.

Finally, when you have narrowed your choices, compare attorney fees. You'll have to weigh your wants and needs against your financial capabilities. An attorney who specializes in real estate, remains informed about the market, and conducts his business with integrity is not going to be cheap. Talk to your financial advisor about what you can afford, and be specific when asking your attorney what you can expect for your money.

Do I need a tax accountant?

Absolutely. If you are looking to save money and think that doing your own taxes is a good idea, please reconsider. As a new business owner, you are opening yourself up to a whole new area of taxes. Even if you understand the basics of taxes, which are complicated as it is, the laws are constantly shifting. You want to take full advantage of all the tax benefits, shelters, and deductions that are available. As someone new to the business, you just aren't going to have knowledge of what is available, and you could end up costing yourself a lot of money.

A tax accountant and an attorney work hand in hand on your team. There are often areas of overlap, and having two capable professionals who are working with each other to meet your goals is a critical part of your investing business's success. Your financial advisor will help you devise a process so that your portfolio makes you as much money as possible while costing you as little money as possible. The latter part of the equation is where your attorney comes into play.

Tax law is complicated. Real-estate tax law is very complicated. You need a knowledgeable advocate who can work with your attorney to set up the right type of ownership structure for your business and advise you on which paperwork needs to be filled out to maximize deductions and take advantage of tax breaks. Considering that you are a new business owner, you may be responsible for sending out the proper W-2 and 1099 forms to any independent contractors who work for you. Your accountant can help ensure you are staying on top of your paperwork and can help you understand your own financial statements. When you start a financial venture having been set up for success, you will have a much easier time than if you have to backtrack and make repairs due to neglect or ignorance.

Your tax accountant is a part of your team year round, not just during tax season. These experts are well versed in bookkeeping, audit preparation, and financial planning. While fees will accumulate with each additional service you use, it is good to know that someone is on your team whose skilled services can expand in conjunction with your investment portfolio. The more income properties you add to your name, the more money you risk losing if you do not have a full-time team member dedicated to protecting your asset accountability.

Are there tax accountants who specialize in investing?

Yes. When seeking out the referrals of your friends and colleagues, keep this following list of questions and answers handy, as you'll want someone who has experience with building a business in your field and is prepared to offer you a personalized structure for your goals.

Are you working with other new real-estate investors who are just beginning to build their property portfolios? As always, you want to know the level of experience and expertise this professional is going to offer. Ideally, your tax accountant has worked with clients from their start-up phase through the expansion of their business and can speak to you knowledgeably about what is on your horizon.

Will I always work directly with you? This is an important question when you are interviewing accountants affiliated with larger firms. You do not want to enter into a relationship where you are constantly being staffed out.

How should I organize my paperwork for you? As you are new to investing, your accountant should spell out for you exactly what to save and give you a system for organizing your materials. As everyone should be working on computers, an automated system that is easily shared between sender and recipient would be ideal.

What ideas do you have for my business? As a paying client, you should not have to constantly solicit advice from your accountant. You want to work with someone who comes to the table with fresh ideas and money-saving strategies.

How do you stay up to date on the changing tax laws? Many accountants from smaller firms now issue newsletters, and larger firms periodically host lectures to keep their clients informed of the tax changes. Look for evidence that your accountant is keeping abreast of the latest changes and has a system for keeping her clients in the loop.

A tax accountant who can help an investor move from nervous beginner to confident veteran will be a welcome addition to your team. Look for someone who caters to the needs of a novice and has the knowledge necessary to manage an old hand.

Do I need additional insurance policies to protect my new interests?

Your financial advisor will be instrumental in helping you to determine which insurance policies will best protect your assets. Of course, the most common protection is homeowner's insurance. While most mortgage lenders will only require that you carry enough insurance to match your outstanding mortgage, there is no minimum liability. Therefore, you should work with your financial advisor to determine the right amount of coverage.

Most homeowners are insured against fire, theft, and other natural catastrophes (although flood and earthquake insurance policies are almost always regarded as extras), and the policies cover the home and its contents. "Contents" are usually assumed to be about 10 percent of the home's worth. Since you are purchasing an income property, your insurance concerns will differ from that of primary homeowners. There are such policies as property damage insurance, protecting you if your building is destroyed by fire; public liability coverage, if someone is hurt on your property; and rent interruption insurance, which insures that you do not lose money from a rental property while you make necessary repairs caused by a covered catastrophe, such as a fire. Each of these policies has its own set of specific inclusions and exclusions and should be discussed with a knowledgeable insurance professional.

Generally speaking, the more assets and wealth you have, the more protection you will need. Since your property will be used by other people, you must protect yourself against claims from third parties. Unfortunately, we are living in a litigious society, so protection is not an indulgence, it is a necessity. You are using your precious time and money to develop a lucrative business. Take the necessary steps to protect its integrity so you can continue to focus on its prosperity.

How long should it take to assemble my team?

It will take as long as it takes. We're sorry we can't be more specific. When you think about what you are trying to accomplish—organizing the collaboration of several professionals who will work toward your real-estate investing goals—you should realize this is not an overnight process.

Even if you are able to save time by following through on every one of your referrals and signing on with these specialists, it will still take a few deals to solidify the relationship. You may find that the Realtor you thought was going to be fully accessible and high energy seems to be preoccupied with other commitments. It may be more difficult than anticipated to get your accountant on the phone. For reasons such as these, you may find yourself reinterviewing for team positions you thought had been filled.

As in any interview situation, prospects are going to put their best foot forward. Unfortunately, this sometimes means that you end up working with someone who oversells and underdelivers. While this can be discouraging, it is part of the growing pains of launching a new business venture. While we have given you strategies to limit disappointing hires, occasional dissatisfaction is hard to avoid. You cannot evaluate how your team is doing until they have actually done something. Then it will be time to take a look at how each player performed.

You may be surprised at the answers. Sometimes the person we think will take the team lead is the weaker link, while a less-hopeful colleague really makes a difference in getting things done. As a business owner, it is your responsibility to constantly monitor your team's efforts and results. While you cannot predict the future, you can weed out subpar performers and replace them with more appropriate choices.

The more experience you have, the more sure you will be of your own expectations. Right now you are making the best decisions you can with the resources you have. After one or two deals, you'll be more confident in your abilities and better able to serve yourself and your business. Assembling the team is only the first step. To manage a cohesive team takes time, energy, and experience.

Scenario: I really liked the Realtor who sold me my first home. Would this be a good person to work with on purchasing investment properties?

Let's take this scenario step by step. When you say "liked," what exactly do you mean? If your Realtor was a nice guy who is new to the real-estate profession and sold you a house in a booming market, that's great. But will his limited expertise transfer to your business plans? If, on the other hand, you worked with a seasoned professional who returned your calls, arrived promptly and energetically for your appointments, and navigated you through your first home-buying experience with kindness and competence, he may make a nice addition to your team. Having experience to draw on is always an added bonus when assembling your team. Refer to your home-buying experience as you look back over the suggested interview questions, and see if this agent could be a contender.

Your previous real-estate transaction was a primary residence and therefore reflected your personal taste. You were probably concerned about schools, commuting, or area attractions. Perhaps you had always wanted a wraparound porch or acreage to secure your privacy. Now that you are shopping for business, your needs have changed. You'll want to work with someone who appreciates those changes.

If your Realtor has experience working with investors, has investments himself, and can speak knowledgeably on the differences between being a primary homeowner and a cash-flow property owner, he may be someone you want to work with again. If this Realtor insists that he already knows what you like, be wary. Clearly communicate your current investment intentions and how they differ from your previous needs. If this Realtor doesn't seem to be paying attention, he may not be an ideal team player. There is a huge difference between buying for yourself and buying for your business.

Real estate is competitive, and good Realtors covet repeat clients. When a Realtor knows he has a serious buyer, he will be motivated to close another deal. Consider this Realtor a referral you are making to yourself, and follow through with the appropriate procedures.

I don't have time to interview dozens of different people. How can I find the best people in the shortest amount of time?

Instead of focusing on how much you can get done in the least amount of time, concentrate on how you can make the best use of your time. The difference in this type of thinking is subtle but important. We don't want to see you rush into anything, so the best course of action is to be as well prepared as possible. Make each step count so you can avoid backtracking.

Start by talking with a professional you already hold in high esteem. Ask this person for her recommendations on who can best serve your new business interests. Since you already have a business background with this person, she is already familiar with your preferred style and may know of someone whose own business practices would be complementary.

Make each initial interview as thorough as possible. Research your referrals online from the comfort and convenience of your own home. Is his Web page user friendly and informative? Is his company's philosophy posted? Are there customer comments posted? Get a feel for your referral before reaching out.

Have your bare-bones business plan in place, and be ready with your list of interview questions. There is nothing more frustrating than having no time to waste then realizing you are the one who is wasting time by being unprepared. Do not take shortcuts when writing out your business plan or assume that you'll just go with the flow on the phone. You will not be able to thoroughly assess your potential team player unless you can articulate exactly what you are looking for. When you are ready, clear time in your schedule and make your phone calls.

Take note of your initial contact attempt. Was the phone answered in a timely and polite manner? If you had to leave a message, was it returned promptly? Did you receive the referral's full attention on the phone or were you suspicious that he was simultaneously checking e-mail? A first impression can go a long way in helping you to form an educated opinion about your prospects. There is no denying that a new business venture takes time, but with solid planning you can avoid wasting time and reserve your most precious asset.

I now have all the right people in place. How hands-on do I need to be?

You need to be completely hands-on. Your money is going to work exactly as hard as you do. Having the best people in place is critical for your business's success, but it is not an excuse to take a backseat to your interests. Even the most committed colleagues are not going to take care of your financial portfolio in the way that you will. You are the driving force behind each deal and must always be sure to keep both of your hands on the wheel.

While having a Realtor who is actively helping you to look for your next property is imperative, you must educate yourself about housing market shifts, changing rental fees, and area business trade. Your parameters may change as you learn more about neighboring towns, and you'll want to keep your agent informed of your findings. Your attorney and accountant can walk you through the specifics of tax law and legal issues, but it is always a good idea to network with other investors who can share their experiences from the trenches. An educated client is a highly desirable client. It is your responsibility to live within your budget, be consciousness of your credit standing, and follow the guidelines of your financial plan. If you are not hands-on, if you are not actively managing your portfolio, you will not be successful.

Your real-estate investing business does not have to take over your life, but in the launch phase it will demand considerable amounts of your time. Your effort is an investment in your future. Use the people on your team to help get you to the next level, but don't expect anyone else to carry your weight for you.

Chapter Three Financing Your Investment

How do I begin the process of financing my investment?

Now that you have your bare-bones business plan completed, have compiled your financial paperwork, and are starting to assemble your team, it is time to move forward with the financing portion of your real-estate venture.

As we mentioned, your credit is going to affect the types of financing programs you are eligible for. The stronger your credit history, the less risk you are to the bank. But even with a solid credit score, an investment property purchase usually requires that you come up with a higher down payment than if you were buying a primary residence. You may also pay higher interest rates. Why the additional costs? Simply, an investment property purchase is a bigger risk to the bank. Lenders know that if you find yourself financially strained you are more likely to miss payments on a rental property than miss a mortgage payment on your primary residence.

Since obtaining investment funding already costs more, a solid credit footing is a necessity for investors. If you have fumbled your credit in the past, work with a reputable lender whose in-house credit rehabilitation staff can help you get back on track then continue the application process. If you have stellar credit and are prepared to make application, take time to consider the amount of cash reserves you want to have on hand before proceeding.

We recommend having a considerable cash cushion before purchasing your first property. Determine how much money it would take to maintain your current standard of living for the next six months. List your monthly expenses, including things such as mortgage payments, recurring bills, and everyday expenses. When you are beginning a new business deal, it is important to give yourself a financial pad to fall back on should the need arise. You don't want to find yourself with a primary mortgage payment, a vacant investment property, and an unexpected medical emergency all at the same time and realize you don't have the funds to meet your financial responsibilities. The added security of savings is important when you are about to make a significant financial purchase.

In addition to your six-month reserve for cost-of-living expenses, we recommend setting aside one to two months' rent for each property you intend to own. This way, if you find yourself with a vacancy or need to pay for unexpected repairs, you have a fund to tap into that will not affect your primary investment budget.

While it may seem like a daunting task to save these excess monies, this is a good indication of how financially ready you are. If you get into real-estate investing without any cash cushion, you are setting yourself up for disaster. Take time to secure your reserves before making an additional financial commitment.

What is a mortgage?

Mortgages are contracts between financial institutions that lend money and individuals or entities who borrow the money and pledge the property to be purchased as security if the loan isn't paid back under specific terms and within a specific time frame. The most common lending institutions are banks and mortgage companies. Mortgages make it possible for people to buy and live in homes without having to wait until they have the entire purchase price available. The buyer only need come up with some predetermined portion, or down payment, of the entire sale price, and the mortgage covers the rest. The amount needed for the down payment is based on a review of documentation that the borrower provides. This allows the bank to assess its risk position in the whole transaction. The bank determines the willingness of the borrower to repay the loan and prepares the mortgage repayment terms.

The lender charges interest. Typical loan repayments are principal plus interest, and payments are usually made on a monthly basis. Most mortgages are front-loaded with interest payments. This means that the monthly payment will be mostly interest in the beginning and very little principal. As the years progress the amount of interest in every payment decreases, and the amount of principal paid increases. For example, if you borrow $200,000 at a rate of 6.0 percent for a thirty-year period, your payment would be approximately $1,200 per month for 360 total payments. The principal and interest breakdown of the first payment would be $200 principal and $1,000 interest. The second payment would be $200.11 principal and $999.89 interest, and this would continue every month until approximately halfway through the eighteenth year when your payment would be $600 principal and $600 interest. After that, the majority of your payment would pay down the principal.

When trying to determine how much of your payment is actually going to pay down the principal on the loan, you can always review an amortization schedule from your lender. This schedule shows you the principal and interest breakdown of every payment. In addition, your lender will provide you with a truth in lending statement. This form lists the amount of the loan and the amount of the total interest payments so you know the total payback amount of the loan. If you prefer to reduce your total interest obligation, you may be interested in prepaying your mortgage, something we'll address a bit later. You will want to discuss the best loan programs for your portfolio intentions with your team mortgage consultant.

Why should I contact a mortgage representative before searching out properties?

We recommend that you contact a mortgage representative and obtain a preapproval letter before beginning to look at properties. This will protect your most precious assets: time and energy. Many potential real-estate investors neglect this advice, and the results can be detrimental.

While it is much more enjoyable to go house shopping than mortgage shopping, the latter should be done first. We know many buyers who insisted on looking at the area's inventory to "get a feel for what's out there" only to find that they had the means to shop for more expensive properties. Others are disheartened to find that their perfect property is out of their financial range.

Both scenarios waste time and energy. If you know that you cannot afford something over a certain price, you will insist on seeing inventory within your limits. However, if it turns out that you can afford more, you'll have to backtrack, recanvassing neighborhoods you already considered. If, on the other hand, you set the bar too high, you'll be disappointed that you have wasted so much time and may be let down when you see what you really can afford.

You will also have wasted your team Realtor's time. The successful Realtors we know will not even take clients out on the road until they have their client's up-to-date mortgage letter in hand. No Realtor worth her salt is going to waste weekends with a client who is guessing at his buying power. Since you are a serious real-estate investor who has taken the time to secure your financial footing, you want to be ready to make an offer when the time is right. A letter from your mortgage representative can act as a negotiating tool when the opportunity presents itself, especially if you face competition over a property. Your Realtor will be able to show that you have the buying power you say you do.

How do I apply for a mortgage?

When you apply for a mortgage you will be led through the origination process, the procedure by which your lending institution decides if you are a safe risk to the bank.

When a borrower makes application, she submits personal financial documents relating to her financial history to the underwriter. The underwriter verifies the documents and determines if additional paperwork is necessary. These additional submissions are referred to as *conditions*. Since it is the underwriter's responsibility to meet the institution's lending criteria, he must ensure that all conditions are met. Some banks offer "limited doc" or "no doc" loans, which require less paperwork, but a slightly higher interest rate may be assessed or a stronger credit background may be required.

While the process can seem long or tedious, it is necessary to ensure that both the borrower's and the bank's interests are protected. Once these additional documents are produced, submitted, and verified, the conditions are considered cleared, and the procedure can continue.

Your credit score will be used as a means of measuring your likelihood of repaying the loan. A higher score will most likely mean more favorable interest rates and more access to different types of loan programs. As lower scores suggest higher risk for the bank, you may have a higher interest rate or be required to come up with more money down to obtain the loan you need.

If you work with a direct lender, as we recommend, several professionals will work to move your loan from origination to approval. If bumps come up along the way, these people will contact you and help you make the necessary adjustments and meet the additional requirements. No one is guaranteed a loan, and no one is entitled to a mortgage. Remember, you are asking someone to lend you money. Becoming agitated because your lender, the one at risk, asks for proof that you are credit worthy is not good business. Provide the necessary documentation and any additional requirements in a timely and professional manner.

Obtaining a mortgage will be a key objective in your real-estate investing business. Work with your lender to make the process as smooth as possible.

What paperwork do I need to apply for a loan?

Now that you appreciate the necessity of reaching out to your mortgage representative, here is a list of items you are going to want to have on hand to expedite your application and help you obtain your preapproval in a timely manner.

- Full name, two-year address history, date of birth, and social security number of the mortgage applicants. If more than one person's credit will be used when applying for this mortgage, be sure to have the following information for both applicants. E-mail address, home and business phone numbers.
- Gross income amount, secondary income sources, current position, and employer's address. Don't underestimate the significance of a part-time job or supplemental income. Fully disclose all of your earning power including incoming alimony, child support, and social security and disability income. All can

be used to help you obtain a loan. You will need to verify two
years of employment and income.

- Asset information, including savings, checking, and 401(k)
  accounts, money markets, pensions, and annuities.
- Current expenses, including current mortgages or rents, credit-
  card balances, auto and personal loan payments, and child
  support, if applicable. Include any other financial obligations.

Having worked with your financial advisor, you may have a price range you are considering. Your mortgage consultant will help guide you from here. He will make recommendations about your estimated down payment and help determine how much money you will need to put down on your investment property purchase.

These last two points can be determined with your mortgage representative as he considers the information you are providing. Do not feel obligated to make up an answer. A lender is happy to help you figure out the answers to your questions.

It is not enough to merely tell your lender about this information; you will often need to provide documentation. As we previously discussed, the origination process is when all of these financial papers are collected, reviewed, and verified. Therefore, do not guess on these answers. Your lender trusts that you are providing accurate information during your conversation, and having to backtrack to fill in the right information will waste everyone's time and energy.

Throughout your application process, be sure to ask questions when they arise, request clarification when you need it, and be up front about any concerns you have. The more forthcoming you are during the mortgage process, the better you will be served.

What is a preferred lender?

A *preferred lender* is a mortgage representative, or its parent company, that has already established a solid reputation with referral sources such as builders, Realtors, attorneys, financial advisors, and homeowner associations. A preferred lender has a proven track record of customer service, unique program abilities that include reduced fees, and can often facilitate a smoother transaction. In your situation as a real-estate investor, you will most likely be encouraged to use your Realtor's preferred lender. While there is no legal obligation to do so, there are several benefits in going this route.

When a Realtor finds a mortgage representative who can make a deal happen efficiently and productively, the Realtor wants to work with that individual. After all, unless a deal closes, no one gets paid. When builders, Realtors, or homeowner associations recommend a lender, they are basing it on that representative's track record or on the company's overall commitment to customer satisfaction, loan programs, and financing options. Professionals who make a living in real estate want to do business with lenders who specialize in their particular niche, be it new construction, renovations, or commercial properties. Mortgage representatives who earn the title of preferred lender want to continue cultivating that relationship and will go above and beyond the call of duty to maintain this profitable relationship. For the real-estate investor, choosing a preferred lender can be a win-win situation. You will receive top service from your lender, and your lender will cater to your Realtor's needs.

Once banks establish themselves as preferred lenders, there can be even greater benefits. Full-service lenders, for instance, are interested in being your lender for life and offer additional benefits for using their branch. You may be privy to equity enhancement programs, biweekly payment scheduling at no additional costs, notification of free rate reductions and refinance opportunities, or rewards for making timely payments. You could receive incentive packages for having all of your financial needs, including home-equity loans, credit cards, and insurance, met by this one institution. You may also be able to take advantage of additional bank services, such as reduced fees or rates, when you open a savings or checking account in your local bank branch.

Despite all of these benefits, you must still find your representative a competent, compatible professional to work with. A preferred lender is perhaps the highest-tiered referral you can receive, especially when you consider how many mortgage representatives exist. We strongly suggest interviewing a preferred lender and finding out if this is the type of professional you'll want servicing your mortgage needs.

How can I most efficiently compare lenders?

Using your referrals, especially any recommendations for a preferred lender, will give you a starting point for conducting your search. You can further equip yourself for this decision by investigating the finances behind the representatives.

While we have encouraged you to find a compatible mortgage professional to work with, we also want to offer strategies for comparing mortgage programs. Since the goal of real-estate investing is to make money and enjoy financial security, do not underestimate the necessity of reading the fine print.

Familiarize yourself with a commonly used loan, like a thirty-year fixed mortgage. As this program is used by most lenders, it is a good source of comparison. Simply defined, a thirty-year fixed mortgage will have a fixed interest rate for the life of the loan, meaning your interest rate will not change for thirty years. Instead of trying to compare all the different programs each lender offers, focus on getting the numbers for this widely used program.

You may find that rates and fees may vary greatly among organizations. Ask about the loan's interest rate, points, and fees, like origination and closing costs. Until you are locked in, you cannot assume that these initial quotes will be valid at a different time, but you can keep track of each lender's offer and chart the comparisons, giving you a better idea of which company's program suits your financial needs. Don't be afraid to ask for the best deal possible and inquire about the means of assessing fees and costs. Remember, though, that this comparison is used as an overview to narrow your choices. When the time is right you'll have the opportunity to work with your mortgage representative to choose the best loan.

If after you have compared the loan programs and fees each lender has to offer you still prefer the personality and work ethic of a representative whose costs were slightly higher than the competition, contact this person and discuss your concerns. No one wants to lose business, especially when it is over a matter of a small amount of money, and many lenders will waive junk fees if you ask.

If you indicate to a lender that you're seriously considering that institution, chances are they'll give you additional incentives to borrow from them. This call back can get you the personality you want at the price you can afford.

Can I trust Web quotes and e-programs?

Web sites and online mortgage programs can be a good source for research, helping you learn about the direction the market is moving in and offering interesting and informative articles. But when it comes to up-to-the-minute accuracy, reliability, and customer service, you may be better off working with someone you can contact directly, such as a mortgage consultant, rather than a toll-free number.

E-programs cater to the masses. They are designed with the typical 5 to 20 percent down payment, owner-occupied property in mind. Their loans may require copious paperwork and can take up to ninety days to close. That's a problem when time is of the essence. While low interest-rate numbers may flash across the screen, always read the fine print. Closing costs, rates, fees, and points can all add to the total amount of the purchase. In addition, the information you are reading is only as accurate as the last time it was updated. What you are looking at may not reflect the most accurate quotes.

Most direct lenders have up-to-the-minute quotes available to best service their customers. They have access to a wide range of investor-friendly loan programs, and as we mentioned, you should work with an individual who specializes in this market niche. Direct lenders will have shorter closing times, enabling you to free up money and proceed with your next transaction. That's an important feature when pursuing investment deals in a competitive market.

As a new investor you are bound to have many questions and concerns during the process and are going to want a responsive customer service-oriented individual to address those needs. When it comes to sealing the deal, who will be able to navigate you through a difficult situation if something unexpected arises at the closing table? With a room full of anxious, expectant real-estate players, is this the time to trust an 800 number and a dot-com address?

Web programs may seem like a quick way to skip a few steps, avoid having to track down a referral, and circumvent the interview process, but the truly successful know there is no benefit in omitting necessary work. We want to help you build a team of finance professionals who will grow with your business. The level of commitment we are interested in cultivating will be less likely with a Web-based mortgage broker. While we encourage you to familiarize yourself with those sites and read up on your new market, we recommend that you establish a relationship directly with a reliable mortgage consultant to get the job done.

Is there a difference between preapproved and prequalified?

There is a huge difference between shopping with a preapproval letter and a prequalification letter. Having the right paperwork before beginning your property search can make a world of difference in your real-estate investing experience.

A prequalification letter is a simple courtesy letter from your mortgage lender. It lets you know approximately how much money you will be able to borrow from the bank based on what you have told your mortgage consultant. While this may seem helpful, it isn't really worth all that much since often credit and income have not yet been reviewed. Even if you've supplied all the information required, no one has yet verified it. Therefore, you have not met any origination requirements. Quite frankly, a prequal has about as much merit as a note from your mom explaining what a nice person you are. While it is a step in the right direction and comes complete with the lender's letterhead, it is not a sure thing. As a serious real-estate investor, you want to shop for properties with a reliable recommendation of your buying power in hand. For this reason, we recommend obtaining a preapproval letter.

A preapproval letter is a written agreement that your lender will let you borrow up to a certain amount of money, once certain conditions are met. This means that, based on the paperwork that has been collected and verified, you have met the basic requirements necessary to borrow the stated monies. Usually you cannot obtain an actual mortgage commitment before beginning your property search because there is no real estate on which to conduct a title search and appraisal, two necessary steps. Some mortgage companies will issue a full preapproval with the property to be determined, after obtaining a (usually) refundable fee. Check with your lender to see which preapproval options are available. Either way, having submitted the paperwork necessary to begin meeting requirements makes you a more serious buyer. Your preapproval letter is a commitment from the bank and is like shopping with cash.

Also, making a preapproval inquiry provides an excellent opportunity to see your mortgage consultant in his element. It is a great time to discuss new product developments, your overall buying power, and to discuss different possible scenarios that may come up. Since you are no longer speaking in hypothetical but in practical terms, you can better discuss the specifics of your projected investment timeline, including your immediate and long-term goals.

Take time to obtain a prequalification letter and relax in the knowledge that you are pursuing properties in the appropriately targeted range, as opposed to wasting potential time and energy concentrating in the wrong areas.

How do interest rates affect my cash-flow potential?

Interest is the cost of borrowing money. As we said earlier, a mortgage makes it possible for people to buy real-estate property without having to come up with the entire cost of the home in cash. But there is a fee for that privilege, and it is assessed as interest. Depending on the financial market, you may be paying a lot of money for that privilege if interest rates are high or be charged less if interest rates are low. Because these rates fluctuate on a daily basis, they are one of the more temperamental aspects of real-estate investing. Be sure to speak with your mortgage lender about locking in your interest rate when the time is right and inquire about the cost of this service. A lock-in freezes your interest rate for a predetermined amount of time, protecting you against sudden market changes. Working with a knowledgeable lender will help you determine when is the right time to lock, but once you lock, typically you cannot relock if rates drop suddenly. Some lenders will allow you to lock in for protection against an increasing rate and will offer a float-down option if rates decline. This typically has a fee associated with it, but it may be a good bet in a volatile market

As an investor, you want to generate the most positive cash flow from your property as possible. To capitalize on profit, you are going to be interested in finding a low interest rate. The higher your rate, the more it costs you to borrow money to own your property and the more profit you stand to forfeit. Consider an interest rate of 6 percent where your mortgage payment is $1,000 a month. You are charging $1,400 a month rent, therefore, pocketing $400 a month in profit. But if your rate were to climb to 7 percent, your payment would increase to $1,100 a month, leaving you with only $300 profit. Over the course of a year, you will have lost out on $1,200, a substantial figure. So of course, you want to work with your lender to find the best programs and best rates for your portfolio. This does not mean that you should wait for low rates until you buy, because savvy investors know there are opportunities to purchase in any market.

An investor knows that in the big scheme of things interest rates are only one factor in purchasing property. Instead of looking for the best interest rates, look for the best real-estate deal. Working with your lender, you can find ways to finance the right property using different programs. Keep in mind, too, that if you have to buy when rates are higher, you can always refinance once you build equity into the home and rates drop. While everyone wants to talk about rates, and it is an important conversation, it is not the only one.

How much money should I be prepared to put down?

There is no easy answer to this question because there are so many variables. While the generally accepted down-payment parameters for investment properties are between 0 to 20 percent, there are no hard and fast rules about what your requirements will be. Here are some of the reasons down-payment requirements fluctuate.

Different types of loans will have different down-payment requirements. As we've said, down payments can be anywhere from 0 to 20 percent or more of the sale price of the property. While some 0-percent-down loans may seem inviting, such programs often have fees or higher rates associated with them. You can expect to pay a higher rate if you choose to put less money down, due to the increased risk to the bank. Work with your lender to decipher all the costs and contingencies of using such programs.

Different types of properties also require different down payments. An investment property carries additional risk for the bank, as you are most likely to pay your primary mortgage before any other real estate should you run into financial hardship. Knowing this, banks want assurance on their investment, and that will be reflected in the required down payment. While several different kinds of loans are available to investors, the type of property you are buying and the intended use of the building has a lot to do with the terms of the purchase. Finally, your credit will affect the kinds of loans you qualify for. The stronger your credit score, the more likely you are to pay back the bank. With this track record comes financial privileges, such as lower down payments. As you can see, taking your credit seriously will benefit you throughout your investing career. If your credit history is subpar, work with your lender's credit rehabilitation team so you can take advantage of all the mortgage opportunities available.

How much cash should I have on hand?

At the beginning of this section we talked about the cash cushion you should have in reserve before beginning your property search. Our recommended three-to-six-month cushion is designed to keep you and your family living at the same standard of comfort if a hardship presents itself. Along the same lines, you should have money reserved for the actual purchase of your real estate. Some money will be paid out upon purchase, while other funds will remain available for incidentals.

You will need to cover the cost of your down payment, determined by your loan choice, property type, and credit score. This amount of money is required to purchase the property and is usually listed on the contract. You will also usually be required to pay closing costs. These fees can vary greatly among lenders, especially between direct lenders and mortgage brokers. At the beginning of your purchase process you will receive a good-faith estimate, which we will detail shortly. This will indicate the anticipated cost to close your transaction. While some homebuyers hope for, or count on, a seller's contribution to these costs, typical investment property contracts only allow for a 2 percent seller's contribution. You should be prepared to write a check at the closing table.

Lenders can also make their own separate list of requirements. For example, some lenders will want to see documentation that you have between two and six months' mortgage reserve to cover principal payments, interest rates, taxes, and insurance. This is added assurance that you have not begged, borrowed, or scraped together your last few dimes to make this deal happen but instead have a means of making payments. Since your intention is to rent the property at a rate that will cover the mortgage, this required bank reserve could end up being a fund for incidental real-estate needs, such as unexpected repairs or vacancies. While the bank may require the money, you are the one who ends up benefiting from such an account. The amount of cash you are required to have on hand will vary according to your lender's preferences and fee schedule, but it is prudent to plan for various financial requirements at the time of closing.

Are there specific loan programs that can save investors money?

Banks are concerned with protecting their interests. When they lend homebuyers money, they want to do so in a way that minimizes their liability. For this reason, lending institutions have designed loan programs for investors that service the client while safeguarding the financial organization. These loans are usually more expensive to carry and require greater amounts of documentation. But this does not mean that you are shut out of the property-buying market. There are options to keep your costs low.

One alternative is to seek out specialty lenders who have the means to take on a bigger risk. Subprime lenders are institutions that service individuals who have weaker credit scores or have limited financial resources on hand. Those with damaged credit may benefit from working with this group of lenders who cater to unique circumstances. These lenders may accept a smaller down payment in exchange for a higher interest rate. You can benefit from working with a well-established lending organization that has the means to help you get started.

The subprime market has changed a lot over the past year. The irresponsible lending and borrowing that became prevalent several years ago fortunately has passed. If making your purchase with a subprime lender, as with any lender, ask all the necessary questions to protect yourself against prepayment penalties, ARM adjustments, or caps. Your trusted mortgage partners can guide you into safe subprime loan programs that have many benefits to the investor with limited cash or credit profiles.

Another option is to fund your financing through the seller. Using an attorney to protect and assist both the buyer's and seller's interests, you can draw up a private note between the two parties. In this alternative means of financing, the seller actually becomes your bank, as you will be making your payments to him or her. Since this is a private note, the down payment and interest rate could be lower than if you went a more traditional route.

Finally, an excellent means of saving money while creating cash flow is to live in one of your rental units. The property is now owner occupied, and the mortgage is no longer considered an investment loan. As a result, the guidelines are more relaxed, meaning less documentation and increased loan options, because when you purchase this home you will now have a tenant who will help contribute to the mortgage monthly and lessen your obligation. This anticipated income coming into the property is income that the underwriter can use to help you qualify. Your lending status and capability to pay back a higher loan will also change as you can usually afford more home with this projected higher income. This is a great way for new investors to get into the market. In addition to these ideas, your mortgage team specialist may have several more suggestions for getting the most bang for your investment buck.

How risky are nontraditional approaches to investment financing?

Real-estate investing is only as risky as the investor. Just because something is new or different doesn't make it dangerous. Working with your mortgage consultant and financial advisor to determine your comfort level, both emotionally and economically, you can come up with several alternate approaches.

Banks are not in the business of owning real estate, so of course they are going to write loans in their favor to protect themselves. On paper, a thirty-year fixed mortgage is going to appear safer than a one-year adjustable rate mortgage (ARM) because there is less change with the traditional thirty-year mortgage. But just looking at the loans on paper does not take into account the needs of the consumer, especially if that consumer is looking to build a lucrative real-estate portfolio. For those investors who are interested in flipping a property in two years' time, a one-year or three-year ARM could actually be more beneficial. These short-term adjustable rate mortgages typically have attractive low interest rates as opposed to long-term, seven- or ten-year ARMs that have higher rates much nearer to thirty-year fixed loans. The benefit of the lower rate could lead to cash flow sooner or less carrying cost on the property and needs to be discussed on a case by case basis with the investor. Nontraditional approaches are many and varied. This is another reason you should work with an experienced mortgage representative who can walk you through the intricacies of each possible loan option.

Regardless of what each loan can do for you financially, check your personal comfort level. Ask yourself: Do I want the lowest monthly payment or the most consistent loan program or the greatest amount of principal reduction?

What you want will greatly influence the type of loan you should apply for. Consider, too, the goal of your mortgage. Are you looking to get in, renovate, and get out? Are you more interested in finding a steady-earning property in which you can build equity? Again, it is more than just looking at a few loans laid out on the table; you must consider what each loan has to offer you and your real-estate investing career. Before charging forward, take time to revisit conversations about your financial security concerns and emotional well-being, then find the loan program that best serves your goals.

How can I learn the language of lenders?

There are few things more frustrating than feeling like you are left out of the conversation, especially when it comes to discussions involving your money. Instead of faking your way through the conversation, you can find ways to better communicate with financial professionals so you can make more informed choices.

Remember, your lender originates mortgages for a living. He is a paid professional who must be an expert in his field to best service his clients. You do not need to know everything that he knows, but it would be wonderful to understand everything he is talking about. Instead of concentrating on becoming a mortgage expert so you can speak his language, concern yourself with working with a lender who speaks your language.

We have found that the more comfortable a professional is with his products and services, the better he will be able to communicate with you. Using metaphors, analogies, and personal anecdotes, a lender can lead you through the sometimes-complicated process of application, processing, and approval. Instead of the conversation being one-sided, your expert will draw you into the discussion, making certain that you are not just agreeing with what is being presented but that you are fully able to digest and decide on the best course of action. For instance, when we were having difficulty understanding a new plan of action our financial advisor was suggesting, he picked up on our hesitancy and drew a parallel between our portfolio and a game board. This simple shift in language helped us grasp a new concept.

On the other hand, those who are less certain of their business practices will stick with jargon. When clients ask for more detail or another explanation, these lenders are apt to merely repeat themselves instead of giving a fresh perspective. Frustrated, clients usually just nod in approval so they can move on and hope that things make better sense later on. Often, this does not happen. More beneficial than knowing the language of lenders is seeking out a mortgage lender who appreciates your financial comprehension level and speaks to you accordingly.

What kind of loan should I apply for?

As a real-estate investor new to the business, of course you are concerned about making the right choices. It would be very comforting to have someone tell you, "This is the program that will maximize your cash flow and limit your liability." However, there is no single right answer. You should consider several factors before applying for a particular program.

When trying to answer this question, you will most likely talk to the people who are closest to you and solicit their opinions. This is a good time to reiterate who is qualified to give investment advice. While your best friends may encourage you to stick with a traditional fixed-rate mortgage, they may not know the benefits an alternative loan program can offer property investors. Make sure that you are talking to trusted individuals who have experience in real-estate income properties.

Of course, the number-one person you want to discuss your mortgage options with is your lender. Since she has access to all the different types of loans you will qualify for, she is an invaluable source of information. Instead of asking your lender, "What loan should I take," ask, "What loan would you recommend an investor in my position take?" In essence, you are asking your mortgage consultant to draw on her own experience and narrow your options based on what she has seen work for other investors. This approach empowers your consultant to speak candidly and gives you the opportunity to hear the pros and cons of different programs.

It is most beneficial to lay all your plans out on the table before trying to determine which approach to take. While some may pressure you to decide on the type of loan you want before contacting a lender, this advice, while well intentioned, is often harmful. Since you have never done this before, how can you predict what will work? This is an excellent chance to rely on the experience of an expert.

The kind of loan you are going to apply for will be determined by your credit score, property type, intended use of the property, down payment, and time frame. It is a good idea to familiarize yourself with common types of mortgages, but do not feel pressured to make a decision until you have all the details necessary to do so.

What is a fixed-rate mortgage?

A *fixed-rate mortgage* is a traditional mortgage program. As you would suspect from its name, a fixed-rate mortgage fixes the interest rate for the life of the loan, meaning your monthly principal and interest payments stay the same. These loans are usually set for fifteen, twenty, and thirty years, although there have been instances of different terms.

There are several benefits to having a fixed-rate mortgage. For those homebuyers who plan to stay in their properties for a long time, a loan like this can make sense. You will appreciate knowing what your payments will be for the life of your loan and will not have to worry about any interest-rate changes that could result in expensive surprises. You may experience increases in your payments if your property taxes or insurance rates go up, but your repayment schedule toward the principal and interest will remain the same.

If you are buying real estate when interest rates are low, it could be a good time to lock in this rate with a fixed mortgage and take advantage of your good timing. If you are buying when rates are higher, it is always possible to refinance your loan once you build equity in your home and rates drop.

For those homebuyers who are living on a fixed income or do not expect an increase in their wages, being able to count on a consistent mortgage payment can be helpful. Owners of rental properties with a fixed-rate mortgage know rents will cover the mortgage because the mortgage payments will not change.

Since fixed-rate mortgages are geared toward homebuyers who plan on keeping their homes for a significant amount of time, be sure to discuss your investing plans with your mortgage consultant and financial advisor. If you are interested in purchasing a property that you will only hold for a short time, other loans may better suit your needs.

What is an ARM?

An *ARM* is an adjustable rate mortgage, also called a variable rate mortgage, whose interest rate changes periodically. The rate will be set for a predetermined time, then reset based on market conditions using a predetermined margin and index. The index used is typically the U.S. Treasury note (T-bills) and/or the London-based LIBOR index. For example, a one-year ARM is a thirty-year amortized mortgage. The interest rate is set for the first year. It will adjust every year for the remaining twenty-nine years on the anniversary date of the loan. The adjustment will go up or down based on the index and margin and usually follows market conditions.

There are many different types of ARMs. More common are 3/1, 5/1, 7/1, and 10/1 ARMs. These are intermediate ARMs, since the interest rates are fixed accordingly for three, five, seven, or ten years. The "1" signifies that there will be an annual adjustment after the original locked-in period. For example, a 7/1 ARM will be locked for the first seven years then adjust at the start of the eighth year and continue to adjust for the remaining twenty-three years of the loan. ARMs typically have lower rates than fixed-rate mortgages, and often these ARMs offer other options such as interest-only payments, which we will discuss later on.

These loans may sound intimidating because you cannot predict what the market will be at the time your mortgage rate is going to reset. But because you are essentially sharing in the risk with the bank, you benefit from better rates to start with. This can be a good opportunity for those investors who are looking to save money in the short term or who know they are only going to have this property for a short time, usually less than ten years.

Recently, because of a wave of foreclosures across the United States, ARMs have been receiving quite a bit of negative press, which can make potential real-estate investors wary of investigating such a program. While it is true that an adjustable rate mortgage will change, that does not mean it is inherently unsafe. We always recommend you work with an experienced lender who can fully explain the details of your program so there are no surprises. A nontraditional program such as this may be the right loan for your investing needs.

What is an option ARM?

An *option ARM* is a mortgage program that allows for several different types of mortgage repayment options throughout the loan's term. These loans, also called *exotic ARM loans* by the media, have been used in the most recent real-estate boom as a way of purchasing expensive properties with low monthly payments. For property investors, these loans offer several advantages.

A mortgagor (the borrower) can request a different repayment option as his needs change. The repayment plan's choices are interest only, principal and interest, or a minimum payment. The minimum-payment option is at a very low rate, in some cases 1 percent, and is usually based on a market index. These indexes are usually MTA (monthly treasury average), LIBOR (London interban offered rate), COSI (cost of saving index), or COFI (cost of funds index) with a margin added on. The loan can be amortized over a fifteen-to forty-year period with up to 100 percent financing depending on the borrower and property qualifications.

Option ARMs have risks associated with them. For instance, when the minimum payment is selected, the attractiveness of the starting rate or payment should be seriously considered. In most cases the 1 percent rate that keeps the payment manageable also has a drawback of negative amortization, meaning the payment is low, but if it does not cover the indexed rate the difference is added onto the principal amount of the loan. This results in the principal of the loan growing rather than reducing. For instance, if the payment is based on a 1 percent rate and the indexed rate is at 5 percent, the 4 percent difference is added onto the mortgage payoff. This is the biggest drawback of this type of loan.

On the flip side, borrowers are attracted to the benefits of an option ARM. If the property is located in a high-appreciation area, the impact of the negative amortization could be limited as the property value grows quicker than the negative amortization of the loan. This allows for more leveraging, as it allows for more monthly cash flow. For investors who are detailed managers of their financing or have irregular incomes, it can be a great way to take the monthly burden of a large payment off their mind since it allows for prepayment in large amounts in more prosperous times or during seasonal rentals. Homeowners may find this especially helpful if they receive salary bonuses or have commission incomes. The option ARM allows for a low payment in times when money is lean, but you can benefit from prepayment when income is greater. Discuss the pros and cons of this loan option with your mortgage consultant.

What is an interest-only loan?

Typical loans are paid back with principal and interest (PI) in the monthly payment. However, *interest-only* (I-only) loans require that the borrower only pay the minimum monthly interest and no principal. The interest payment is based on the outstanding balance of principal remaining on the mortgage and is recalculated monthly. Only when you pay more than the required minimum monthly interest will the money be applied to principal. This can sound like a bad idea at first, but this type of loan feature can greatly reduce the monthly obligation and allow the investor more monthly cash flow or profit. Likewise, when the properties have greater cash flow you can apply principal reductions.

I-only loans also have advantages that PI loans do not. For instance an I-only loan will reamortize when the loan is prepaid. This is another reason I-only loans are appealing. Prepayment of a PI loan reduces the principal, but the payment remains the same. For example, let's say you borrow $150,000. At current interest rates, the payment will be $974 PI per month. For an I-only loan it will be $843 per month. If you pay $10,000 toward your mortgage at one time, the monthly payment on a PI loan following that pay down would be $974. In an I-only loan the pay down would lower the payment the following month to $787 for the life of the loan or until the next time you pay principal. I-only loans reamortize every time you pay above the minimum. Such payments do not have to be in large amounts; they can be as little as $100 per month. Investors who like to prepay their mortgage or like to see the impact of their prepayment immediately usually benefit from the interest-only features.

Usually interest-only loans are a feature of ARMs, but many banks offer fixed-rate interest-only loans. For example, on a thirty-year fixed or 10/1 ARM, both loans would be interest-only for the first ten years. Both allow for monthly interest payments, and both reamortize when additional monthly principal is paid. Both loans in year eleven convert to twenty-year PI payment plans. However, the ARM rate will adjust in the remaining twenty years of the loan, while the fixed-rate mortgage will remain the same during the interest-only period and the PI period of the loan.

Going the interest-only route is currently a popular option for many borrowers. Since you are not required to pay principal, this frees up more of your money. This can be an important feature when you are launching a new business venture or concerned because your investment property may have vacancies and you want to keep cash on hand. You can use the extra money to develop other investments, allow for repairs or maintenance, or save for your next purchase. These lower payments can give you additional buying power, especially useful in higher-priced markets.

A nice feature of the interest-only loan is your ability to pay down capital when it is convenient for you. If you are self-employed and know there are some months that are more profitable than others, you can send in additional monthly mortgage payments during those months. This way, when you have the extra money, you use it toward your mortgage, and when you don't, you keep making the manageable interest payments. This can be a good loan for those who like to maximize control over their cash flow.

What is HUD?

The U.S. Department of Housing and Urban Development is commonly known as HUD. HUD's mission is to regulate the housing industry through preserving communities, expanding homeownership, and operating its offices with integrity and accountability. It is the responsibility of HUD to supervise the Federal Housing Administration (FHA), the largest mortgage insurer in the world. HUD itself does not issue loans but rather directs borrowers to the FHA to see if they qualify for HUD housing and/or FHA loans.

Because HUD supervises the FHA, when a borrower defaults on his FHA mortgage and can no longer make payments, the lender will foreclose on the home and HUD will assume ownership. As HUD has no interest in owning real estate, the department will secure an appraisal on the home and offer it for sale at market value. HUD usually prefers owner-occupied offers. If no such offers are made, they will open up the sale to any interested buyers, including investors. These homes usually sell faster as they are prime investor opportunities. You can work with your team Realtor to put together an offer as long as he is registered with HUD (and most are). If the contract specifies it, HUD will pay the Realtor's commission fee, as he will be negotiating this contract as he would any other transaction.

While there are some nice opportunities to purchase a HUD-owned home, keep in mind that these are usually distressed properties. Do not skip steps during the process. Even though there is no homeowner with whom to negotiate repairs or credits, you must still treat this purchase as you would any other. As a professional real-estate investor you should never forgo a home inspection; to do so in a HUD home would be an even bigger mistake. These properties are sold as is; the agency does not make repairs or handle maintenance issues, and it does not issue home warranties. Therefore, it is critical that you know exactly what you are getting into and if you can handle it. A deal that will end up costing you a new roof, new electric system, and new plumbing when you haven't budgeted for it is no deal at all.

If you are interested in HUD properties, inquire as to your Realtor's experience with these transactions. We also suggest talking to your mortgage consultant about renovation and construction rehabilitation loans, as these programs may give you the means to repair a distressed property.

Can I qualify for an FHA loan?

The Federal Housing Administration has created loan programs intended to increase homeownership by making the purchase of real estate less expensive than with other mortgage programs. With reduced down-payment requirements, no financial reserves necessary, and regulated closing costs, many people are finding the real-estate door opening for them. There are, of course, guidelines for an FHA loan, but they tend to be more flexible, more forgiving when it comes to negative credit, and more attainable than other programs.

Some requirements for eligibility include two years' steady employment with consistent or increasing income, a new mortgage payment of no more than approximately 30 percent of your income, flexible credit requirements that can allow for an approval with limited or no credit history or one that has some derogatory or recent improvement to a previously credit-challenged history, and down-payment and closing costs that may be gifted. These loans are federally regulated and are designed to help low- to moderate-income buyers or credit-challenged buyers own a home with little money down.

Because HUD and FHA loans are intended to help people become homeowners, these programs are only available for owner-occupied properties. But do not be discouraged. For the real-estate purchaser who is interested in a multiunit property, this flexible financing program may be just what you need. In order to qualify for the loan, you must live in one of your units for at least a year, and the rental income from the other units will count toward your income and your qualification. This is a great way to make an investment purchase with manageable funding, build equity in your property, and, when you are ready to move out and rent your unit, add an investment property to your portfolio.

If you are interested in this approach, ask your lender what your state's FHA loan limit is before looking for properties. While there is no cap on the sale price of the home you can buy, there is a limit to how much money will be lent to you. Multiunit properties have higher loan limits, and these income-producing properties can be purchased with the FHA-required 3 percent minimum investment. FHA loans even allow for commercial mixed-use properties that have storefronts and apartments above. This is a great way to build your portfolio of homes before moving to investing in the single-family home of your dreams.

What is an FHA 203k loan?

As discussed earlier, the FHA provides financing for many buyers with limited money and with limited or damaged credit. The FHA typically requires the homes it finances be in a safe and habitable condition. If a property is not approvable, the repairs will have to be completed prior to closing. Often the seller is not willing to do the repairs; therefore, the FHA has a provision, called the 203k section, that allows it to bend its rules. Under the conditions of a 203k loan the home can be in distress, and the purchase can still close with the repairs to be completed afterward. A 203k loan allows the cost of the repairs to be escrowed at closing and included in the total loan amount. The loan amount is based on the property value as if the property were repaired before the closing even though it will not be repaired until a later date.

For example, you find a home that is selling for $120,000. Inspection of the property finds the roof needs to be repaired, the carpets and windows require replacing, and the house needs to be painted. The estimated cost is $20,000, but once the repairs are completed the appraiser tells you the property would be valued at $150,000. This looks like a great opportunity since the appraiser is telling you that you can build $10,000 in equity just by repairing the home. Under 203k guidelines, the FHA would be willing to lend you the money to cover the purchase and repairs because the home will have additional value added by the repairs. This program is ideal for fixer-upper listings and in cases where buyers have limited money for a down payment and little or no money for repairs. It is possible for a buyer to purchase with as little as 3 percent of the total acquisition cost, sale price, and renovations.

Besides the FHA, many lenders have similar renovation loans. Unlike the FHA, these can be used for the purchase of second homes and investment properties. These loan programs are designed just like the 203k loan and will allow for the property to be inspected up front and a list of repairs prepared. Money for the repairs will be escrowed and dispersed back to the homeowner or her contractor as the work is being done. The terms of the loan are based on the value of the home after repairs are completed.

These loans are great for updating existing housing stock and can allow equity to be built right into a property by rehabilitating it as you purchase it. These types of loans are usually limited to specialized lenders, and your mortgage consultant can guide you to an expert in this lending field.

How do I buy with no money down?

If you are looking for a no-money-down, 100 percent financed loan on an investment property, it is best to speak to your financing team. Comparing the monthly payments and cash-flow potential of the proposed property is imperative before even contemplating placing an offer. Generally speaking, it is difficult to find the properties in some areas that will allow for positive cash flow with no money down, and your team can help determine if this will be the case. Keep in mind that investment properties pose greater risks for banks. Applying for a no-money-down loan further exposes the lender to risk. The lender is often willing to take the risk on qualified buyers but will do so only after passing that risk onto the borrower via higher interest rates and fees. So be prepared. Typically you must have good credit scores and cash reserves to qualify for these loans.

Mortgage lenders will offer several options for the no-money-down loan investor. These may include some of the following:

- The 100 percent loan. This is one loan for the entire sale price. This will have a higher interest rate than the prevailing rate. In most cases the resulting mortgage payment will be so high that the owner cannot use the rents on units to turn a profit. This option also may or may not have private mortgage insurance (PMI). PMI is a requirement from most lenders in a case where you put less than 20 percent down. Typically loans with less than 20 percent down have higher default rates. The lender arranges for a PMI company to share the risk and charges you a monthly fee for this insurance. In the case of 100 percent financing, the PMI company helps take on this risk until the loan is paid down to the 80 percent mark. This could result in a deterrent to the overall purchase, as the PMI will add more to your monthly payment obligation.

- A 90/10 loan. This is really two loans, one for 90 percent of the purchase price and the other for the remaining 10 percent. The interest rates on both these loans typically are higher than the prevailing interest rate, and there is a good chance that it may involve PMI due to the fact that the primary loan is at 90 percent of value and you have less than 20 percent down. The mortgage payment again is usually too high for the investor to turn a profit.

- The 80/20 loan. These are two loans that result in 100 percent financing with no PMI. Since the primary loan is at 80 percent of the total sale price, the need for PMI is removed. This is a much better option. Both loans usually have higher interest rates than the prevailing rate. However, the interest rate for an 80/20 loan will be lower than a 90/10 or 100 percent loan. Structuring payment this way will allow for many investment properties to have some cash flow and thus warrant an offer for purchase. Again, since cash flow is the goal, a discussion with your lender will guide you to the best program.

- Leveraging. This uses the equity from one property to finance the purchase of another property. If your investment cash is not readily available, look at the equity in your primary owner-occupied home. If there is enough equity in your home to cover the purchase price of the investment property, you can draw on a home-equity line of credit. Using money from the equity line, you can pay the down payment the lender recommends. The bank through which you have the home-equity loan will then finance the remaining cost of the investment property. Thus the property is 100 percent financed with no money out of pocket.

Since you have money down on the investment property, the bank will offer you a lower rate on the loan. Since you're drawing the down payment from the equity loan, and it is on your primary home, the rate for that loan will also be lower. The net result is you will have created a beneficial position for cash flow by having the lowest rates and best programs available. The rents on the investment property will have a better chance to show profit.

The final consideration is to work in a seller contribution for closing costs when you place your offer. With most lenders the maximum is 2 percent of the sale price on an investment property purchase. With the addition of these monies, you may end up closing with absolutely nothing out of pocket.

Do these investor loans have hidden fees?

Fees aren't really "hidden," because all fees have to be disclosed on good-faith estimates and truth in lending statements from the bank in order to be charged and collected. We have seen many lenders claim to have mortgage programs with no hidden fees. In fact, if they're reputable, it should not be possible for them to have hidden fees. Are there unscrupulous exceptions to this rule who will hand you a last-minute bill and demand you pay a fee to close? Yes, unfortunately. More likely what people are referring to as hidden fees are changes in their overall qualification status that affects their costs.

If you have a credit-approved loan, your rate and fees hinge on your credit and other factors. If between your loan process and property closing your credit drops, your income changes, or some other change takes place, your fees or rates will reflect that. If you are assuming that the interest rate and subsequent monthly payments you discussed with your lender last month are still in effect today, you could be disappointed. Rates may have climbed along with your payments.

When it comes to locking in an interest rate, some borrowers prefer to wait it out, hoping for a better deal. Some borrowers do not know they can lock in a rate. Ask your lender when you can lock your rate. Most direct lenders will allow you to do this at application, regardless of your approval status. Rates change every day, so if your lender says you cannot lock your loan until you are approved a few days later, you have reason to be wary.

Reputable lenders will discuss the benefits of locking in and give you your locked rate in writing, usually on your commitment. Your commitment is a document issued by your lending institution that states you have been approved for a loan and outlines the loan's conditions, called stips, or stipulations. These are the conditions that must be met for you to close on your loan. They usually include clearing the title, having the property appraised, and gathering other paperwork.

Typically, a standard lock in is sixty days, long enough to meet all of the necessary conditions and get to closing. However, some lenders will lock much longer. If you are waiting on new construction, some lenders will offer a one-year lock at no additional fee. Other lenders will allow you to lock for two years with a fee, giving you time enough to finish the project. Make sure your rate lock will last long enough to get you to that closing date, otherwise you may be surprised. Your good-faith estimate and truth in lending states all of your fees and should be relatively accurate with a locked-in rate, thereby avoiding the hidden fees problem.

The more you know about your mortgage stipulations, the better prepared you will be to meet the costs of home buying. Working with a seasoned lending professional who clearly explains the process will go a long way toward giving you peace of mind.

What if my investment property doesn't appraise?

Typically, in order for your loan to be approved, your intended property must be appraised. An appraiser is a licensed individual who is paid by the buying party to evaluate the property's worth. He is an independent contractor who will give his opinion on the value of the home, based on its highest and best use.

The highest and best use means the most profitable and probable use for the property and takes into consideration if the intended use is legal, physically possible, and can fulfill a marketplace need. It is not necessarily the property's current use. The appraiser will also take into account the current fair market value, resale value, and anticipated improvement value, if applicable.

Before sellers determine how much to list their property for, they will have consulted with their real-estate agent and reviewed a current comparative market evaluation. This evaluation is a breakdown of similar homes in the area and what they have sold for. Sellers who seriously consider the price at which homes are selling will price their homes comparatively and have a much better chance of avoiding any appraisal issues. As a buyer, you can work proactively with your team Realtor and take a look at these sheets as well. This is another way to familiarize yourself with your market and avoid falling in love with a property that is overpriced.

An appraisal is usually mandated by your lending institution so that the bank can avoid overlending, and you can avoid overpaying. If the property does not appraise, meaning, the appraiser thinks your intended loan amount cannot be justified, do not panic. First, get a complete copy of the appraisal and check for any inaccuracies. Also look at the *comparables* (properties similar to the one you are looking at) that were used. Sometimes not all of the information from an area is readily available. Appraisers who are not familiar with your area may be unaware of additional comparables that could be included in their evaluation. If you find any discrepancies or see an area of opportunity, tell your Realtor, who can pass the information to the seller's Realtor so you can all work toward a solution. Remember, the seller wants to sell and should be open to fixing a problem that will get her to closing.

If the appraiser's report is accurate, speak with your loan officer about other options. You may need to come up with a larger down payment, pay PMI (private mortgage insurance), or negotiate a lower selling price. In some cases, you could choose to have a second appraisal. While no one wants to go to contract with a property that doesn't appraise, it happens. Your lender probably has experience dealing with similar problems and may be able to help you get the financing you need. If not, it was not the right deal, and you can take this learning experience and move on.

What is a good-faith estimate?

A good-faith estimate (GFE) must be issued by your lender within three days of your application for a loan. This information usually appears with your commitment letter and covers your loan terms and the anticipated costs of closing. While it is not an exact number, it should be a reliable estimate.

The loan terms section of your GFE should include:

- Property address
- Closing date
- Sale price
- Loan amount
- Type of loan you are applying for
- Interest rate
- Term of your loan
- Monthly payment, including principal, interest, taxes, home insurance, maintenance agreements, and private mortgage insurance

Remember, until you are locked in, your interest rate—and therefore your monthly payment—can change.

The GFE will explain loan origination charges, the cost to have this loan processed, and a charge or credit for any interest-rate discount points. *Points* are a percentage of the loan paid to secure a lower rate for the life of the loan. This fee is usually rolled into the closing cost and due when the loan closes. Other settlement costs that will be listed on the GFE include lender fees, attorney fees, state fees, title services, title insurance, taxes and homeowner's insurance escrow accounts, and prepaid interest. Your particular lender may have additional required services that you must pay for, but these must also be disclosed.

The reason that this document is called a good-faith estimate and not an exact payment document is that some charges can change. A locked rate will stay the same, but things such as taxes, insurance, and third-party required services can change. But the real frustration for buyers comes in the form of jargon. This is why it is so important to compare lenders.

A lender may advertise that she does not charge an origination fee, and you may think this is a good way to save money. Yet her processing fee, higher rates, and lock-in fee may actually make her services more expensive.

Fees can be manipulated to include numerous things that quickly add up. A good-faith estimate should list all fees, giving you the opportunity to see exactly where your money will be going so you can make the most informed decision possible.

Do I need private mortgage insurance (PMI)?

Private mortgage insurance can be optional. It is intended to protect the lender. Lenders like the security of knowing that a third-party insurance company is helping to share in the risk of possible default on loans that have limited down payments. There are no real benefits for the borrower; therefore, we favor loan programs that do not require PMI.

Banks used to require a 20 percent down payment on a home. However, many aspiring homeowners couldn't come up with this down payment because of the amount they were paying in rent. They could come up with a down payment of 5 percent. Analyzing the situation, banks determined that for most of these potential customers, the amount they were currently paying in rent was equal to the amount they would pay on a mortgage. The banks therefore relaxed their guidelines to allow borrowers to purchase with only a 5 percent down payment, but this opened the bank to greater risk. The bank shared this risk factor with PMI companies until the bank gained a 20 percent equity position (the position they would have had if the homeowners had made a 20 percent down payment).

PMI is a federally regulated loan insurance policy that can help lessen down-payment requirements, making it seem as though you have more buying power. PMI is typically required when a borrower intends to put less than 20 percent down on a loan. Instead of saving for years to come up with a huge down payment, PMI makes it possible to purchase a property with 5 to 10 percent down. For instance, if you were required to put 20 percent down and had saved $40,000, you would be able to purchase a property priced at $200,000. But with PMI, a good credit standing, and a reliable income source, you could use the same $40,000 to make a 10 percent down payment on a $400,000 property. But this privilege costs money.

Borrowers usually pay a monthly fee for the PMI, included in their mortgage, in addition to their principal and interest payments. The fee is paid to the lender, who transfers the payment to the insurance company. There are several ways to finance PMI:

- Annuals. The first year is paid for at closing, then the borrower makes monthly PMI payments.
- Monthly premiums. The borrower makes monthly payments beginning at closing, but it is not necessary to come up with the entire first year's payment at closing.
- Singles. A one-time premium usually financed through the mortgage by increasing your rate.

The monthly premium plan seems to be the route most borrowers are choosing. However, this is an added expense and one that can be avoided. Since we are most interested in protecting an investment and making the most out of every purchase, let's take a look at a program that makes lower down payments possible but does not require PMI.

What is an 80/20 loan?

Another option to discuss with your mortgage consultant is an 80/20 loan, which does not require the additional expense of private mortgage insurance. On an 80/20 loan, the borrower takes out two loans on one property, the first for 80 percent of the sale price, the second for the remaining 20 percent. This option is especially advantageous for those who have solid credit and excellent income but have not had the chance to accumulate a substantial amount of funds for a down payment.

Commonly known as a piggyback loan, the borrower's main loan is for 80 percent of the sale price, while the piggyback loan is for the remaining 20 percent and does not require a down payment. The 20 percent loan thus effectively becomes the down payment on the property. Other loan combinations along these lines include 80-15-5 loan, or an 80-10-10 loan, both of which have a main mortgage, a piggyback loan, and a down payment amount, in that order.

Usually, the piggyback loan has a higher interest rate than the first mortgage, but the combined payments usually still end up being less than they would if you had one loan and private mortgage insurance. Consider also that while you may deduct mortgage interest on your tax returns, in some cases you may not deduct private mortgage insurance.

Lenders can structure these loans in several different ways, making it possible for a real-estate investor to purchase a property with little or no money down, leaving only closing costs to worry about. Good credit and cash reserves are usually required for this type of loan. Discuss with your mortgage professional if a loan structure like this would be beneficial to your portfolio.

Can I use the equity in my primary residence to purchase an investment?

Home-equity lines of credit have become an increasingly popular means to finance investment ventures. A home-equity line of credit uses your home as collateral. Lenders will consider your credit standing, outstanding mortgage, and income, among other factors, to determine how much money you can borrow on a home-equity line. You will also need to have an appraisal done on your property to determine its current market value. Lenders may allow you to draw out up to 100 percent of your home's value, minus the amount of money owed on your current mortgage.

Since you are pursuing a home-equity line of credit to finance an investment property, be aware that some lenders require down-payment money. This money usually sits in an account for thirty to sixty days. This requirement, called *seasoning*, shows your responsibility in handling money. As time is always of the essence when investing, you can begin this process as you are forming your team. Work with your lender to follow rates and be ready when conditions become favorable. Even before you decide on a property, you can draw money out and let it mark time in a separate account. When you are ready to purchase, your money is already seasoned and available for immediate use.

Once the amount of money you can take out has been determined, be sure to ask some of the following questions:

- Will my account be accessed through credit cards or checks?
- Is there a limit to the amount of money I can access at one time?
- Is there a time limit by which I must use the money in this account?
- What about the repayment schedule?

As with any home loan, compare lenders, looking for the best rates and most advantageous programs. Discuss rate, points, prepayment penalties, and closing costs. Inquire as to whether you will have a fixed or variable interest rate, as this will affect your monthly payments. Be prepared to pay closing costs that are usually lower than your original mortgage. You will benefit from the set of disclosure standards outlined in the Truth in Lending Act, which requires a good-faith estimate of all costs. Speak with your mortgage consultant about the pros and cons of home-equity lines of credit and see if pursuing this line of financing today could best set you up for purchasing success when the time is right.

Can I purchase an investment property before I buy my own primary residence?

Sometimes you have the opportunity to purchase an investment property before you have bought your primary residence. Generally speaking, this is a manageable proposition, but as you will probably not have had any prior experience in buying real estate, check your motivations. Remember, if something seems to be too good to be true, it usually is. Make sure that this purchase fits in with your business plan, is supported by your team players, and makes sense on paper. Opportunities can appear at all different times, and your first real-estate transaction may very well be an investment project. By reviewing the recommendations and strategies offered in Chapter One, you can decide if this is the right move.

If you and your team think it is time to move forward, work with your mortgage professional to determine the type of financing this property will be eligible for. Since you are most likely renting and do not intend to live in this purchase, you and your lender must discuss the property's occupancy intentions. But just because you do not intend to live there full time, you can still qualify for more than investment programs. Your experienced mortgage consultant can help you determine the best use for your property and may be able to offer different financing suggestions.

For example, second-home financing is usually more favorable than investment financing. Since you plan on living there at least part time, there is less risk that you will default on the payments. Let's say you live in Manhattan and plan on buying a home on the Jersey Shore. It makes perfect sense that you would have a vacation home at the beach that you would rent out while you weren't using it. You would therefore meet the requirements of a second home without having to own a first home. You could benefit from more relaxed qualifying requirements and stand to profit from an income property.

On the other hand, if you live in Manhattan's Upper East Side and want to finance a property on the Upper West Side, you would be hard pressed to prove this second location was a second home. Credit scores, down payments, and rates not withstanding, a loan has to make sense. In this case, you would be purchasing a property as an investment and would need to meet the lender's more stringent requirements. With so many programs available, each with its own set of requirements, it makes sense to explore all the available options with your lender to determine the best course of action.

What does owner occupied *mean, and how will it affect my loan?*

Owner occupied means that you own and occupy a primary residence. Your intention is to live there for at least one year. When applying for a loan, your occupancy status will help determine which loan programs you are eligible for. Each lending institution will have its own set of criteria to qualify you for owner occupancy, but generally it is the property you live in most of the year and is usually a property in a state in which you file your tax returns as a permanent residence. Investment property purchases are nonowner-occupied properties. This means you are not living in the property, and you will be drawing rental income on the property.

When the lender is underwriting loans on properties that are investments, he is able to use the anticipated rents to help qualify you for your loan. In cases where you are buying a multifamily property as an owner-occupied property, the same underwriting criteria applies. If you are buying a two-family property to live in and the second unit will be rented for $1,000 a month, the lender can use a portion of that rent as income to help you qualify for the loan. These loans are considered owner occupied since you will be living there even though a portion of the property is nonowner occupied.

The other option besides owner occupied or an investment loan is a loan on a second/vacation home. Second-home loans are loans on homes you intend to occupy only part of the year. For example, you may live in Washington,

D.C., year round but have a home at Virginia Beach where you stay during the summer months or certain weeks during the year. The Virginia Beach property is a true second home but may draw a rental income when you are not there if you choose to rent it. It is still considered a second home, not an investment home, because it is occupied seasonally. An investment home is one the owner does not occupy at all. Qualification for a second-home loan may be a little harder, so it is best to preview your potential purchase with your lender.

When you are consulting your mortgage counselor, discuss the differences between owner-occupied homes, second/vacation homes, and investment properties. The lender needs this vital information to determine what program best fits your needs. It will also determine what information the underwriters and appraisers will request.

At the time of application and at the time of closing you will sign documents that state your intentions regarding the property. It is not advisable to sign a mortgage for a property as owner occupied when your intention is to use it as an investment.

Is it a good idea to buy and rent new construction?

Finding a new development to buy and rent can be a nice way to begin building your real-estate portfolio. If you live in or around an area where new homes are being built, investigate the development as soon as possible. Many new construction sites have on-site staff to help answer any questions, explain the features of each unit, and tell you the anticipated time to complete a project. Ask about starting prices, upgrades, delivery schedule, and lot choice, if applicable. Inquire whether the properties will have an association board or bylaws that could hinder or prohibit your renting the property. Be up-front with your intention to purchase as an investment, as your contracts will not be written as owner occupied.

When looking to invest in new construction, sooner is often better. Builders want to get qualified buyers into their properties and know that people can be hesitant to be the first buyers in a new location. Take advantage of your timing by purchasing a unit in the beginning of development to get the lowest "starting at" price, have your pick of the lots, and perhaps even take advantage of some favorably priced upgrades.

When negotiating your contract, ask that your property be built toward the end of development. By the time your unit is built, prices may have risen and you will have already built equity into your home. Again, it makes sense to complete a business plan, have your prequalification in good standing, and have your cash reserves in savings so when an early-bird opportunity such as this comes along you are ready.

Once the property is complete and you are ready to rent, you will be advertising a brand-new unit. Depending on the area and your renter pool, you may have chosen to install a washer and dryer and/or dishwasher. These time-saving conveniences, coupled with a sparkling unit, can bring in a handsome rent. Maintenance issues should be at a minimum, and if things do arise, you can count on your warranties to cover the cost. As your property has never been lived in, you will have little argument over a security deposit as any damages would be the fault of the only tenants.

We have bought new construction for investment purposes four times, and twice the tenants have approached us about purchasing the property. New construction can have many benefits if you are equipped for the opportunity and have a good sense of your market.

Is it a good idea to buy a fixer-upper?

When you think of making repairs, are you envisioning a fresh coat of paint and new window screens? Or are you talking about replacing the roof and adding a bathroom? Each investor has her own idea of a fixer-upper. Be clear about your own, then consider the following recommendations.

You are going to have a home inspection done on your property, but this does not mean the inspector will give you a detailed account of any and all problems, the cost to repair them, and the time involved in making such repairs. A home inspection is a qualified opinion about a property with recommendations for what issues deserve further investigation. If your home inspector recommends having the electrical system upgraded, hire a professional electrician to give a professional analysis of what needs to be done and how much it is going to cost.

If you have a home inspection done with the intention of making repairs yourself, check your own qualifications. While you and your brother-in-law may enjoy fixing minor projects around your home, rewiring an older property and bringing it up to code can become overwhelming. Since your intention is to be a landlord, you have a responsibility, both personally and professionally, to provide your tenants with safe living conditions. There is a huge difference between a weekend project and renovating a home. Be honest about your abilities and resources.

If you are interested in finding a fixer-upper, we recommend doing so only if you are partnered with professional contractors. Remember, buying investment properties is not your full-time job, at least not yet. You are building a team, financing a new venture, and still working your current career and spending time with friends and family. Add to those commitments a hefty renovation job and you could be setting yourself up for disaster. There are several loans that cater to rehabilitation projects, and we will discuss those shortly. But these programs work best with investors who know their limitations, have licensed professionals on their team, and appreciate what a commitment it is to make these projects profitable.

Should I look for properties that are in foreclosure?

Properties go into foreclosure when a homebuyer cannot pay his mortgage and the lender has taken ownership of the property. As banks are not interested in being real-estate owners, they sell the foreclosed properties at auction. Just as you would expect, the property goes to the highest bidder. Before you go looking for these diamonds in the rough, consider the following.

While it's true that foreclosures tend to sell for lower than market value, you could end up paying a great deal of money to make the property habitable. Owners who know they are being evicted have no vested interest in the home and can harm the house. At the very least, you'll have to plan on several cosmetic projects such as painting, carpeting, window replacement, and appliance upgrades. You could also be looking at structural issues, plumbing and electric neglect, and general mistreatment. Unfortunately, homeowners in foreclosure are most likely not going to let you into the property to look around, and if the property is vacant lenders may or may not grant you access, making it even harder to assess the situation. Expect to do a lot more work to find foreclosures also, as they are not advertised in the real-estate sections but in the legal sections of newspapers.

Legally speaking, foreclosures are no walk in the park. If the home is still occupied, you could end up having an eviction nightmare on your hands as you try to secure a cleared title. As these properties are sold as is, you may also be responsible for back taxes. All bids are final, so if you win there is no backing out. While laws vary from state to state, you are usually expected to have 10 percent of the selling price on hand and pay the balance within thirty days. There is no second-guessing. You must have access to cash or a substantial credit line to pursue these purchases.

If you still want to pursue foreclosures, we suggest a few dry runs first. Familiarize yourself with an area that has foreclosed properties. Speak to your Realtor about her experience in this niche market. Attend auctions to familiarize yourself with the proceedings, and meet seasoned foreclosure bidders who can offer you some pointers. Ask a lot of questions.

For a beginner real-estate investor, this option has too many variables and too many risks for us to recommend it. Instead of trying to obtain a property under market value, we suggest becoming an expert in your particular market and creating your own opportunities.

Can I take a renovation loan on an investment property?

Some lenders offer renovation loan programs for investment properties, and these little-known plans can be an excellent way to finance your fixer-upper. There are programs that allow a qualified buyer with a minimum down payment to finance the purchase price of the property plus the cost of the renovation. You could also finance the purchase and renovations together, with the loan amounts reflecting the postremodel value of the home. The lender distributes money to the renovation professional or homeowners in phases as work is completed. An inspection is usually made as phases are finished, then the bank releases funds in accord with a contract. The benefit of this approach is that you are using the bank's money to finance your project, not your own. Instead of filling up your Saturdays with construction projects, you can hire professionals to complete the job while benefiting from tax-deductible interest.

Most people do not know about this type of financing, so they approach a fixer-upper as if they had only their own financial resources to use. Having guesstimated how much work needs to be done, they buy the property then try to figure out how to pay for repairs. Unaware that a mortgage lender can help on an investment property, they turn to high-interest credit cards, personal loans, or drain a cash fund. Or they tap into several resources and still need to take out an equity line on their existing home. Most of these options cost money, have no tax benefits, and can come attached to risky, variable rates. A renovation loan, on the other hand, combines the purchase price of an existing property with cost of repairs. Instead of funding your project piecemeal, you have one tight, financially beneficial package.

Different loan programs are available based on the size of the renovation. Usually, homeowners have to wait to build equity into their homes before they can draw on this resource. But renovation loans consider the assumed value after the changes have been made. So you get credit for the equity the home will have once you've updated or replace the electric system, septic system, plumbing, and sheetrock. Working with your mortgage consultant, you can also find renovation loans that can be applied to complete knockdowns, adding an entire second floor, or bringing a 1940s house up to date.

Renovation loans are available on owner-occupied properties, second homes, and investment properties. Such programs can make projects that seemed unattainable a reality.

What is Section 8 housing?

Section 8 housing is a government rent-subsidy program that helps low-income families secure safe, decent housing. As a real-estate investor, you can determine if you would like to participate in this program as a landlord.

While entire properties used to be termed "project based," no new projects have been developed since the early 1980s. Today, tenants apply for rent vouchers based on their income. A tenant who qualifies for rent assistance can expect to pay about 30 percent of the rent out of pocket, with the remaining amount paid directly to the property owner by the local housing authority after it has been approved. The unit must be reasonably priced, reflecting a fair market value as determined by the Department of Housing and Urban Development (HUD), and the landlord must agree to accept the vouchers and maintain the unit to HUD's standards. The agreement is maintained as long as the tenant meets the financial criteria and has a contract with this landlord. The rent subsidy stops when the tenant moves out.

There are pros and cons to becoming a Section 8 landlord. On the positive side, you are guaranteed a portion of the rent each month. In slower markets with more vacancies, this can be a comfort. On the downside, you have someone renting your unit who cannot afford it without government help. If you need the security of knowing your tenant can manage the complete payment on his own, this may not be a good option for you.

If you are interested in becoming a Section 8 landlord, contact your local housing authority. Let them know that you welcome Section 8 renters, and mention this feature in your advertising. If you are contacted by interested parties, proceed with your interview and credit check as you would any other potential tenant. Despite any financial subsidies, you and your tenant must still see eye to eye on your lease. Do not use this program as a chance to skip steps. Treat this tenant responsibly, and make sure you have found a good match.

What if I default on my investment's mortgage?

We have mentioned several times that a bank assumes a great risk when lending you money for a home, especially for an investment property. To help protect their interests, they are very clear about the terms, conditions, and obligations of your mortgage and take careful measures to list these terms in your contract. If you default, there are serious consequences.

When you default, you breach the contract, meaning you violate an agreed-upon condition of your mortgage. This can happen if you stop making mortgage payments, neglect to have the appropriate amount of home insurance, or refuse to pay your property taxes, to name a few common violations. As you have agreed to use your house as collateral for the loan you have borrowed, it is your responsibility to maintain the property for the bank as you make your repayments. If you do not keep up your end of the bargain, the bank will take steps to protect itself.

Your lender will send you written notice of your breach of contract and recommend that you remedy the situation immediately to prevent further prosecution. If you do not, you will be sent a demand letter, which requires you to settle any discrepancies immediately. For example, it may demand you bring your loan payments up to date immediately. If you refuse, the bank will begin foreclosure proceedings, by which they will take possession of the property for sale at public auction. A foreclosure will remain part of your financial records for seven years and greatly influences the type of credit you are eligible for.

If you see that you are headed into trouble with your investment property, face the problem as soon as possible. Do not treat an investment property as a less serious matter because it is not your primary residence. The bank will not take nonpayment as a light matter. Reach out to your lender to discuss your payment options. Talk with your financial advisor about proactive solutions. Speak with your Realtor about the market and ask that a comparative market analysis be done on the property, as selling the unit may be your best option. If no mutually acceptable solution can be reached, contact your lawyer to help you prepare for a difficult time.

Do not go into real-estate investing thinking that defaulting on your loan is a benign option. Take the recommendations in this book seriously, work closely with your investment team, and become involved in deals that make sense.

Scenario: I am looking at investing in either a single-family or a multifamily property. Will different loans apply depending on my purchase?

Yes, some loan programs may only be available for certain types of properties and may vary from state to state. Working with an experienced mortgage consultant will help guide you in determining which one is best. Typically banks will provide residential mortgages for properties with four units or less and commercial or other types of loans on properties with five or more units. When discussing a single-family purchase versus a multifamily purchase, your lender will discuss what each bank requires and guide you through the tangled web of underwriting.

For instance, lenders may only require a 5 percent down payment on a single-family home and 10 to 20 percent on multiunit properties. This could be a big consideration when determining the amounts of money you have available to make your purchase. Some lenders will have portfolio loans that will allow for 5 percent down on all one- to four-unit properties, but in these cases, your credit must usually be excellent. Keep in mind that if there is more risk on the bank's side—meaning less money down—you will end up sharing in that risk via higher fees, higher rates, or both. Another hurdle to clear is if the property has commercial mixed usage, that is, residential and commercial together. This could further complicate things.

Often the size of the loan will dictate how much you need to put down on the property. For example, in order to qualify for a loan of $500,000, lender guidelines may require the maximum risk the bank will take is 80 percent or less of the property's value. This means that if the sale price was $620,000, you would have to put down $120,000, or 20 percent. This also means that if you only wanted to put $100,000 down on the same $620,000 purchase, you would not qualify for that loan program.

In determining your loan qualification and what is the most appropriate loan, consider the following questions:

What is the sale price of the property?

How much do you intend on placing down?

How many units does the property have?

What type of property is this?

What is the monthly rental income per unit?

What are the yearly taxes and home insurance?

In which state is the property located and how is it zoned?

Is the property attached or detached?

Is the property in need of repair?

Be prepared to answer most of these questions when you start narrowing down your property choice.

I have the opportunity to buy an investment property, but I'm planning on buying my own home. Can I do both, and is it a good idea?

The answer depends on the individual. The reason many people shy away from buying an investment property first is fear that they will not have enough money to purchase a primary residence when the time is right. But with proper financing and financial foresight, such an opportunity may be worthwhile.

Many lenders will give you 100 percent financing on your primary home at little or no additional increase in fee or rates. To take advantage of this option, you will have to first make sure that you meet the guidelines for zero-money-down loans. Typically, this means having strong credit, a reliable income, and money in the bank. If you meet the criteria, you can plan for two purchases simultaneously.

For instance, let's say you have $20,000 in the bank or accessible through such savings as a 401(k) program. You plan to use this as a down payment on your first home, but you have a team-endorsed investment deal that has come up first. You may think that you have to choose between the two, but you may have more options. Theoretically, you could finance your investment property and your owner-occupied property with the same $20,000. Working with your mortgage lender, take a look at the way the numbers add up.

If you were to pass on this investment opportunity, thinking that you need all of your $20,000 to purchase a future primary residence, you may end up with a loan that would cost you $120 a month less than financing 100 percent, based on current rates. But if you work with your lender to put zero money down and pay the "extra" $120 a month, you will not need to save that $20,000 in the bank. You could use it now to buy that investment property. To get an idea if this equation would work for you, consider your current rent payments. If you have been paying $1,500 a month in rent, you can afford a $1,500 mortgage payment. If saving your entire $20,000 for a future down payment would only reduce your loan payment to $1,380, you may want to consider other options with your lender, such as limited money down rather than 20 percent down, or other loan programs that can reduce the interest rate or overall payment with limited money out of pocket. This keeps your money free for an investment opportunity.

When trying to decide the best way to finance your investments, be sure to consider your own comfort level. Your Realtor, financial advisor, and mortgage consultant can help you prepare for different scenarios, offering their professional insights, but if this is not the right time for you to be buying an investment property, do not try to convince yourself that it is.

I've just come into some substantial money. Should I pay cash for my investment property or take out a mortgage?

Even if you have the cash, borrowing money from the bank may not be a bad idea. Mortgages have beneficial tax deductibility, and you should consult with your tax accountant and financial planner about this. These advantages can be especially helpful if you own a property that is producing enough income to warrant taxes on your profit. The mortgage can be a helpful tool to help offset these taxes. See Chapter Six for more on taxes, but suffice to say, the more benefits you can take advantage of, the greater part of your rental income you'll be able to retain.

Remember, once you turn your cash over for a consumable product, be it food, electronics, or a real-estate property, you have used up that money's potential. You have traded a liquid asset for a product, and all you have left is the product. On the other hand, if you finance a property, perhaps only tapping into your cash for a sizable down payment to help bring down your mortgage rate instead of paying the entire amount, you are retaining cash for other purposes. You could choose to buy another property, hire a property manager, or pad your savings for upcoming maintenance.

Having cash on hand also tends to be more comforting than spending all your savings on one venture. For a real-estate investor, unexpected costs always come up, be it an extended vacancy or an unanticipated repair. Having a cash cushion can help give you peace of mind.

If a property is especially cheap, you can make a stronger argument for paying cash. For example, a unit bought at $50,000 bringing in $500 a month rent has the potential to earn $6,000 over the course of a year, which is about a 12 percent return on your money, a substantial figure. We advise enlisting the services of a tax accountant, but usually a happy balance between your cash contribution and a favorable mortgage will be the best-case scenario for your money.

Chapter Four Acquiring Real Estate

How does buying an investment property differ from buying other real estate?

When most of us think about buying real estate, our first instinct is to imagine our ideal home, be it a residence on a cul-de-sac that our family can enjoy or a vacation spot near the beach or lake. We have probably mentally decorated the space and can talk lovingly about our plan for living there. But when we talk about investment properties, we need to worry less about our own preferences and concentrate more on the business of real estate.

Approach buying investment properties from a more analytical perspective. Of course, you want to find a comfortable, aesthetically pleasing space, but your list of priorities is going to shift. In short, you should remove the emotional element. Since we are used to looking at real estate with an eye toward our likes and dislikes, it will take some practice before you can concentrate on the business side of homeownership.

When looking for an income property, concentrate on its income potential. This means accurately calculating a unit's cash-flow potential. If you have a $1,500 a month mortgage and charge $1,800 a month rent, you will make a $300 profit. But can you get $1,800 a month? What are you offering tenants to justify this amount? Consider access to commuting highways, available appliances and utilities, parking, and heating and cooling units. While you may not need air conditioning to be comfortable, chances are tenants are going to look for such features. And if you don't offer it, someone else will. Prioritize your property's features from the point of view of a tenant to get a much better handle on what the home needs to make money.

Your home's value is based on appreciation, equity, and also your personal interests. It is a place to spend time with friends and family, create memories, and lay your head. Many primary residence sales are made with an emphasis on this type of emotional content. When shopping for your income property, remember that you do not have to love the unit—you have to be able to make money on it. A seasoned real-estate investor approaches every deal without emotion. Work toward making decisions based on income potential and manageability instead of personal preferences, and you'll be more likely to secure a profitable portfolio.

How much money should I spend on an investment property?

This will be determined with input from your mortgage lender and financial advisor. Getting prequalified will help you determine how much money you should be spending on your investment property. Having this number before you set out to look at available real estate will go a long way in saving you time and money.

Whenever you consider an investment opportunity, always do your research. Real estate is just like buying stocks, and you can lose or win big. Rely on your market data and input from the experts; crunch the numbers so you are certain your purchase with the intended money down will allow positive cash flow every month. Investing money you don't have is not advisable, and risking your hard-earned savings on hot tips is often foolish. Many experienced investors will not buy a property that loses money monthly, since that defeats the whole principle of buying the investment. However, there are some exceptions to the rule.

Working with your lender to determine the best types of loans for your purposes will be instrumental in setting search parameters. Many of the loans that investors favor use programs that require minimum down payments. Focusing on loans that require less up-front cash has given investors such as us additional buying power, broadening our prospective inventory. For a negligible amount, we can go from looking at $200,000 homes to looking at $300,000 homes. While the monthly rent may only vary slightly, despite this $100,000 difference, cash flow will probably work out to be about the same, and we will benefit greatly at the time of resale. While both of these homes will appreciate at about the same time, a 10 percent gain on a $200,000 unit is $20,000, while a 10 percent gain on $300,000 is $30,000. Financing that helps you get into a higher-priced house could have significant gains later on.

Which types of real-estate properties are available for investment purposes?

There are many types of properties available for real-estate investors, and while all share common elements, there are also some key differences. It is important to consider your own strengths and weaknesses, then share your thoughts with your mortgage consultant to best devise the most effective course of action. You want your first experience to be as positive as possible so that you stay with this new venture instead of becoming frustrated and quitting after one transaction.

The most popular real estate to purchase and rent as income properties are single-family homes, condos, townhouses, multifamily units, commercial properties, apartment complexes, and raw land. Deciding which properties to pursue is both a matter of personal preference and financing options. Your lender can walk you through the different types of loans available and outline the qualifying criteria necessary for each.

Other investment opportunities available are individual "ground up" new construction or general "tract" new construction, where preconstruction prices are often lower. In large tract where construction will happen in phases over a few years, there may be advantages to buying in phase one versus phase ten. The builder often discounts the first phase to stimulate interest, then slowly raises the prices as the work progresses. By the time the construction project is over, the value of the first phase usually increases to the selling point of the last phase, building instant equity for early birds. This also adds an instant rental pool for you. As people are waiting to move into the community, they may need short-term rentals while their house is being completed and you may ask for a rental premium. By the time it is all over you may be flipping the property for profit to latecomers who greatly desire to live in the community but have missed the boat since all the home sites have already been sold.

You can also purchase properties in need of rehabilitation, properties that have been foreclosed on or are bank owned, or properties that are not distressed but ideal for renovations. All of these scenarios may need work and foresight but can lead to greater profit later when sold.

How do I decide which type of investment property is best for me?

Having considered the types of financing available for different properties, you should speak with your mortgage lender and financial advisor about which loans would best suit your portfolio's needs. But in addition to the financing of your investment properties, you'll want to think about your preferences before deciding which types of properties to pursue.

What is my comfort zone? Most beginning investors will be most comfortable with what is familiar. This means sticking with rentals that are indigenous to your neighborhood. Having close proximity to your investment property can give you added security. You are close by to address any issues that come up, you know the area's demographic, and you have a firm handle on current market values. While purchasing a multiunit property may seem like the most profitable route for you to go, if the nearest available property is fifty miles away you may be better off sticking with what is offered in your town.

How will I manage my properties? It's important to develop tenant relationships, check in on your property, and keep a close account of your cash flow. However, many new investors can become nervous when it comes to picking up rents, addressing tenant issues, or feeling as if they are on call. Think about how you will strike a balance between being an active part of your developing portfolio and best servicing your tenants. If you are uncomfortable being in charge of multiple units, you may want to consider hiring a property manager. As the landlord, you must be honest about your abilities to care for your investments and make the necessary accommodations to do so.

What is my market doing? Since we want to become experts in our own immediate areas, it's important to know what is happening in our local real-estate market. Is Main Street undergoing revitalization with new businesses moving into town? Perhaps this would be a good time to pursue commercial financing and take advantage of this trend. Has a local college just expanded, increasing its enrollment? You may want to consider a multifamily unit to rent as off-campus housing. Having a good idea of your area's development can help you decide which direction to lean toward.

How much rent will this bring in? Again, knowing your market can help you determine the most profitable properties to pursue. A new corporate building means new employees looking for housing. A single-family unit geared toward this corporate expansion could be a target for success. If Main Street is littered with commercial buildings for rent, you may want to refrain from adding to the available inventory. The goal of real-estate investing is to make money. Look for properties that have the potential to do that for you.

While favorable loans will help to sway your opinion regarding the best investment opportunities available, don't underestimate the importance of choosing inventory that also makes good sense.

Which type of property tends to be more profitable: residential or commercial?

There are no hard and fast rules when it comes to this, but there are certainly substantial differences when we compare owning a residential property versus a commercial property. In general, commercial properties tend to cost more money then residential properties and usually involve loans that require larger down payments with higher interest payments. The documentation necessary to secure such loans is often extensive, and the approval process can be much more involved. It's likely that your commercial property will have to meet more extensive code requirements, such as mandatory fire escapes and handicap access. In many areas, commercial inventory is usually less abundant than residential, and the sale prices can be dramatically higher. If the economy takes a turn for the worse, vacancies can become a lengthy problem. While these points may seem discouraging, owning commercial properties has advantages.

Realtors who specialize in commercial transactions tend to take their business very seriously, as smaller inventory and longer closing processes makes it a niche that requires careful oversight. If you pursue commercial real estate, you will most likely work with an agent who prides herself on professionalism. While leases are much more complex, the landlord can make far more specific requirements and can expect more state help should there be a breach of contract. State laws tend to be more favorable toward commercial landlords than toward residential landlords, empowering them to lock out delinquent clients. Commercial leases are usually signed for years, instead of month to month or only one year, so you will have less tenant turnover. And, of course, commercial rents tend to be considerably higher than residential properties. So while the up-front costs and conditions may seem bothersome, the long-term benefits may be worth it.

For the beginning investor who does not have a large cash reserve, coming up with a more substantial down payment may be a challenge. Even if you do have the funds, consider how you can make your dollar stretch the farthest. For example, you could buy one commercial property with a 20 percent down payment or two residential properties with 10 percent down payments each. Instead of putting all of your money into one commercial project, you could search for a manageable residential property, cultivate your cash flow there, then parlay that into a second residential property while having a nice cash reserve. Commercial investing can be a lucrative business but one that you may be better off looking at after you've built your confidence and portfolio a bit.

What is a net, net, net lease, and could I benefit from it?

A *net, net, net lease* is most commonly used in commercial rentals. When units are rented in a strip mall, they usually come with a net, net, net lease. This unique lease has financial requirements separate from the rent. The tenant is responsible for paying monthly rent, of course, but he must also pay for a portion of the complex's insurance, a portion of the landlord's taxes, and a portion of the maintenance fees; hence the three nets. A unit's portion is determined by its individual square footage unless all units are comparable, in which case the portion is divided equally among the units. For instance, if there are ten equally sized units at 2,000 square feet a piece, each tenant will pay 10 percent of the net, net, net lease. This money is collected in addition to the tenant's rent. For the commercial landlord, this lease is good protection against rising costs and helps ensure that serious businesspeople will take occupancy of the units, as the tenants are sharing in the landlord's risk and expenses. Having successful businesspeople renting your commercial property helps keep the overall unit occupied, attractive, and lucrative for all and can cut down on the hassle of tenant turnover.

As a residential landlord, you can apply this same principle to your own properties. If your taxes go up, the tenant's net lease pertaining to taxes also increases. This is added insurance for the landlord, as you do not have to wait until the lease renewal to ask for additional money. You will have the benefit of screening more serious tenants, as this lease is more expensive than a standard rental agreement. However, in a market that is rich with available properties and low on prospective tenants, you will want to weigh a net, net, net lease against the chance of vacancy. If you ask for more, you need to provide more. Making your property more desirable than the competing units, with incentives and upgrades, can help ensure that you have a rented unit in any market, under the conditions that you deem most favorable. A net, net, net lease serves commercial landlords quite well and, if thoroughly evaluated, can have benefits for residential real-estate investors as well.

What does mixed use mean?

A mixed-use property is real estate that has more than one use. The most common example is a commercial/residential property where a commercial storefront occupies the first floor of the building and tenants reside upstairs in a residential section. The business and residency are in the same location, and one loan is written to cover both units. As both the business and residency are intended as income properties, the mortgage is most typically written as a commercial loan, but in some cases it can be a residential loan.

Many investors like the idea of mixed use because it provides two means of income, giving a temporary residential vacancy less impact. The strength of the business unit usually carries the rentals. It is important to scout out the area's potential, taking into account your rental pool and the need for commerce. Consider the following points:

Know your neighborhood. What needs does the neighborhood have that can be satisfied by this mixed-use property? When you are dealing strictly with residential income properties, you must know how much rent the area demands, who your potential tenants are, commuting accessibility, and conveniences and attractions. If you are concerned with commercial real estate, your focus shifts toward the area's demographic and whether the business can be sustained by the neighborhood residents and area consumers. With a mixed-use property, you need to have a firm grasp on both sets of questions, making your job more involved. Mixed use requires two separate leases as you will be landlording two separate projects simultaneously. Working with an experienced mortgage consultant and Realtor is critical for this type of undertaking to get off on the right foot.

Know what you are getting into. What is the current commercial lease? What is the current residential lease? Do you plan on renewing this business's lease or do you have another business lined up? Chances are you are inheriting someone else's leases, so you need to review the leases currently being used and determine if these are stipulations you can live with. Usually, you will not be able to alter current contracts until they expire. So if the rent will not cover your loan, do not assume that once the deal is done you can automatically raise your tenants' rents.

Know the long-term goals of the area. Is this neighborhood expanding the schools, roadways, and municipal building to compensate for the growth in population? Can a business and tenant be supported by this community? You always want to purchase in an area that is developing. While it is fortunate to be ahead of the curve, buying low and benefiting from a big industrial and residential boom, do not be so far ahead that you spend the first year with an expensive vacancy. As we encourage new investors to build an investment portfolio where they live, you should probably have a pretty good handle on what is going on in your neighborhood. But town hall will be able to tell you what big projects, if any, are on the horizon. You may also want to talk to other area business owners, this time not as a consumer but as a colleague.

Mixed-use properties have more complicated terms, but a well-established, manageable unit does not have to be out of reach.

What is a spec house?

A *spec* house is a property built on the speculation that someone will buy it. Suburban housing developments, for example, are usually constructed by professional builders and general contractors who obtain financing from the bank to begin the project. These major companies may build anywhere from 100 to 500 homes once they have purchased the necessary land to do so. They are responsible for obtaining all of the building permits, making sure each home meets all safety codes, and usually have a model home or trailer to meet and greet prospective buyers. Smaller builders may focus on a parcel of land and minor subdivisions, choosing to build anywhere from one to ten homes. They also apply for financing, obtain necessary municipal paperwork, and build homes with the intention of selling them for a profit.

There are several ways new real-estate investors can break into this market. The one that makes the most sense involves pairing your assets with an experienced, reputable builder. Perhaps you have land in your family, and you'd like to build a home and sell it. Maybe you live in an area where developable land has just been made available, and you see a nice opportunity to profit in your expanding community. Either way, you'll want to solicit the help of an experienced contractor. There is lengthy paperwork that must be filed, inspections that must be conducted, and complicated codes that must be met. Even an experienced builder can run into the occasional snag, but she knows what to expect. Trying to go it alone doesn't make good sense.

This is especially true since you are not tapping into a rental market but are looking to sell the home. Spec houses are not built with the intention of renting them. If a home does not sell, it can quickly become an expensive problem. While you will benefit from a quick and profitable return on your investment, a vacant home can wreak havoc on your finances and sanity. For these reasons, you want to build a solid home in a timely manner. Treating a spec house as a weekend project can quickly drain your finances. Building a new home can be a profitable way to invest in real estate, but success is more likely if you are part of the investment team.

Is land a good investment?

Buying raw, undeveloped land was once touted as a sure thing in real estate. Buy a piece of property now, at the current market value, hold onto it for a time, sell it, and reap the cash benefits. This is still a good tactic, based on the fundamental truth about land: They're not making any more of it. But there are several variables to consider.

As more and more people begin to realize what a precious commodity land is, there is increasing pressure to preserve what we have left. In our area, we have seen zoning laws go from three-acre zoning to ten-acre zoning. The investors who bought two acres of land, hoping to sell it to a builder twenty years from now at a huge profit, may have to rethink their strategy. While zoning changes usually have grandfather clauses, meaning the legislation that was on the books when you made your purchase will still be honored, you may still have a long, tedious road ahead of you. You may have to appear in front of the planning board several times to have your zoning requirements and variances resolved, and you may have to take action within three years of a legislative change. In some states, holding onto a parcel of land for twenty years and waiting for the price to rise might not be feasible.

Purchasing undeveloped land can still be a good investment as long as you approach it proactively. Keep in mind that your land will cost you taxes and maintenance and generate no income. If you follow the buy-and-hold method, make sure that the end result will be a profit, not a loss.

Instead of merely buying what you can, where you can, then doing nothing until you are ready to sell, work your land. Become an active member of your town's planning board so you can stay involved in upcoming changes. Join your area's open spaces committee to learn which lands are being preserved and which areas will remain developable. Maintain your land purchase as you would any other property in your portfolio, and you will be able to make better choices regarding your investment.

Can I buy a large piece of land with a house and subdivide some of the land?

You find a single-family home on a parcel of land that is fifteen acres in a town where the minimum zoning requires five acres to build. The cost of the home is $150,000, and you plan to subdivide the current parcel into three five-acre parcels. The two five-acre lots without homes would become buildable lots valued at $50,000. Often this is a great way to invest your money, although you may want to add a few more members onto your team.

Add an engineer to your list of team members as well as someone who is familiar with zoning requirements in your town. This situation differs from buying raw land. In that case you would have expenses every month without an income, which could be a burden. Here the home on this parcel can be rented and will help defray costs as you make your way through the zoning changes and requirements for the subdivision.

Once the property is subdivided, the next hurdle is the company that currently holds your mortgage. Since the mortgage is a contract, and the contract is on the fifteen acres and house, selling off the five-acre parcels will technically void the contract. You will have to notify the mortgage holder of your intention, and the company will let you know what is needed in order to keep the mortgage contract valid. Usually what happens is the mortgage company will require a partial release of that portion of the mortgage that relates to the acreage and renegotiate the loan terms. The mortgage company will assign a value to the acreage; in this case let's say it is $20,000.

This means that when you sell the subdivided lots for $50,000 each, the mortgage company will require when the new lot is deeded over to the new owner that your existing loan is paid down $20,000, leaving you with a net gain of $30,000. You invested $150,000 in a property, chopped off two lots that sold for $50,000 each, and were left with the original property and home valued at or near the original purchase price of $150,000. All the time you were planning this, your tenant was paying rent in the single-family home.

Should I buy a property in a vacation destination?

Many investors are drawn to the idea of purchasing in a vacation destination. The idea of owning beachfront property, a unit near a theme park, or a tropical island sanctuary sounds appealing, and it can be. The thing to keep in mind with vacation homes is the small print. There are many differences between owning a time share and a single-family unit. Knowing exactly what your rental intentions are will help you make better decisions.

If you opt for a vacation home near the lake, theme park, or the like, you will work with your mortgage representative who, depending on your qualifications, may suggest financing this as a second home if you plan to use the property part time, or an investment property if you intend to always rent the unit. Finding a home in a vacation destination may be a bit trickier, as you are not the only one who has had this idea. As a beginning investor, it is a good idea to broaden your horizons. Instead of beachfront property, you may want to consider a property that is within walking distance of the beach. If the beachfront homes are priced out of your range, but you are set on your property being waterfront, consider a bayside unit or a lake house. Your first investment vacation purchase does not have to be your last. It is more important to purchase a solid building within your budget than to stretch yourself to the max just to have the view you have always dreamed of. The view will still be there in a few years.

When looking outside familiar territory, ask your Realtor for a referral if possible. You want to work with a local agent who can familiarize you with the seasonal changes in renters, counsel you on what your property should offer, and help you decide the best way to furnish your unit so you can maximize sleeping accommodations. Many local Realtors will also help you find renters for a fee and can offer suggestions on security deposits, going rates, and incentive packages to keep your unit occupied in the off season.

Buying in a vacation destination is a lot like buying artwork: Buy what you like so you can enjoy it, and chances are others will enjoy it too.

Should I buy real estate in a town I just visited on vacation?

Once you get yourself in the mindset of real-estate investing, you'll never overlook a For Sale sign again. Everywhere you go, you'll find yourself thumbing through the local paper's classified ads and checking up on the area's prices. You'll never take a vacation from this business so to speak, so when you are traveling you may spot potential opportunities that pique your interest. If you are handing over your hard-earned income to vacation in this area, it's very likely others are also. Buying a second home to take advantage of tourist season is a popular investing idea, and one that can be quite profitable. But before you cut into your sightseeing tour to call a Realtor, keep the following things in mind:

- You are on vacation. You are probably more relaxed and more pampered than usual. Good weather, friendly service, and a break from the office can go a long way toward soothing your nerves and making you more open to enjoying your surroundings. You may think that purchasing a real-estate property here will help you capture this feeling and provide a long-term sense of relaxation. It is important to remember, however, that you're not buying a vacation; you're buying an investment property. You're turning your retreat into a job. Tenants will want to use your unit so they can take advantage of all the available amenities, amenities you must supply and maintain.

- You are most likely visiting this area during its high season. We have vacationed during all parts of the year and have fallen in love with the Old World Christmas charm of Newport, Rhode Island, during winter and basked in the sun at the shore in New Jersey when shops are open, restaurants are serving daily specials, and the nightlife and sightseeing tours make for great photo ops. It can be hard not to fall in love with a new town. But when you buy real estate, you become a part of the community year round. The "show" you are currently enjoying could come to a screeching halt when the seasons change. Will this area look as tempting then?

- Tourist towns are in the business of advertising. They want their place to look great so it will draw vacationers and entice visitors to return. But no town is a utopia. Whether it's corrupt local government, a high teacher turnover in the schools, or the sanitation department threatening to go on strike, all towns have problems, even vacation towns. Do not let your business judgment be clouded because you are having a great time.

Visiting new locations can be a good way to see what else is out there, and we will discuss in further detail what to do if you are serious about purchasing in unfamiliar territory. Remember to always make financial investment decisions with your head, not your heart.

What do I need to know about buying in unfamiliar territory?

If you decide that a new location could make a nice addition to your investment portfolio, place a call to your mortgage consultant and ask about updating your preapproval so that you are looking in the right price range from the start. Inquire about any specific financing procedures particular to this area. For example, some states require that you use an attorney at closing instead of a title company.

Know what to expect. Talk to your financial advisor about what this unplanned additional expense would do to your portfolio. Review your short- and long-term plans to make sure this project fits in with them.

The easiest way to do a little detective work is with the local papers. Tourist towns usually have various real-estate magazines available at convenience stores and rest stops. Look through them, and if your impression is a good one, reach out to your team Realtor back home. Let her know where you are and what has piqued your interest. Your Realtor can access information via the computer and let you know what real estate is selling and renting for. It is quite possible that she will have an affiliate office in the area and can call ahead to set up an appointment for you with a local Realtor. Your business will be taken much more seriously with a referral than if you walk in off the street. Even if this turns out not to be the right time to buy, you have made another professional connection.

When meeting with your new Realtor, make sure that you ask the same questions you would if you were looking at a home in your neighborhood: schools, community events, police and fire departments, local hospitals, commerce, and so on. Of course, you'll want to know about the town's population, what it swells to during tourist season, how long the season lasts, and what the effect of weather, economics, advertising, special events, or a combination of these things, is on tourism. Also inquire about real-estate practices and regulations in the area. How long is a property usually on the market? Are you in a flood zone? How strong is the rental pool? Since this is an unknown area, make sure you cover all of your bases.

As a new real-estate investor, we feel you're best off to begin with an area you know intimately. If, however, you feel drawn to another location, activate your team before making any financial moves. If you do not have the support of the professionals who have helped you design your portfolio plan, we recommend proceeding with caution.

What, if any, are the advantages of buying a time share?

If you buy into a time share, you must do your homework when it comes to selecting your portion of the property. Time shares have become a catchall phrase for a host of different vacation options. Work with a reputable, well-established firm that can answer your questions and provide you with everything in writing so you can make an informed decision.

Instead of being locked into certain days at certain locations, you now have more flexibility in where you vacation and for how long. Many time shares work on a point system or a color system based on investment amounts and location. The greater the investment and the more popular the season, the higher the points or the better color is allocated.

When shopping around at the different kinds of time-share programs available, keep in mind luxury never goes out of style. This is not the time to nickel and dime your investment. There are many vacation options for families, singles, and couples. What does your unit or location have that will bring people in and allow for trade? A good rule of thumb is to purchase at the level of comfort that you vacation at. How much do you vacation and plan on vacationing in the future? If you have children and want your unit to come equipped with a kitchen, separate bedrooms, and an indoor pool, keep those items in mind when deciding on your property location. If you wouldn't stay there, why would someone else?

The conditions under which you can rent your time to others is a matter to be discussed with your time share's association. There are usually other fees associated with time shares, such as monthly maintenance fees. The terms of your purchase are unique, as you are buying into a property that is deeded but you do not own the unit outright.

Speak to your mortgage representative about the best kind of financing for this venture. A time share often can be purchased with little money down, and leveraging a home-equity loan from your primary house for this purchase may be the ideal option. Your time-share representative may also suggest you speak with an in-house lending institution that is familiar with this unique property type. Finally, consult with your tax advisor and financial planner, as there may be tax benefits associated with your purchase as well. Your ownership is deeded to you and can be passed to your heirs or deeded or sold to others.

Can any type of property be rented?

You might assume that once you own something it is yours to do with as you please. But as many homeowners will attest to, putting an addition onto your house, erecting a backyard shed, or updating a home in a historical district is not just a private matter. Permits, municipal approval, and appropriately filed paperwork can all be required to make changes on your property. Similar issues can come up when you are looking to rent a unit.

Many townhouse developments and condominiums have rules prohibiting absentee landlords. Homeowner association bylaws are written to protect the integrity of the development and are often considered stronger than municipal laws. While renting a single-family home may be perfectly legal according to the town's laws, a private condo development can prohibit such a setup. If they do allow renters, they may limit the amount of time the unit can be occupied by someone other than the owners. A retirement community in Florida, for instance, may permit a unit to be rented out part time while the owners attend to their home up north, but these short-term arrangements are carefully monitored.

Gated communities have all of their rules and regulations available in a homeowners' association handbook, and you are well advised to read the information before making a purchase. Aside from rules involving renters, the handbook may also have rules concerning the selling of a property. Many developments prohibit displaying For Sale signs, making a for-sale-by-owner option very difficult to pursue. Associations can also dictate, among other things, what, if any, satellite dishes are permissible, whether you can drive a motorcycle through the property grounds, and if you are allowed to park a boat in your driveway.

As you choose to live in these carefully regulated communities, do not expect to do whatever you want without repercussions. Before deciding if a gated community such as a townhouse or condo development is right for you, read through the homeowners' manual and ask specific questions regarding your intentions with the property. We would hate to see any new investor buy a rental property with the intention of using it as an income property only to find out that such a scenario is not permissible. Make sure that you are buying in the right place for your portfolio.

Doesn't all real estate appreciate over time?

When property owners speak of certain real-estate appreciation, they are most likely referring to their primary residence, which they intend to live in for thirty-plus years, build equity in, pay off their mortgage, and cash out into a smaller home when they are ready to retire. While this generally works, it is important to know that in today's society most homeowners do not stay in the same house for more than seven years, so capitalizing on thirty-odd years of equity and appreciation may not be realistic. While real-estate profits are made in less time, to accurately assess your profit, consider both appreciation and inflation.

If you buy a property with the intention of holding onto it for a long time, it can appear that you have made a huge profit through appreciation. But if, for example, you bought a three-bedroom, two-and-a-half-bath property at $375,000 then sold it seven years later at $750,000, using that money to buy your next three-bedroom, two-and-a-half-bath home on the same block, you have not doubled your money. The price of your home has inflated, but the value of the home has not appreciated. In order to truly capitalize on the appreciation of your first home, you would have to move your money into a home where your dollar was worth more.

There are ways to increase the likelihood of selling your property at a profit. If you made renovations, upgraded the infrastructure, or added amenities, you will probably see a nice return on your investment. You do not want to depend on time and appreciation to afford you a real-estate profit. You want to begin generating a profit on your property as soon as you take possession of it through steady income while enjoying tax advantages. Having worked your property and drawn financial security all along, you can then look at appreciation as the icing on the cake. Real-estate investors who purchase income properties may have an eye toward appreciation, but they would be well advised to focus their energies on making their property profitable right now.

Are certain rental properties more lucrative than others?

The golden rule of real estate—location, location, location—is true here. It is also true that it costs money to make money. Here are some suggestions for targeting properties that could be a nice addition to your portfolio.

If you are looking to buy a property with a low sale price in hopes of saving money up front, you have to be certain of the areas you are targeting. If you buy a distressed property in a neglected area that shows no signs of revitalization, you could be opening yourself up to a lot of headaches. Buying a rundown unit, making no improvements, and concerning yourself with finding anyone whose rent can just cover the mortgage may not be a sound investment. For starters, you will most likely not enjoy your own project, which can result in further neglect. This will make it difficult to cultivate a sense of ownership among tenants who see from your own disinterest that this property is not to be respected. In areas where there is a predominance of absentee landlords, we usually find it takes longer for the values to rise since property upkeep is limited, and the housing stock sits or deteriorates.

Part of building a lucrative property portfolio is becoming a vested part of a community. You are better off targeting a neighborhood that is on the rise, with new businesses and new landlords making renovations to existing buildings and planning for future additions. While buying in this area could be marginally more expensive, you will most likely enjoy your project more, making you want to stick with investing. The longer you stay with a business, the better at it you'll become.

Once you target an area for solid investing opportunities, evaluate how much money you can afford to spend. Risk what you can lose, but remember that this is an investment and nothing is guaranteed. Calculate your monthly income, and from this number subtract all of your monthly living expenses. Take the remaining number and see if it is enough to cover a full month's mortgage on the investment home if it was completely vacant. If you don't have the ability to cover it from your income, analyze how much savings you have and how much of a burden the potential vacant home would be. Is this an acceptable risk? The guidance you receive from your professional counselors and the calculated risk you are willing to take based on your research ultimately determines if you should purchase the proposed property.

How can I calculate my income potential?

One of the goals of investing in real estate is to achieve a positive, consistent cash flow by means of rents. Your profit is the amount of money remaining after you pay all the necessary expenses associated with your property. These expenses are usually the mortgage payment, taxes, insurance, home association dues, water, sewer, and utility bills that are in your name, plus repairs, maintenance, lawn care, snow removal, Realtor fees, and other miscellaneous operating expenses such as a property manager's salary and travel expenses to inspect the property. In order to generate a positive cash flow, the rent must cover these expenses and still have funds remaining for you. When you consider how much money a real-estate property can cost to maintain, you can better understand why this type of investing takes patience and persistence.

When deciding which property to buy, keep in mind the likelihood that the unit will rent, what you can reasonably expect to charge for rent, and the amount of money it will take to maintain and upgrade the unit. Once you have narrowed your focus to a potentially profitable neighborhood with a strong client pool, calculate your income potential.

If purchasing an investment property from another investor, it's a good idea to request the seller's yearly operating costs. Since you are purchasing a business, the seller often is willing to disclose his previous year's profit and loss. If this information is not available, you can start by adding all of the anticipated expenses previously mentioned and create a business plan or profit-and-loss calculation. Take the number of units and the anticipated income or actual rents and total them for a one-year period. Assume your rental will be fully occupied 75 percent of the time (since it will take some time to find new tenants once the old ones move out).

Now compare your total expense column to your adjusted total income revenue column. If income exceeds expenses, this is a potentially sound investment opportunity. If expenses are more than income, recalculate assuming 100 percent occupancy. Does income now exceed expenses? If it does, now what?

Your instinct and research of the marketplace need to become part of your decision. If the rental pool is strong and chance of long vacancy is limited, it still may be a potential purchase if at full occupancy you show a profit. But if the property does not make money even with 100 percent occupancy, you should consult with your accountant and financial advisor to determine if you should purchase this property. The sometimes unseen bigger picture of a changing neighborhood or speculation on future gains in the next boom area is best discussed with the professionals who are most familiar with your financial capability to carry a losing investment and the potential gain from future profits.

How can I find out what other area properties are renting for?

As a smart businessperson, you will not have purchased a property without having first familiarized yourself with the rental market. Working with a local Realtor, you will already have an idea of what kinds of rents are being charged.

But since it takes time to close a property and you could be coming into a slow season, it is a good idea to take a look at what is currently happening in the marketplace.

Scan the paper for rentals and see which descriptions sound closest to your unit. You can call the owners to ask about amenities, payment schedules, and maintenance agreements. You may also want to ask how long the property has been vacant to get an idea of the current rental pool. You will find a wealth of information online and can usually get more information from a Web site than from a classified ad. Look for pictures in color. These will help you get a feel for the property and note its curb appeal. Be objective when comparing your unit against others, and keep your fact-finding mission localized. In some areas the towns to the north warrant much higher rents than the towns to the south (or vice versa). Make sure that you are looking at a similar demographic so you can make the best decision possible.

Talk to your Realtor. If she has seen the same properties sitting vacant for a number of months, now may not be the time to push the rental fee envelope. Work with your Realtor to determine what strategies you can implement to best portray your property. If there is a high demand for rentals, do not consider this easy money and look to cut corners. Instead, see what you can do to maximize your property's desirability, drawing in numerous potential tenants. The more desirable your unit, the better chance you'll have of finding the occupant who best accommodates your business plan. Taking advantage of a strong rental market does not mean skimping on amenities or charging excessive amounts of money for subpar conditions. It means setting yourself up for success so you can negotiate a profitable fee and reduce tenant turnover.

How much rent should I charge?

Having done the market research, you may think you have all the facts necessary to hang your For Rent sign in the window and begin making money. But there are a few more things to consider before coming up with a final number.

Let's say your residential property is very similar to the other available units, and right now nothing is moving. If vacant properties are renting at $1,500 a month, you can offer a $50 discount for turning in the rent one week early. If you are pressed for time and concerned about landscape maintenance and upkeep, consider lowering the rent $50 if the tenant takes responsibility for snow removal and lawn care. Knowing that you want to build these incentives into the rent, start with a number that gives you room to negotiate. Without having to show your hand, you can choose to advertise your unit with "tenant incentives." This may pique the interest of renters who would make a good match for your needs.

If you are a commercial investor, you may be surprised to hear how different rents can be, even in the same neighborhood. While it seems safe to assume that the going rate per square foot is comparable, this is not always the case. Personal relationships, tenant timing, and market changes can all affect the terms of a commercial lease, especially as commercial leases are written for longer periods of time. Your lease is a contract between you and your tenant. The terms of the contract can be negotiated to make the most amiable relationship possible. Before deciding on a monthly rate, consider who you want to be renting your unit. You know your neighborhood and your market. What type of business would fulfill a need? In a slower market you may have fewer tenants to choose from, but in any situation you should consider the likelihood that this tenant will be successful. Just as banks take on greater risks when financing commercial properties, commercial landlords also have unique risks. You do not want to sign a lease with someone who will not be able to pay his rent. Just as you will choose the residential tenant you feel most comfortable with, choosing the commercial tenant who helps you sleep at night makes good sense too.

There is more to consider than just numbers when determining what you should charge for rent. Balance your financial situation with your market sense, and ask for input from your investment team to make the best choices possible.

How do I find a qualified Realtor in my area?

As we talked about in Chapter Two, there will be quite a few Realtors to choose from. The strategies and interview questions in that section are designed to help you narrow down your list of potential team Realtors. Now that you have given greater consideration to the direction you want to go in and have discussed different options with your financial advisor and mortgage consultant, we can further strategize about connecting with the right Realtor.

Having balanced the financing options available with your comfort level, you have probably decided on the best neighborhood to target, one that has the commercial, residential, or mixed-use properties available for your needs. Now it's time to do some footwork (literally). Having decided on the area, you'll want to drive around and scope it out. Write down the names of the Realtor signs you see. Who has the greatest market share? Whose names do you see over and over again? You will most likely see local Realtor signs affiliated with local offices.

When looking for investment properties, we want to stress the importance of working with a local Realtor. Simply put, local sells local. For the real-estate investor, local also rents local. You want to work with a Realtor who has his ear to the ground and his finger on the pulse of the neighborhood. The people who work where they live will know when the school is going to expand (more homes being built), whether the commuter train line is going to be approved (more rental opportunities), or if taxes are on the rise (higher mortgage payments).

A strong local presence is only possible when an office is in the area. Just about every town in America has a Main Street or town center. Your Realtor's office should be in the middle of this action, an active member of the local chamber of commerce and an ally of the community. She should support the Little League baseball team or help fund new band instruments for the high school. Why are these qualifications so important? Because the difference between building a relationship with a local Realtor and a long-distance Realtor can be the difference between money in your pocket or not.

Use the suggestions in Chapter Two to narrow your search of local Realtors, then research their business online, talk to homeowners who have worked with them in the past, and call the offices to get a feel for the staff. Local agents can help keep you ahead of the game and become valued colleagues in your business venture.

What questions should I ask my Realtor about his expertise?

Add these questions to the interview recommendations outlined in Chapter Two.

Why have you chosen to focus on commercial/residential/multiuse properties? With all the different types of properties available, you want to inquire about this agent's motivation. The best answers will include a personal anecdote, which involves her own investment experience with this type of property. It would be most beneficial to work with someone who has had a positive experience dealing with the types of properties you are in the market for. The worst answer will sound like "I don't know; because it was there."

Since I am purchasing this property to rent it, how will you help me do that? Even if you try to rent your property on your own, it's good to know you have choices. Find out what marketing tools this agent uses and if he has a pool of renters available to him, meaning his office is well known for successfully matching tenants and homes. The more experience this Realtor has as a landlord, the more strategies he'll be able to offer for filling your vacancies.

What mistakes have you seen other real-estate investors make? You can benefit from other professionals' experiences, as well as your own. Though you'll be hard pressed to find a Realtor who hasn't had to work with someone who was impatient, unrealistic, or unprepared, this shouldn't turn into a gossip session either. A Realtor can offer insights on problem transactions or clients without naming names. Even if a deal was disappointing, each client's identity should be protected. You will want the same courtesy extended to you.

What deal are you most proud of? Answers will run the gamut from first experiences to tough deals that finally closed, but all should share a common thread of enthusiasm and excitement.

What would your ideal investment property be? Drawing on his experience, your Realtor can give you a mental sketch of what his idea of investing success looks like. Is this a community-minded individual who wants his success to work hand in hand with his neighbors, or is this investor hoping to have the town renamed after him once his monopoly of the community is complete? Matching business motivations will help you both see eye to eye down the line.

Combining broad-based and focused interview questions can help you choose a professional whose professional style and personality complement your own.

What questions should I ask when looking at properties?

Whether you are looking at your next potential home or working to add an investment property to your portfolio, take an active role when looking at real estate. When we are in new territory, we can sometimes clam up, hoping others ask the right questions and keep our best intentions in mind. While your Realtor can help keep you on track, having these questions at your fingertips will give you a point of reference while searching properties.

Since your time frame is more flexible than that of a person searching for a primary residence, you can afford to be discriminating. However, this does not mean you should wait until you find the perfect piece of real estate, as perfect does not exist. What it does mean is that you can look past the cosmetic features and focus on issues pertaining to structure and location. While you will have a thorough home inspection done by an accredited company, you can ask about the history of the building you are buying and the community where it resides. Some questions to help you get started:

- How old is the property?
- How old is the roof?
- Have there been renovations or upgrades to the home?
- Who built the home or did the upgrades?
- Has the house ever been treated for termites or other pest problems?
- Are there any zoning restrictions, easements, encroachments, or liens against the property?
- How old is the hot water heater and oil burner? Have they been regularly maintained?
- If applicable, what is the condition of the septic tank, and has it been properly maintained?
- Is the home well insulated? Are the windows insulated?
- Are there signs of water damage or mold (bubbling wallpaper, soft window frames, smell of mildew)?
- Is the electrical wiring up to code?
- Is the house efficiently heated and cooled?
- What are the conditions of the surrounding homes?
- Is it located near excessive noise such as railroads, airports, or heavily traveled roads?
- Is there convenient shopping and commuting?
- What is the crime rate?
- Are there local police and fire departments?
- Where are the fire hydrants?

Some of the questions and answers will be covered in the seller's disclosure form, and some will be available in the listing agreement. But we would recommend asking these questions if you tour the home with the sellers or their agent present. Many times you will get further insight into the property and hear things, good or bad, that are not available on the marketing material. If you and your agent are looking at the property alone, make sure you give him a copy of these questions, which you have every right to have answered in a timely fashion.

How does my wish list change since I'm not living there?

If you were looking to find a new residence for yourself or with your family, you would compose a set of criteria before looking at properties. You would decide the size of the home you need, the number of bedrooms and bathrooms desired, optimal acreage, ideal neighborhood, and local community services, including schools. But you would also have the feel of a home in your mind. Do you want a big bay window over the kitchen sink or a turret to display your Christmas tree? Have you always wanted a wraparound porch or a garden for summer vegetables? Because of the feelings involved, buying a residence is an emotional purchase. As an investor, you want to focus on the needs and not be overly swayed by the feelings.

Again, as this is not a rushed purchase, consider the marketplace. If now is not the right time to buy due to financial or personal encumbrances, do not try to talk yourself into a property. Many primary home shoppers are forced to do this when they are under the pressures of a schedule, but you have time to find the right real estate for your needs. You want your money to go as far as possible, so waiting and researching properties with profit potential does not mean you are dragging your feet. Do not become so excited by the idea of becoming a landlord that you lose sight of the criteria that will help make you a successful business owner.

When deciding which criteria is most important to you—number of units, location, age of the building, amenities—do not allow emotion to influence the mix. Of course you want the unit to be comfortable and clean. After all, if you wouldn't live there, why would someone else? But remember that you are not buying a property with the intention of finding a renter who thinks this unit is her dream home. You are buying a unit with the intention of fulfilling a tenant's need for a clean, comfortable, and temporary living space. Forgo ideas of grand spiral staircases or hand-laid stonework and look for a building with structural integrity in a nice location that can command a rent that will make you money. Not only is this not your dream home, it is not your tenant's dream home either. Do not worry about catering to an emotional wish list. You are buying a business opportunity. The most successful investors we know look at a property with the eye of a businessperson, not the heart of a resident.

How important is the neighborhood?

When you buy a property, you are not just investing in the real estate, you are investing in the community. As we have recommended you start with an area you know, you'll probably already have a good idea of what is happening in the neighborhood. But since you are purchasing as an investor, not a resident, you are going to want to further research the area from that viewpoint.

If you are planning to invest in a planned community or gated community, check with the homeowner's association regarding possible rental restrictions. If you favor an older historic district for its yesteryear charm, check with town hall and the historical society to see if there are limitations regarding upgrades and renovations. If you plan to purchase in a city, check in with city hall to see what, if any, major construction projects are on the horizon, such as a new major highway in your front yard.

Ideally, you want to tap into a neighborhood that is gaining in desirability. Working with your local Realtor, ask about your market. If there have been bidding wars or multiple offers on properties, an increase in local homeowners buying bigger and better properties in the neighborhood, or a surge in remodeling projects, you could be looking at a community that is on the rise. This could mean higher rents, fewer vacancies, and the opportunity to see a nice return on your investment.

If you are aware of a neighboring community but do not feel you have an insider's perspective, there are ways to nurture that relationship. Almost every town has a local paper that lists community events, school athletics, and town council meetings. Reading a few issues will give you an idea of what is deemed newsworthy by the community. Lunch at area restaurants, make a purchase at the local gift shop, and visit the library. Drive the back roads to see what is happening behind the scenes. The more time you spend acclimating yourself to the businesses and their patrons, the better you'll be able to assess the neighborhood.

Where you choose to build your investment business is not a decision to be taken lightly. Look at each potential community with a discriminating eye, and you'll have a much better chance of finding a neighborhood that can grow with your portfolio.

How important are the schools?

Some real-estate advisors lump this question in with the previous one, assuming that when we talk about neighborhoods school status is assumed. However, we want to make sure that you appreciate the importance of good schools, even if you don't plan to use them.

If you have a family or are planning to start one, chances are you'll want to purchase a home in a community that values its children's education. You may opt to visit the schools, attend a board of education meeting, or research school statistics, including grade point averages, athletics, and college-bound graduates. While there is no guarantee that the schools will stay the same, good or bad, for the next eighteen years, starting off in a district whose education style complements your own can be a comfort.

If your intention is to rent properties to tenants using a standard one-year lease, you may be tempted to forgo any school research. We recommend against this. First, potential renters could have school-age children. Second, even though you are buying a property with the intention of renting, you always want to keep an eye toward resale. School staff turnover and the intentions of the board of education cannot be predicted, but as you are looking into solid neighborhoods, you can safely bet that a school will grow with its community. Even if school is not on your radar, it could be very important to the next property owner.

To get an insider's feel for the schools, talk to the parents who use the system. Local moms' clubs are an often-overlooked avenue of investigation. These groups usually have a contact person listed in the local paper. You can reach out to these parents and get a firsthand account of what raising a family in the area is really like. These parents can also tell you about local shopping, traffic, parks, and community events. As a businessperson, you not only want to look at what needs you have but how your investment can best serve the next owner when you decide it's time to move on to your next project.

What is a seller's market?

A seller's market is exactly what it sounds like: a real-estate market that favors the seller's intentions. This situation happens when there are a limited amount of homes available. Low housing inventory cannot meet the demand, and prices are driven upward. A seller then has the luxury of waiting for the asking price she wants and setting a closing date that is most convenient for her. Just because prices are higher doesn't mean that buyers can wait it out. Buyers often cannot wait until the market shifts in their favor.

In this market, homeowners may put their house on the market to test the waters. It may have not been a planned move, but they are open to selling if the price is right. Since selling is not a necessity, these homeowners will leave little room for negotiation. After all, if the property doesn't sell, they haven't lost anything. For a buyer, it can be more challenging, though not entirely impossible, to find a good deal.

For a seller, putting your residence or investment property on the market at this time can be very profitable. For those looking to sell their own homes, this market is an ideal time to sell high and change locations. For example, cashing out in New York and moving to Maryland, where the market favors buyers, can get you more home for your dollar. People who are nearing retirement or had planned for a relocation in the future will often move up their plans to take advantage of such a scenario.

If you're a real-estate investor who is holding onto a property that is much desired, this could be nice chance to sell and reinvest your profit into multiple properties or to expand your portfolio to include a different type of property. Residential homes may be selling at a premium, but the price of a mixed-use property may still be manageable. This would be a good time to conference with your team players about your next investment move. Even if you decide not to sell, knowing your options and making an informed decision is always the preferred method of operation. As a property owner, a seller's market should, at the very least, prompt you to take a look at your financial situation and see if your portfolio could benefit from a sale.

What is a buyer's market?

In a buyer's market, the market is in a decline. There are plenty of houses for sale, and the high inventory has driven the prices down. A saturated market has a surplus far exceeding the demand. This puts potential buyers in the driving seat. Homeowners who are forced to sell in this market will have to make their homes stand out. They may invest money in cosmetic repairs or upgrades, hoping to capitalize on curb appeal, offer to pay Realtor incentives for bringing in a contract, or inconvenience themselves to suit a buyer's closing-date requirements.

In this kind of market, you are far more likely to find browsers who are just curious to see what is available at what price. They have no great motivation to actually buy. Since they have the upper hand, they may bring in a contract far below asking price or require a laundry list of repairs and upgrades be made just to see if the sellers will bite. For the investing businessperson, it is good to remember that more important than the time you get in the market is the time you spend in the market. Even if you have to sell in such a market, you should not assume it will be at a loss.

You can make money in any market. Investors who have built up equity in their properties, have good credit, and have a capable finance team in place will be able to strategize the best scenarios. This may be the time to look into adding another property to your portfolio or temporarily moving into a multifamily unit to provide yourself with a residence while still offsetting your mortgage costs with supplemental rental income. Upsides to this kind of market are financing programs. Sellers are more likely to accept offers with lower down payments or seller contributions for closing costs, making it possible for first-time homebuyers to take advantage of lower sale prices, even if their credit is not superior.

Real estate is a living, breathing market that has peaks and valleys. As a long-term investor, you can assess each market for what it's worth, talk to your team about your best plan of action, and make informed, profitable decisions.

Which market is more challenging to make money in?

Just as it is possible to make money in any market, it is also possible to lose money in any market. If you wait for the ideal circumstances and the ideal market, you'll never build a portfolio. Real-estate investing is a vehicle to meet your financial goals, and that is possible whether you are in a buyer's or seller's market. Those people who lose money in real estate are usually not looking at the big picture.

In a seller's market, home buyers with poor credit or low income can feel shut out of housing opportunities as the shoppers competing against them may present a more compelling financial package. These buyers would be well advised to seek the counsel of a reputable mortgage consultant whose in-house credit counseling and numerous loan programs could help level the playing field.

Investors who lose money in this market usually do so because they become greedy. Instead of being satisfied with a generous profit, they hold out, wanting to make a killing. When bragging rights take precedence over your portfolio plan, you can lose sight of your intentions; resist the counsel of your team, and you may miss out on a favorable market. Everyone wants to make money. But a savvy real-estate investor knows this is only one measure of investment success.

In a buyer's market, homeowners who have to sell because of a job transfer or other extenuating circumstances may be pressured to do so at a loss. Time constraints often put buyers and sellers at the mercy of the market, and a loss, or at the least a disappointing sale price, is sometimes unavoidable.

But for investors, a loss is usually a result of leaping before you look. Getting into the market at a favorable time does not ensure that you will know what to do when the tide turns. Without the input of experienced team members, investing colleagues, or personal education, investors often panic in this market and sell at a loss, convinced that something is better than nothing. These circumstances can be avoided if there is a plan in place.

There is no guarantee that you will make money in real-estate investing, and adverse market trends can be tricky. But an educated consumer who can keep her eye on the big picture can fare successfully in any circumstances.

Can I hold onto a property too long?

We have mentioned the strategy of buying real-estate property and waiting for it to increase in value over the years, then selling it at a profit. We covered the pros and cons of this strategy, citing zoning changes, community shifts, and location desirability as variables that should be considered. Instead of just hoping that one great choice will be enough on which to bank your future, we encouraged you to cultivate each investment opportunity so that you can maximize your profits along the way. This can mean selling your property in preparation for your next step.

Real-estate investing is a process, with each new opportunity built upon the last. When investors are new, they often become complacent, and, pleased with their profits, they resist moving on to the next project. Buying real estate, renting it, maintaining its value—all these things take considerable time, money, and effort. Selling a "sure thing" and putting yourself back into a vulnerable position can feel dangerous, but there are several things to consider.

- You only have to be a beginner once. After that, every transaction provides you more and more experience.
- Almost nothing is as frightening the second time. While it may feel like a do-or-die situation the first time around, you are more apt to have greater confidence in your abilities and the procedures than you did in the past.
- When it comes to investing, if you are not moving forward you are moving backward. Markets, communities, finances, and tenant pools all change. Hold on to a property as long as it is working, but don't despair when it is time to move on. As businesspeople, we must try to keep our emotions out of our transactions. Becoming overly attached to a unit that has finished serving its purpose is bad business.

Check in with your financial team to make sure that you have a balanced perspective on all your properties. Nostalgia is welcome in your own home, but it can cloud your judgment when investing. You wouldn't want to miss the next right opportunity because you were afraid of letting go of the last one.

Can I give up on a property too soon?

Not only do investors give up on properties too soon, they give up on real-estate investing too soon. The term *investment* implies a time commitment, yet many investors become aggravated and walk away from what could be a lucrative portfolio.

Usually when investors are quick to get out of real estate, it's because they were too quick to get into it. In recent years, media coverage has made the housing market seem like an easy way to make substantial profits with little effort or aggravation. As we have discussed several times before, making easy money is not a business plan. While it may be possible to get lucky once, or even twice, those who build strong financial portfolios do so by committing themselves to education, learning from their experiences, and looking for the right deals, not quick deals. Those who hope to cash in on a hot market will most likely find out that this approach lacks staying power.

Instead of holding your breath and waiting for the ideal time to get in and out of the real-estate market, spend your prepurchase time building your team, connections, and confidence. When you do become an active player, you'll have people to bounce your ideas off of and solicit feedback from. Discussing your frustrations with veteran investors will go a long way in calming your nerves and helping you to see your plan through. There are no new experiences, just new investors.

For those looking for instant gratification, this kind of long-term strategy can be frustrating, but the rewards can be worth the growing pains. A farmer who plants seeds on Friday night and rips them up on Monday morning because they have not yielded a crop should probably look for another line of work. In the same way, investments must be cultivated before you can enjoy the fruits of your labor. We encourage you to balance your long-term financial goals with short-term targets to help you stay on track and not become discouraged.

How can I spot a great opportunity?

There are three things that can make an opportunity great for you.

1. **Comfort.** Always start with your comfort level. The better you know yourself and what you can handle, the more likely you'll be able to assess whether you should move forward on an opportunity. If others are trying to convince you to get on board, or if you are ignoring your gut and trying to convince yourself, this is not the deal for you.

2. **Use.** A great opportunity is useful to you and others. You do not have to get on the ground floor of the next big thing (although it would be great if you could), but you should purchase with an eye toward the future. What needs will your property fulfill? What will it add to your portfolio? What will it add to the community? If your property is one unit among many in a saturated market, you may want to stop and think

a bit. If, on the other hand, you see a niche that can be filled by your property, your portfolio can profit while you bring something essential to the neighborhood. Everyone wins.

3. Price. Some might put this first, but if you're not comfortable and if the project is not useful, the price really doesn't matter because it is not a valuable deal. Getting property dirt cheap may sound great, but when the vacant unit remains vacant because the market cannot support another rental or when renovations are costly and inconvenient, there is little to brag about.

Once you run through these three factors and determine that the opportunity really may be great, run your ideas past your financial team. If everyone is on board, you know you are on the right track, personally and professionally.

When is something too good to be true?

Almost always. All real-estate investors want to make money. Each of us hopes to stumble upon that diamond in the rough that catapults our portfolio from merely making money to earning millions. But there are several red flags that go up when we hear people talk about something being too good to be true.

Common sense must prevail here. As a novice investor you must think to yourself, "Why would I be privy to this deal, having done none of the necessary work to earn such an opportunity." Down the line when you have several substantial connections, have walked through a few transactions, and have tweaked your team, learning about a promising up-and-coming project will seem reasonable. While luck plays a part in life, it is not something on which to hinge your financial future.

If you are being pressured by someone who throws around terms like "once-in-a-lifetime deal" or "for a limited time only," take care. While some real-estate transactions move more quickly than others, pressure to hand over money is never a good sign.

Finally, always talk to your investment team about such potential transactions. A great deal should never be based on one person's opinion. If things look good, your attorney will confirm that all contracts are in order. Your mortgage consultant can help you find a loan program that suits this project. Your financial advisor can let you know his take on the proposition and draw on his own experiences to offer you advice. Your Realtor will have his ear to the ground, getting a feel for what is going on. If all these people agree, consider moving forward. But chances are when a great deal is examined by multiple parties who keep your best interests in mind, it will seem less than perfect.

As investing is a process built on experience and education, we will be ready when the right time meets the right place. Keep your eyes and ears open for great opportunities, as they are usually the result of hard work and diligence, not luck.

How can I increase my chances of being at the right place at the right time?

As we just mentioned, being at the right place at the right time is most often a result of diligence, not luck. Is there such a thing as a charmed life? That we don't know, but in our experience if you want to have a magic touch, you will have to remain a hands-on investor. For example, this book is just a steppingstone in your education and experience as a real-estate investor. There are always more people to meet, more conversations to have, more knowledge to gain. Being a hands-on investor means appreciating that there is no finish line.

The best way to find the right place is by asking directions. If you want to know how other investors have claimed their success, you need to ask them. This is not something that is done at a first networking meeting any more than you would ask someone to marry you after a first date. You'll want to network with a variety of investors until you find those people with whom you want to build relationships. In the process of building relationships, sharing ideas, and trading information, you will have the chance to see what habits are worth emulating and which approaches can help put you further along the road to success.

Many people are fond of saying that timing is everything. This implies that there are only a finite number of deals to be made, only a few coveted spots at the top of success's ladder. But in real estate, and, arguably, many other professions, staying power is much more lucrative than a perfectly timed hit. The chances of accidentally having the right finances, the right team, and the right deal appear at the right time are slim to none. Taking the necessary steps to help ensure that you start slowly, build momentum, and stay on track is a much more reliable approach. The right place at the right time is a location available to those who are willing to pursue their professional endeavors with patience and perseverance over time.

Do I need a home inspection?

Having a home inspection is a bit like taking a new car out for a test drive. While it may look great on the showroom floor, you want to know how it will perform when it is in use. Cosmetic upgrades can help a unit look its best, which is great, but you want to know how the house is running. To find out about the plumbing, electric, and heating and cooling systems, enlist the help of a qualified home inspector.

Web sites such as the American Society of Home Inspectors (*www.ashi .org*) can put you in touch with an experienced inspector who is part of a professional organization insisting on qualified and ethical inspectors. You can also ask other real-estate investors for their referrals. Those who stand to benefit from the sale of a property, such as the seller's Realtor, may not be the best source for an inspection referral. We encourage you to stick with recommendations made by third parties to avoid any conflict of interest. You want someone who can give you an unbiased opinion of the property you are looking at. When checking home inspection referrals, ask former clients if any major problems were found after closing and if they would use that particular inspector again.

Be sure and ask the inspector what his inspection will cover and point out particular areas of concern you may have, such as an outdated electrical system or an older roof. If problems are found, ask if the inspector will make the repairs or if this would be a conflict of interest. Different states and organizations take different lines on this. Make sure you know how much the inspection will cost (typically between $300 and $500), when the report will be finished, and if you can attend the inspection. It is a good idea to see your potential unit though the capable eyes of an expert and learn about what makes this property tick.

Your Realtor will help you put a contract together that protects you if a home inspection is done. If substantial problems are found, you can negotiate with the seller about fixing the problems, lowering the selling price, or giving you the money to make repairs. A home inspection is not intended to kill a deal; rather, it is a tool to assess the home and make recommendations for repairs and upgrades before signing the contracts. This way, both the buyer and seller have peace of mind.

Do I need homeowner's insurance?

Like most real-estate investors, you will likely be financing your purchase using a mortgage. Your lender will require you to carry homeowner's insurance to make sure the institution's investment is covered. Homeowner's insurance can offer you certain reassurances, but it does not protect you from everything.

Typically, homeowner's policies cover damage done to your home, most commonly by fire or theft. Different policies and different fees will determine how much of your home and how much of your personal property is covered. You will have policy options such as replacement coverage or actual cash value. While actual cash value policies tend to be less expensive, they take into consideration depreciation of the real estate and your possessions. Weigh the pros and cons of both policies.

Most homeowner's insurance policies do not cover a renter's possessions. Encourage your tenant to protect himself with personally funded renter's insurance.

Keep in mind also that floods, tornadoes, hurricanes, and earthquakes are not typically covered by homeowner's policies. These disastrous acts of nature can do considerable damage. If you are buying a property in an area prone to such catastrophes, consider buying additional policies to cover these added risks. This is especially important when you are buying in an unfamiliar area, such as a vacation location. Check with your Realtor and mortgage consultant to review which policies they would recommend.

It's a good idea to shop around for insurance and see which policies and prices are most advantageous. If your unit has carbon monoxide detectors, smoke detectors, or a flame-retardant roof, you may be eligible for discounts. Also, consider a policy with a higher deductible, which can greatly affect your premium. Talk with your financial advisor to see which option works best with your finances and ask for a referral. Make sure you ask how much insurance to purchase so you cover your risk.

Scenario: I have seen so many different properties and received so much information my head is spinning. How can I keep everything straight?

When the time comes to look at different properties with an eye to purchase, it may seem as if you are seeing the same property over and over again. That's especially true if you are clear about what you want and are sticking to a price range. To make the most of your time on the road, be as organized as possible.

Don't head out for an appointment without pens, highlighters, a folder with pockets, paper, and a camera. When you meet with your Realtor, you will most likely be given copies of the home's information sheet, available online at sites that use the Multiple Listing Service. This sheet will list the property's bedrooms, bathrooms, acreage, age, taxes, and township, among other things. Take time to read through the information, highlighting details you want to investigate further (for example, whether a multiunit property has ample parking), and familiarize yourself with the home's details. When you arrive, you should see an advertising brochure at the site. This is a good supplemental piece of information that usually has details such as commuting distance and whether there is natural light in the kitchen or hand-crafted molding. This can provide a nice overview of the property.

Once inside, take notes as you move through the property. These notes are not going to be seen by others, so write what is helpful to you. If the bathroom wallpaper is lime green with pink flowers, make a note of it. That can act as a defining visual to help you recall the house. Write down other things you like or dislike: great closet space, small functional kitchen, laundry hookup in the basement. Ask if you may take a few photos to refresh your memory when you get home. You may think you'll remember what you see where, but after a few properties things will tend to look the same.

When you are finished viewing the home, sit in your car and talk over some of the property's details with your Realtor. He may have noticed additional things such as a water stain on the ceiling or hardwood floors underneath the carpeting.

Conversing about the property while it is still in sight and taking a few moments to organize your thoughts on paper will help you assess your findings later on.

Searching for real estate can feel overwhelming. But by keeping your folder with your personalized details organized and accessible, you will stay on track and avoid having to backtrack or guess about what you saw. 🏠

What can I do to avoid becoming too emotionally attached to my investment?

This is a common concern in real-estate investing and a problem that will most likely dissipate as you gain experience. When most of us think about real estate, we think about our own homes and the memories we have built there. There are probably things you love and hate about your house, so when the idea of buying a new property comes up, you naturally refer to your preconceived ideas about what a home should or should not have. Also, whenever we are at the beginning of a new experience, we tend to become more emotionally involved, wanting everything to go just right and be just so.

No property is perfect, and no transaction will be either. If you have always wanted a front porch and are looking at a property that has one, it makes sense that you may start thinking about purchasing the home for yourself. Sometimes you can make an unexpected move and prosper from it, but this should be discussed in detail with your financial team. The best course is to stop focusing on the details, step back, and remember the big picture.

Investment properties are just that: investments. You are looking at properties in a price range and neighborhood that suits your investment plan. If you decide to move, you are, in essence, postponing your investment career. Moving is one of the most stressful things you can do. It's not a good time to begin a new business venture.

To stay on task when searching for real-estate properties, set yourself up for success. Before you head out for an appointment, make sure your own home is neat and tidy so that it will be a comfort, not a stress, to come home to. Dress appropriately. You are going to work, so look the part. Take notes and keep a file on the properties you have seen. Keep the file in your home office, as these are business files. When you return home, change clothes, get comfortable, and switch gears from business to casual. Remember that you are looking for an investment that can help you achieve the financial success you want.

Since I don't plan on living in this property, do I really need to spend so much money on inspections and insurance?

The flip side of falling in love with every property you see is not taking enough interest in your new acquisition or looking for ways to save money on your investment by skipping steps. As we have said before, to be a successful investor, it is penny-wise and pound-foolish to take shortcuts. Just because you are not residing in the property does not mean that you do not own it. You will still be responsible for taxes, maintenance, and upgrades. If you want to have a unit that rents well and provides a steady supplemental income, make sure you buy a solid building that is well protected.

A home inspection does cost money, but the cost of not having one can be much greater. Usually, the most expensive problems are behind the scenes. Granted, when you flip the switch the light goes on, but faulty wiring doesn't usually rear its ugly head until the problem is full blown. A home inspector knows where to look and what to look for. She can give you an unbiased, unemotional view of what the house needs. These reports can become an important negotiating device, saving you time and money down the line. To avoid a home inspection is foolish.

Homeowner's insurance is mandated by your lender, so there is no way to avoid this cost unless you plan to make your purchase in cash. You may think about passing on additional insurance, believing the chances of a flood or earthquake are too small to warrant another policy. You can discuss supplemental insurance with your local Realtor to get a better overview of what is necessary. In the next chapter, we will discuss your liability and risk as a landlord and help you devise a plan to best protect yourself. Whether you are buying your primary residence or an investment property, treat the transaction with the same level of ownership and make your purchase one you can be confident about.

Chapter Five Renter Relationships

Why are the Fair Housing laws so important to a landlord?

There are so many important things to know about being a landlord, such as creating and negotiating leases, collecting rents, maintaining your properties, and building strong tenant relationships. Throughout this chapter we will offer suggestions on how to navigate these areas, but we want to start with the Fair Housing laws because knowledge of the rules of renting is critical to your investment success.

The Fair Housing laws are a result of the Fair Housing Act, Title VIII of the Civil Rights Act of 1968, and are enforced by the Department of Housing and Urban Development Fair Housing Enforcement Center. The Fair Housing Act says landlords must choose tenants based on valid, reasonable, pertinent criteria, which are applied to all applicants. Such standards include a reliable income, letters of reference, and credit history.

Landlords may not disqualify an applicant based on any discriminatory criteria such as race, religion, color, sex, nationality, disability, or family status. Thanks to the Fair Housing Act, everyone in the United States is protected from landlords discriminating based on any of these reasons. Also, landlords cannot modify their practices to alienate or eliminate those in protected classes.

Examples of these wrongdoings include raising the rent for certain tenants, refusing to accommodate the reasonable needs of handicapped tenants, and enforcing stricter policies and terms for some tenants. A landlord must treat all occupants fairly and apply all rules, requirements, and rental fees equally.

If an applicant or tenant feels that they have been discriminated against, they have the right to contact the area's HUD office and file a complaint against the landlord. HUD will notify a landlord that a complaint has been made and begin an investigation to determine if the Fair Housing Act has been violated. If such a breach has been determined, HUD will work to remedy the situation, either by facilitating an agreement that both parties sign or by referring the issue to the state or local housing authority for investigation, or, in emergency situations, by authorizing the attorney general's office to intervene on the prospective tenant's behalf. If an investigation shows reasonable cause to believe a violation has occurred, a landlord can be taken to court and sued for damages and attorney fees. We strongly suggest that you visit *www.hud.gov* for a complete set of laws and regulations, as well as contact your local HUD office to familiarize yourself with the laws that pertain to your state and your properties.

What accommodations must be made for disabled tenants?

Contact your local HUD office to make sure that you are in compliance when renting to disabled tenants. A landlord may not refuse to rent to handicapped applicants or to a family whose members have disabilities. Physical or mental disabilities can include hearing or visual loss, chronic mental illness, AIDS, or mental retardation, to name a few. You may also not refuse occupancy if the applicant has a history of disabilities, such as alcoholism.

In addition, a disabled tenant has the right to make reasonable accommodations to a unit, such as having a Seeing Eye dog in a no-pets property or reserving a parking space close to the door for a physically challenged tenant. When appropriate and feasible, the occupant may be required to return any modifications to their original state upon termination of the tenancy. Check with your local HUD office to see if you can insist upon this.

Since March 13, 1991, buildings with an elevator and four or more units must be handicapped accessible. Doorways, hallways, access ways, common areas, bathrooms, kitchens, and appliance switches and outlets all must be deemed wheelchair accessible. If no elevator is available in the property, first-floor units must meet these standards.

Whether you are planning on purchasing a single-family house or a multiunit property, be sure you are meeting the requirements outlined by the Fair Housing Act. You'll want to know what modifications, if any, will have to be made to a building before you purchase it. If a property needs to be brought up to code, you will want to research the amount of money needed to make the necessary modifications and determine if this cost is within your budget. Never go into a real-estate purchase hoping that you can get away with it. Not only is it dishonest, it is illegal and could end up being a very costly gamble.

How can I make sure I'm following the Fair Housing laws?

The best way is to conduct your business practices based on professional standards, not personal preferences. Concentrate on maintaining legitimate business practices and you will set yourself up for success, not lawsuits. Consider the following suggestions:

Fair Housing laws. While we have outlined how the Fair Housing laws prohibit discrimination, you should visit *www.hud.gov* to review the act in its entirety, contact your local HUD office to make sure you are in compliance, and speak to your team's real-estate attorney about any questions. As a business owner, it is your responsibility to know the law. This means you are also responsible for making sure everyone on your staff, including someone such as a property manager, also know the law and abides by it. You can be held responsible if one of your staff members acts inappropriately.

Background checks. Later in this chapter we will detail how to obtain a credit report on your applicants, the pros and cons of doing a criminal background check, and the best ways to check an applicant's reference. Your application process should require tenants to fill out paperwork for your records and protection, and your process should be the same for every applicant. What you do for one applicant, do for all applicants. This also includes treating no tenant better than any other. If you assess a fee for each day the rent is late, do not waive that fee for the single father unless you plan on waiving that fee for all of your other tenants. You want to avoid all accusations of discrimination, including reverse discrimination.

Business criteria. As a business owner, you have the right to set your own standards, as long as the criteria are based on reason, pertinent principles that can be measured and not just on your feelings. Poor credit histories, no job, negative references, and inability to come up with the security deposit are all valid reasons to turn down an applicant. These reasons can all be documented and are based on relevant finances, not emotions.

As a real-estate investor, you need to treat your business as a business, know the legalities of practicing business, and keep records to protect your business. You do not have to live in fear of breaking the law if you take the necessary steps to ensure that you are upholding it.

Where can I find renters?

Renters can be found everywhere. The good thing about pursuing a business in real-estate investing is that everyone needs a place to live. Having spent time researching your area's community and purchasing a property that serves this neighborhood, you can now target your rental pool.

At the beginning of this book, we encouraged you to have business cards made and to let all of your friends and families know that you are beginning a career in real-estate investing. Now that you are into your first transaction, this is more important than ever. Of course, since you have built an investment team, are networking with experienced businesspeople in the field, and your confidence is increasing, you will have even more people to talk to. It also gives you a great opener for striking up a conversation with potential contacts. Talking about what projects you have on the table and what you are doing with them invites veteran investors to share their experience with you. Word of mouth can go a long way in making business connections and finding tenants.

But since time is of the essence when it comes to filling a vacant unit, you can't rely only on your connections. That is why we recommend advertising. There are many different advertising markets to choose from, and knowing who your client pool is will help you determine the most cost-effective way to reach your prospects. If you have a multiunit property in a college town, you'll want to target the local campus paper, area Laundromats, and community and online bulletin boards. A pricey ad in an upscale magazine would probably not be a cost-effective way to appeal to such a market. If you are hoping to rent a seasonal beachfront unit, the opposite might be true. Knowing who is most likely to be interested in your property will help you determine where you can find them.

What are effective ways to advertise for tenants?

You can use any or all of the following strategies to find tenants for all different types of properties. The strategies range from least expensive to pricey and can be combined to have the most impact.

- Start with a For Rent sign in the window of your unit in hopes of attracting passersby. This works best in locations where there is heavy foot traffic and the building is attractive. Commonly, these signs list a contact name and number, the number of bedrooms, and the rent. If you have a unit in a building that is undergoing renovations and are worried that prospects may talk themselves out of a great apartment before seeing it, you can skip this option. If you have purchased where there is a homeowner's association, be sure to check for the rules and regulations regarding this type of advertising.
- Take out an ad in the community paper. People looking to rent in the area will seek out neighborhood sources to obtain information. For a nominal fee, you can run your ad in the real-estate section.

If you are computer literate, make flyers and hang them in high-traffic areas such as supermarkets, gyms, and library bulletin boards. If your unit has a lovely garden space, consider targeting health-food store bulletin boards. If the property comes equipped with a washer and dryer, hang a sign at the Laundromat. Be sure to include tear-off slips with your contact information and a brief reminder about your unit. Handwritten notices look unprofessional, and we discourage them.

- Do not neglect online listings, which have revolutionized apartment hunting. Check out the free service at craigslist (*www.craigslist.com*), where you can post and search for real estate at no charge.
- Corporate housing offices are a great resource if you live near a big corporation or university where the organization assists employees in relocation.
- Your Realtor will probably be happy to help you find a tenant, but it will cost you a fee that is usually equivalent to one month's rent. If your Realtor has a rental pool to draw from and can fill your unit quickly and efficiently, you may want to pay the fee.
- Property management companies can advertise, interview, and manage your unit for a fee. If you want professionals on call to service any maintenance issues and plan to hire a property manager, you may want to go this route. However, because of the expense it might be best to handle things personally until your portfolio grows and the additional income can help offset these costs.

Ask investment colleagues which strategies have worked for them, and you'll likely find out that their system combined different methods and depended on the location and the property.

Should I rent to friends?

In spreading the word about needing to fill a property vacancy, a friend or family member may tell you he or she would be eager to take advantage of such an opportunity. As a new landlord, you may think that having an acquaintance or family member occupy your property will relieve some of your worries. After all, you already know them, you probably trust them, and you'd like to help the people you care about find a home. But despite your best intentions, and theirs, problems often come up. If your uncle finds himself short on cash, he may ask you to do him a favor and let him slide for a bit. It can be very awkward to enforce the terms of your lease when you know you will be seated across from him in a few weeks at Thanksgiving.

Familiar tenants aren't the only ones who tend to take liberties with rental properties. Landlords can be just as guilty of lax behavior. A call from your cousin asking to talk to you about a leaky faucet or poor lighting may be met with resentment, especially if you know that he is handy and could fix the problem on his own. You may end up putting his request on the back burner or not taking his problems seriously.

If you are convinced that such an arrangement could be advantageous, follow the interview procedures as you would for any other tenant. Complete a background and credit check for your file. Check up on references and recommendations. Walk through the lease together, highlighting the points you want to emphasize. If this process already sounds uncomfortable, think of how challenging it will be to confront your friend or relative for failing to hand over the rent.

Running a business is hard enough. Trying to run a business that is dependent on your friends and family holding up their end of a bargain can be overwhelming.

Should I do a criminal background check on renters?

There is no easy answer for this question, as there is no single source to contact that will give you a complete criminal background check on an individual. Unlike the three major credit-reporting agencies who have compiled information to create a thorough picture of someone's credit history, there is no such tool for criminal histories.

Unless you are a member of a law enforcement agency, you will have to spend a lot of time trying to find information that a criminal could easily conceal from you. If you do find out that a former criminal has made application to rent one of your properties, you may not be able to disqualify her solely based on this. Some states require that there be a direct connection between a past crime and a future threat. For instance, a hospital can reject the job application of a doctor who has been found guilty of malpractice. You could not reject the doctor as a tenant based on the same crime since his past crime poses no immediate threat to you. Of course, you want to have a reasonable sense of security about allowing a stranger to move into your property. You can advertise that you will be doing criminal and credit background checks, which can dissuade criminals from applying for the unit. Be sure to follow up on all references, and require that they represent personal relationships as well as professional contacts.

If you think a criminal background check is necessary, work with your real-estate attorney to determine the best way to proceed in your state. She will most likely be able to recommend reputable companies that handle such inquiries, many of which can be found online. She will also be able to tell you your rights and obligations once you have the desired information in your hands.

There is no straightforward way to resolve this situation. The process can be costly and time consuming, but, as always, you must do what makes you most comfortable.

How can I check a renter's credit history?

As a landlord, you are legally allowed to check a potential tenant's credit report to verify income, employment, previous addresses, and bank account information. Having this report will help you decide which applicant to choose for your unit.

You should obtain a credit report during the interview process. Have each applicant fill out a detailed rental application that includes the prospect's name, address, social security number or individual taxpayer identification number, current employer, income, references, and consent for credit check. With this information, you can contact any of the three major credit reporting bureaus: Equifax, Experian, or TransUnion. All paperwork, including rental applications, credit card reports, and reference check notes, should be kept in a file forever. Never discard these records.

It is likely that all of your applicants will have blemishes on their credit records. Do not become overly concerned with an isolated late payment, but look for a pattern of prompt bill paying. A credit report will not usually indicate rental payments, but it will list bankruptcies or past landlord judgments. You will then have to decide if these more serious delinquencies are grounds for rejecting the applicant. It could be that circumstances out of the tenant's control, such as an illness or divorce, led to such setbacks. If the problems appear to represent a pattern of poor financial skills, however, you may choose to pass over this applicant. If you do, you must inform the prospect why he is being rejected, the name and address of the bureau that has supplied this information (such as credit card companies), and the applicant's right to obtain his own free copy of his credit report within sixty days.

In addition to acquiring a credit report, landlords should follow up on all references, especially previous landlords. Instead of asking previous landlords if a prospective tenant paid the rent, ask the landlord what the terms of the lease were and whether the tenant abided by the contract. If the rent check was to have been received by the fifteenth of each month, you do not want to hear that payment was usually not received until the thirtieth. Not only do you want a tenant who pays the rent, you want to make sure that the tenant pays on time. This is more likely if the tenant has a steady source of reliable income, verifiable through the applicant's employment record and current employer. If this applicant has just changed jobs, contact a previous employer to verify her income.

A credit report is an excellent tool that can help you get an accurate idea of whether this tenant will meet his financial obligation to you in a timely manner. Combining this information with firsthand knowledge of your applicant's financial responsibility will help to narrow down your rental pool and help you choose a dependable tenant.

Would current landlords and employers give false information?

References are not always what they seem, and this is a lesson that many landlords learn the hard way. While most people you will come into contact with during your investing career will be honest, there are a few exceptions. To avoid being taken advantage of, consider the following.

It is unlikely that current landlords will give false information, but they may have biased views. If you are calling about a tenant who has been nothing but a headache to her current landlord, you may hear a glowing recommendation, or at least a recommendation that omits many headache-inducing anecdotes, because the landlord is hoping to get rid of this problem. On the other hand, a landlord who is worried about having to fill a vacancy may emphasize a tenant's bad points or exaggerate problems, determined to keep his own properties filled. Not wanting to give up his great tenant, he embellishes or makes up problems. You will get a more even-handed portrayal from a previous landlord, because his relationship with your prospective tenant has ended.

When you are checking on professional references and contacting employers, make sure that you are actually talking to the supervisor, not just a friend or colleague of the applicant. Instead of calling the direct line number listed on the rental application, call the company's main number and ask to be put in touch with the supervisor. If the company is a small one, check the listed number against the phone book and look for the office online. Even most small businesses have a Web presence that lists contact names and numbers. You can also ask to see current pay stubs. Besides calling the current employer, reach out to a former employer who, again, will have little reason to stray from the truth. These strategies can help make sure that you are hearing the most honest and even-handed information, making it easier to evaluate your tenant options.

Are there red flags I should look for when interviewing potential tenants?

As a new landlord, you will probably be anxious to fill a property since the vacancy is costing you money. But be wary of skipping steps in order to fill the space. Better to take a reasonable amount of time interviewing prospects and following up on their references than choose someone who seems like a nice guy and pay a fortune in eviction proceedings.

The number one red flag to look out for is desperation. If an applicant can't stop gushing about how wonderful the apartment is, offers to pay additional money to move in immediately, or says she has no time to wait for an interview process and must know your answer now, it could mean trouble. While some extra up-front cash might sound appealing, it is likely that this will be the last time you see money from this tenant for a while. Of course it is exciting to get a new place, but excitement and desperation are not the same thing. If your gut is telling you something is wrong, it probably is.

A prospect who encourages you to choose him right away may be hoping that in your excitement you'll overlook checking his credit history or contacting his references. He may have a long list of financial delinquencies or a shallow employment record because he has skipped around and often finds himself between jobs. Knowing that this information could land him on the rejected list, he tries to finagle his way in the door before you have a chance to find out about his background.

As a landlord, you must always protect yourself. If you skip steps and let this tenant move in only to later realize you have made a grave mistake, you will have no paper trail. If you accept this applicant's cash advance, bypass your interviewing process, and reject several other prospects, you could be opening yourself up to a lawsuit. Those prospective tenants who were waiting for your response are entitled to know why they were not chosen. If you do not have the appropriate paperwork to back up your decision, a single mother or same-sex couple could assume that they were discriminated against.

To ensure that you get your real-estate investing career off on the right foot, set a time for interviewing applicants, let them know how long it will take to give them an answer (forty-eight to seventy-two hours is reasonable), obtain credit reports, follow up on references, then make your decision. This way you will weed out the desperate, have documentation to support your decision, and welcome a worthy tenant into your property.

How can I reduce tenant turnover?

After interviewing your applicants and choosing a tenant, you will breathe a sigh of relief when it turns out your efforts were well worth it, as your new occupant is making prompt payments, treating your property appropriately, and has no major complaints or issues. Now you'll want to take steps to ensure that she stays, freeing you up to concentrate on your next project.

Dealing with ideal tenants is as important as dealing with problem ones. As a business owner, consider your tenant a client. You want to keep a good client happy, which in turn keeps your business running smoothly. When it is time to renew the lease, you may see this as an opportunity to raise the rent, but consider if this is really necessary. If you do not need to raise the rent, don't. Your tenant will appreciate paying the same fee, and you will not have to worry about the cost of replacing her should she decide she needs to find a cheaper place to live. If you do need to make an increase, be reasonable. If you only need to raise the rent $50, don't raise it $100.

Throughout your tenant's stay, be timely with your repairs. A well-executed lease will spell out both landlord and tenant responsibilities. When a repair is needed, attend to it promptly. As a customer at any store, you would expect your issues to be dealt with in a timely manner. Having received quick and courteous attention, you are much more likely to return to that store. Extend your client the same level of service so that she will want to stay.

You can also offer monetary enticements to your client. If a responsible tenant has an affection for gardening, you can deduct $50 from his rent for keeping the lawn mowed and the sidewalk shoveled. The tenant will benefit from a price reduction, and you'll have less maintenance on your hands and an occupant who maintains a sense of ownership. It's a winning situation for all parties.

Finally, you can make it easier to stay than to go by booking your tenants for the next lease year. Offer to make a rent reduction in exchange for twelve postdated rent checks. You will cash each of these checks on the first of the month. You now have a year's worth of rent in your hand and a serious tenant in your unit. Keeping tenants happy is a cost-effective way to reduce tenant turnover, build your business, and give you peace of mind.

Is there anything that must be done to the property between renters?

Even in the best circumstances, rental agreements are only temporary situations, and eventually your tenants will move out. When this happens, freshen up your apartment and get it ready for your next occupants. When your current tenants vacate and are ready to turn in their keys and collect their security deposit, walk through the unit with them, checking for damages that are above normal wear and tear.

Even if you're not required to paint before the next renters take occupancy, it is a good idea. Do not paint before the tenants leave but afterward, making the job more efficient. When you show your unit to prospective tenants, you want it to look its best. A tired apartment may be passed up, especially when the market favors renters. Fresh paint looks better, and aesthetics can go a long way in helping you capture the rental fee you are after.

Also not required, but a very good idea, is having the carpets cleaned. Replacing carpeting is much more expensive than having it cleaned. You can either do it yourself with a rental unit or pay the additional expense of having a professional company do it for you. Again, this is a way to present your unit well. If you do not show pride of ownership on a piece of real estate, why would tenants who are only living there temporarily do so?

Finally, change the locks. Even though the tenants who are leaving will turn in their keys, they've probably made duplicates at some point. New locks are a financially reasonable safety precaution that protects you and your tenants.

Once the walls are painted and the carpets cleaned, take pictures of the unit and include these pictures with the new lease your tenants sign. You are documenting the condition the property is in at the beginning of the rental agreement, and you expect, as detailed in the contract, that the unit be surrendered in the same condition, minus normal wear and tear.

Can I offer tenants incentives?

The best time to offer tenants incentives is at the beginning of your relationship. Having worked with your investment team to make the right purchase and having conducted tenant screenings, you can now capitalize on your hard work with incentive programs. Since renters are not bound to your property, you should encourage them to take care of your property the way you would. You need to motivate them in order to make this happen. This is where incentives come in.

When negotiating with prospective tenants, plan your incentives far in advance so you can reveal them when the time is right. The most popular motivation is money. For example, figure out what you want the rent to be then add $50 to the price. Advertise your property at $1,200 a month then offer a $50 rent deduction if your tenant sends you the rent a week early. You can also offer a rent reduction for light landscaping and snow removal.

Tenant incentives must comply with the Fair Housing laws. Do not offer a price reduction to a young college graduate but deny a single mother the same opportunity. Remember, what you do for one tenant, you must do for all tenants. Tenant incentives are proactive methods of building healthy relationships. Successful restaurants and department stores don't stop having sales, giveaways, or coupons because they are profitable; they continue catering to their customers because they value repeat business. You can do this too.

Should I put in appliance upgrades?

The short answer is yes. Why and how this will affect your investment will depend a great deal on your neighborhood. Since you have become familiar with your area, you should know which amenities are standard and which are considered bonus features. Knowing the difference is key to marketing your property.

Your real-estate property is a living, breathing investment that must be cared for. We have spoken about the dangers of trying to make one great deal and ride that out in hopes of a big payday. Nurturing each investment is a much more sound approach. If you do, you will appreciate that in order to receive you must give. The question is how much to give.

The convenience of an on-premises laundry facility is a huge benefit for both families and singles. Given the choice between heading out to the local Laundromat or throwing in a load during a commercial break at home . . . well, the answer is obvious. But you must always know your competition. If this convenience is an area standard, you will have to install the machines at an out-of-pocket cost. If a washer and dryer facility is not the norm, installing such upgrades could help you better market your property. You will have an edge over other vacancies and can probably recoup the cost of installation with a modest increase in rent.

The same considerations apply to cable television and Internet service. If your property is in an area where these necessities are moderately priced and easy to access, you may want to foot the bill for them. These amenities could work well in a multiunit facility where you are living on one side of the building. Since you are already enjoying these things, why not expand the service for a modest fee to include the adjoining rental property? Again, an increase in rent can help defer the cost and bring more prospective occupants to your door.

If you are buying a new construction property, the home will probably be furnished with a dishwasher, microwave oven, and refrigerator. If this is a large complex with several units being offered for rent, you will be right with the competition. But if most people buying here are residents, not landlords, you could be marketing a unique property for the area. This is why knowing your area is so important; it can often mean the difference between breaking even and making excess profits.

An empty property makes no money; in fact, it costs money. If you are charging too much for what you are offering, consider offering more. All residents, even temporary ones, want their house to be a home. Convenient appliance upgrades can help make that happen.

Should I invest in remodeling projects?

Sometimes when you buy an investment property you do so with the understanding that it needs some work. Your mortgage consultant can help determine exactly what "some work" means and how you can finance the project without overextending yourself. Once you have the financial go-ahead from the bank, though, you'll work with your Realtor and a contractor to determine what has to be done. This is where things can get challenging.

Remember: *You are not buying this property for yourself.* Do not start walking around your investment property picturing your family gathering in the kitchen to prepare dinner or you soaking in the tub after a long day of work. As soon as you start mentally moving in, you are much more likely to opt for granite counters and whirlpool tubs, expensive choices that may not be necessary.

It is important to know what the resale value of your unit will be once these projects are complete. Many remodeling projects do not add resale value, and it would be prudent to avoid these choices. Your Realtor can offer you her professional judgment about what kind of return you can expect down the line. Balancing this information with the knowledge gained from a consultation with a remodeling contractor can help you decide how to proceed.

A good rule of thumb is that less is usually more. One of the first room homeowners often look to remodel is the kitchen, and for good reason. A kitchen is the heart of the house and sets the tone for the rest of the unit. If it is tired and awkward, the rest of the unit will feel that way. But the difference between bringing a kitchen up to date and making a kitchen a showplace can cost you a great deal of money, both now and later. For example, refinishing cabinets is more cost effective than replacing them. Midpriced fixtures work just as well as custom-ordered pieces (at a fraction of the cost), and a fresh coat of paint makes much better sense than crown molding with coordinating trim. While the latter upgrades sound more appealing, you will not recoup their costs at resale. You want to avoid projects that take away from your profit line.

Choose remodeling projects to make your unit more appealing and user friendly, but resist going overboard. You can make your investment nice without spending a fortune.

Should I furnish the property?

There are only a few specific rental scenarios that would warrant this expense. Usually when you purchase real estate with the intention of renting it, you are looking for occupants who will be responsible for their own furnishings. But there are a few times when you will be expected to provide the furniture.

If you have purchased in a vacation destination and are renting it out short term, you will furnish your unit. How much money you choose to spend on the furniture really depends on the clientele you will be catering to. If you have a house on the beach that attracts families and groups of friends, high-end furniture is not a great idea. Sand and sun can quickly weather furniture. You may want to opt for brightly colored, midpriced furniture, an excellent grill, and attractive beach chairs and towels. This does not mean you should rest the TV on a milk crate, but it does mean that you can skip the cherry wood cabinets and mahogany bed frames.

On the flip side, if you are hoping to capture tourists en route to national points of interest out west, create an apropos setting. We have decorated our rental cabin in Wyoming with rustic quilts, Native American rugs, and dark wood furniture. Know the intention of your vacationers and you will be able to meet their needs.

In addition to beds, couches, and tables, furnished units often come with linens, plates, glasses, silverware, and so on. Since someone is living there for a predetermined period, these things are necessities. If you mandate that the unit must be cleaned by the renters—common with a summer beach rental— be sure to highlight that point when you negotiate the terms of the rental.

Aside from vacation rentals, there is really no reason to look for short-term rentals. It is a situation that will demand much more of your time and put increased wear and tear on your unit. The only other time you may want to consider furnishing a unit is if you are moving from one destination to another and plan to buy all-new furnishings for yourself when you get there. While this may sound extravagant, it doesn't have to be. For example, let's say that you own a modest home in the north near a college or major corporation. Upon retiring, you decide to move south to a much smaller condo. Instead of packing up the furniture you have owned for twenty years, you take a few items and decide to make a fresh start. You can offer your home for rent, fully or partially furnished, as you have no intention of using the furniture. But, knowing the area, you know that furnished houses are in demand and you can fill a need.

For the most part, furnishing a property is necessary only with short-term rentals associated with vacation destinations or areas of high corporate relocation. If this is an area you are interested in, allow for this expense when you budget your operating costs.

What if tenants want to make repairs themselves?

As a landlord it is your responsibility to make sure that your property meets basic habitability standards. You must provide access to heat, electricity, and water, maintain a structurally safe and sound building, and keep the property sanitary by exterminating and preventing pests. Most local laws mandate that a landlord abide by municipal housing codes, which can mean installing smoke detectors and dead-bolt locks, and making sure electrical wiring is up to code. But once a tenant takes occupancy, who is responsible for damage that she may do on her own?

All occupants have a responsibility to return the property to the owner in the condition it was when they moved in and to take care of the unit while they are living there. If a tenant invites pests into the house due to negligent housekeeping, a landlord can have the unit fumigated and hold the tenant responsible for the bill. So a tenant does not have carte blanche to behave in any way he pleases and keep calling you to fix the problem.

For the most part, though, you will be responsible for making repairs in a timely manner. Any problems that jeopardize a tenant's safety or health, be it a loose steppingstone on the front porch or inadequate weatherproofing throughout the unit, you must address immediately. Often you will have a tenant who volunteers to take care of the problem in exchange for a reduction of rent. Having a tenant make repairs has its pros and cons.

On the plus side, your time is valuable, so if the tenant is capable of fixing that loose stone or installing storm windows, it can save you the hassle. You can knock the price of materials off next month's rent and consider the matter closed. But before giving her the okay, consider these points.

- What is her area of expertise, and yours?
- How do you know if she is capable of making such repairs?
- Are you confident that you'll be able to determine if the problem was adequately fixed?

You don't want to make a situation worse than it is. A $50 problem can easily become a $500 disaster with one swing of a hammer. And you would certainly not want to find out that the electrical repair your former tenants made was merely a strategically placed piece of duct tape. When it comes to repairs, your best bet is to see the job through yourself.

1. It gives you an opportunity to enter the unit and get a quick look at the condition of your property.

2. As the owner, you have a greater motivation to ensure the job is taken care of correctly.

3. If your occupants attempt to make repairs but do an inadequate job, you will have to take care of the problem anyway.

As a landlord, keep on top of your properties by personally addressing any repair issues.

What if tenants want to make upgrades themselves?

This is a little different from the issue of repairs. If a tenant approaches you about wanting to make upgrades to your unit, he will most likely be talking about minor cosmetic changes that would make him feel more comfortable while renting and could improve the aesthetics of your unit.

If a tenant has children and wants to replace your standard switch plates with beloved cartoon light covers, he can make the change and return your switch plates to their places when he moves out. This is an easy request. If a tenant would like an upgrade that he intends to leave behind, there is a little more involved.

For example, tenants may want to limit their utility bills during the summer months by forgoing air conditioning in favor of ceiling fans. You can ask them to purchase a ceiling fan that will be installed and remain with the unit after their lease ends. Ask them to give you the receipt so that you can deduct the price from the following month's rent. You have just added a desirable feature to your unit, and your tenants will be more comfortable during their lease. Everyone wins.

When it comes to more personal preferences, such as a tenant who wants to paint a room a bright color, consider the long-term consequences of this short-term decision. Perhaps you can agree that the tenant will repaint the room a more neutral color when the lease expires. The occupants get what they like while they live there. On the other hand, if the tenants do a poor job, you will end up having to pay for the mistakes down the line. If you negotiate that a tenant return a room to its original color but the job is so poorly executed that you must redo it, you end up costing yourself money, time, and aggravation. Work with your tenants to make upgrades to your unit that can both accommodate occupants' personal preferences and be beneficial to you in the long run.

When should I raise the rent?

There are two parts to this question:

- When can you legally raise the rent?
- When and why are rent increases necessary?

When you first determined the rent for your property, you considered the current market value of comparable properties in your area, looked at what fee you would need to meet your own expenses, and left yourself a little negotiating room so that you could best match your business philosophy to your prospective tenants. Having decided on a figure, you negotiated either a month-to-month or fixed-term lease. The details of your rental agreement dictate when you can make rent increases.

For tenants who are on a month-to-month contract, most states allow you to raise rent after thirty days of giving written notice. If you have negotiated a fixed-term lease, you cannot make changes to the lease agreement unless your tenant approves the changes. Chances are he's not going to endorse a raise in his rent. In both cases, the terms of your agreements may be subject to rent-control laws.

Four states—New York, New Jersey, Maryland, and California—plus the District of Columbia, have rent-control laws. In these states, laws may limit the size of the rental increase, the number of times an increase occurs, or both. If you plan to purchase in these areas, be sure to contact the local rental control board, via the city manager or mayor's office, and inquire about the particular rules and regulations regarding rent.

Once you are clear on when you can schedule rent increases, consider when you want to. There are several reasons to raise the rent:

- Higher taxes
- Increased cost of living
- Unforeseen personal financial burdens
- A troublesome tenant

Typically, landlords raise the rent once a year. You can determine a new rental fee by considering the current market value. If there are several vacancies in town whose rent is comparable to or lower than yours, or if you appreciate how low-maintenance your current tenant is, you may want to make only a small increase. If prices in the area are on the rise and rentals are at a premium, or if a problem tenant is making your business challenging, you may want to consider a more substantial rent increase.

Raising the rent is a business decision that is a means of maintaining your portfolio's profitability. It should be discussed with your financial team.

Should I insist on renter's insurance?

Since you are responsible for your tenants' safety, be sure to obtain the local housing codes to make sure you are taking all of the steps necessary to meet your area's requirements. Usually you will be responsible for installing dead-bolt locks, peepholes, and other safety devices. In addition, you will want to create an environment that does not invite trouble.

Unfortunately, renters can be susceptible to burglaries for several reasons. If your unit is one among many rentals, thieves can move among the properties more easily, as occupants most likely do not know their neighbors or their neighbors' friends. As a landlord, you can be held accountable, to some degree, for making sure your tenant is protected.

Ideally, you will buy investment properties in a crime-free area. But it is a good idea to install motion-detector lights, cut away bushes that hinder a tenant's line of sight, and make sure entrances have proper lighting. Once you have outfitted your property with these features, you can talk to your tenants about renter's insurance, knowing you have done your part to help make your property safer.

Renter's insurance covers losses that occur due to fire and theft. Tenants pay for the amount of coverage that they want, with varying deductibles. Since an occupant's belongings are not covered by your homeowner's insurance, a manageable policy would make sense, especially if the tenants own anything of value.

As a homeowner, you know how important insurance is. Even in the best areas, under the best circumstances, fire and theft can happen. It is not necessary to insist on renter's insurance, as the coverage does not benefit you in any way, but you may want to encourage your tenants to talk to an insurance professional to see how they can benefit.

Why should I collect a security deposit?

A security deposit is usually collected when the rental agreement is signed. Along with the first month's rent, you should require additional money as a security deposit. Most landlords ask for between one and two months' rent, although some states allow you to collect more. This money is held in anticipation of any damage done to the property during occupancy. It should not be considered the landlord's money. It belongs to the tenant and can only be used if the unit is unreasonably damaged. We recommend keeping this money in a separate business account; some states require that the money be formally held in escrow. It is never a good idea to commingle these funds with your personal bank account, and legal repercussions may result if you try to borrow or use these funds for any other reasons. A security deposit is a valuable fund to have on hand, but you will need documentation to prove that damage has been done to the unit if you want to use any of the money for repairs.

Having just expended an extensive amount of time and energy purchasing your property and finding the right tenant to move in, the last thing you probably want to think about right now is the day they're going to move out. But that day will come, and you should set yourself up for a smooth transition. As always, being proactive now is an important step in securing success later.

What are a move-in checklist and an exit checklist?

Several states require that a landlord provide tenants with a move-in statement detailing the condition of the property at the time the rental agreement begins. You can check with your local housing authority to see if this statement is mandated. Even if it isn't, it is an excellent practice. Before signing the lease, walk through the unit with your tenant and use a move-in checklist to note the condition of the property. We have provided a sample checklist and instructions for its use. Taking pictures of the empty unit will provide you with a visual tool to refer to later on. A camera that time stamps the photos is ideal. All parties should sign and date the checklist and the photos. Give the tenant a copy of the paperwork for his files.

This same detailed, dated checklist should be used when your tenant has vacated the premises and wants his security deposit returned. Walk through and look for any signs of damage. If your list indicates that the carpeting was new but now there are several coffee stains visible, you can deduct the cost of cleaning the carpet from your tenant's security deposit. Either way, take new pictures of the property and keep them with this file as part of your paperwork package on this tenant.

A walk-through checklist should be written with your specific unit in mind as to not miss any important, or expensive, features. List all of the property's features, note the condition of the items, and add detailed comments if necessary. If you have purchased new construction, you will certainly want to note that everything in the property is brand new and in good working condition. If your rental has minor cosmetic issues, such as a small window that does not open, note that on your checklist. The document is not a way to get away with something, but a tool to establish a solid working relationship with your tenant. Here is a brief, general overview of things to include on your checklist.

- All flooring, including carpeting, area rugs, wood floors, or tiles
- Stairways and handrails
- Lighting fixtures, switch plates, and light bulbs
- All doors, including working locks
- All plumbing fixtures, noting drips, water pressure, and hot and cold functions
- All windows, including screens and any window treatments
- Any kitchen appliances or laundry appliances that come with the rental
- Miscellaneous items such as garage-door openers or air-conditioning units

As you walk through your unit with your tenant, turn on and off all of the lights and appliances. Check for hot and cold running water in all bathrooms and the kitchen. Turn on heating and cooling systems to make sure they are in good working condition. Take a walk around the outside of the property and check all walkways and steps. Make sure keys and locks work. As you complete this checklist, take this time to get to know your tenant a bit better. You don't want this to turn into an uncomfortable procedure. Let him know that this walk-through is for his benefit also. If there are any problems, cosmetic or otherwise, you want to address them right away. Your dedication to detail and commitment to renting a fully functional unit is a testament to your business practices and can help set the stage for a positive working relationship.

Whether you buy a new property or have restored a historical building, something is bound to break sooner or later. When completing repairs, have your walk-through checklist on hand and add a line for the repair that you are making. Have all parties sign and date that the work was completed in a satisfactory way. This can also help avoid conflict when it is time for a tenant to move out.

When do I return the security deposit?

Tenants will expect to have their money returned to them when they terminate their occupancy, and you must comply with your state's laws regarding these funds. If you do a closing walk-through with your tenants and note that there has been considerable wear and tear to the unit, you can use part or all of the security deposit to remedy the problem. But the term "normal wear and tear" is unspecific and broad, and your opinion of "considerable" could vary greatly from your tenant's. Generally speaking, normal wear and tear refers to the way a rental unit would look after a typically responsible person had inhabited it for the time of the rental agreement. Tenants are required to return the unit in good condition, but this does not mean that they must have bleached, scrubbed, and sanitized every corner of the unit. If you return to your unit and there are smudges on the wall next to the microwave, you will not have much of a case for keeping a security deposit. If there is a hole punched in the wall, that is a different story.

You must return a security deposit promptly or else send a certified letter stating why you have not returned the money and detailing the problems that need remedying. Most states allow landlords to use the security deposit to pay for back rent or to use a portion of the deposit to clean a unit that has been left in unreasonable unsanitary condition. But since the term "unreasonable" is so broad, you should always consult your real-estate attorney and local housing authority before using the money. Most housing authorities require that a security deposit fund be resolved within thirty days of occupancy termination. If you really think you have a case against your tenant, you may be better off seeking legal counsel and addressing the issues in small claims court rather than trying to sort the situation out on your own.

Hopefully, your extensive interview process, well-articulated lease agreement, and care and concern regarding your unit at the beginning of your occupant's stay and during her tenancy will limit security deposit issues. Renting a property in good condition and being an engaged and concerned landlord who makes regular upgrades and responds to repair requests in a timely manner can go a long way in promoting a happy and profitable landlord/tenant relationship.

How hands-on should I be?

At no point in time will your real-estate investing business ever run itself. With hard work, energy, and integrity, you can manage a smooth and successful financial portfolio, but you will always need to be hands-on.

We spent an entire section talking about the necessity of organizing your financial team and highlighted the attributes that each professional brings to your business. As your investing career grows and more networking opportunities are available, your team will grow. But this growth is not a sign that you are ready to turn the reins over to someone else. On the contrary, the bigger your portfolio gets the more attention it will need.

From a financial standpoint, the more people you hire to do the job for you, the less money you will have in hand. No one works for free. Gardeners, electricians, plumbers, and property managers are all hired employees. You will have to weigh the cost effectiveness of doing it yourself or paying for the task to be completed. If you opt to solicit help, which we encourage when the project is beyond your scope of ability, it is still your responsibility to oversee the projects, learn what is involved at each phase, and ensure everything is getting done.

For instance, you may begin working with a home inspector whose expertise you come to rely on. After a few projects together, you may assume that the inspector can evaluate the property without your presence. After all, everything has always worked out in the past. Decisions like these can lead to portfolio deterioration. It is great that you feel confident about your home inspector's abilities. He is someone you can consider part of the team. But this is your investment, your money, and your future. Your presence is an essential component for your success.

We made a point in the beginning of this book that bears repeating. As a novice, you may feel inadequate or uncertain about the next step to take and rely heavily on the advice of other real-estate investment professionals. That is why we believe so strongly in the formulation of a competent financial team. But don't let your inexperience or fear convince you to let others run the show.

Ask for help, evaluate the advice of experts, yes; but always remember that you are the business owner and as such will always need to be hands-on.

Do I need a property manager?

Many would-be real-estate investors shy away from income properties, concerned about how they would handle the day-to-day business of being a landlord. Concerned about having to be on call for repairs or nervous about confronting a tenant about late rent, these potential landlords turn their energies elsewhere, usually unaware that there is a solution to these matters.

Property managers are hired to do exactly what many would-be investors fear having to do themselves. Property managers usually live in close proximity to the property or reside in an adjoining unit and can collect rents, make repairs, and maintain the property's interior and exterior. In addition, property managers can show prospective tenants a vacant apartment, enforce rental agreement rules such as no pets, and can conduct routine inspections of the grounds. The more properties you accumulate, the more reasons you may have to take advantage of a property manager's services.

Your property manager's behavior is your responsibility. For example, if a property manager gives preferential treatment to certain tenants while neglecting the requests of others, the offended tenants have every right to take issue with you as the property manager is your employee. Be certain to hire a reputable individual who understands the rules and regulations of local and national Fair Housing laws and is familiar with such legislation as the Americans with Disabilities Act. After all of the hard work you have done to educate yourself, it would be a shame to jeopardize your new business because of someone else's disregard for the laws. When the time and circumstances are right, a property manager can service your tenants in an efficient and professional manner and can relieve some of the daily burdens of owning several rental properties.

How do I find and employ a property manager?

If and when you are ready to add a property manager to your team, you can look for referrals much in the same way we have suggested before. Speak to your colleagues about property manager recommendations, and check out professional Web sites.

Word-of-mouth referrals can be an excellent starting point when looking for property managers. Since you will most likely be speaking with real-estate investors who are familiar with your area, they can be a great resource. Be sure to ask about the manager's experience, how long your contact has known the manager, what, if any, problems have come up, the kind of properties the manager services, and the responsibilities she is paid to fulfill. As always, conduct your own interview with a referral. Never bring someone onto your team just because she or he has been recommended.

Aside from asking other real-estate investors whom they employ, consider asking one of the tenants who are currently occupying your properties if he would be willing to serve as property manager. Having conducted background checks, verified employment, and enjoyed a positive tenant/landlord relationship, you may have an ideal property manager on location already. You can offer a reliable tenant a role in your business for a reduction in rent. This go-to person can perform basic household repairs, collect rents, and keep an eye on the place.

If you opt to go with a professional company that specializes in income property management, start by visiting the National Association of Residential Property Managers (NARPM) at *www.narpm.org*. This site allows you to search for property managers in your area who are members of NARPM, reflecting their professional designations earned through industry-related education. You can expect to pay more when you solicit the services of an established property management company, most of whom favor serving large accounts. Even if you are just starting out, you can benefit from having a conversation with the specialists who service your area. As your portfolio grows, you can then see if their services match your needs. Property managers can be an asset to your team and should be considered both now and further along in your real-estate investment career.

Who should have a key to the property?

The tenant has been screened, the walk-through completed, the lease signed, and the proper funds paid. It is time to hand over the keys and let your tenant take occupancy. Be sure not to give your tenants the only set of keys, as there are reasons why you and your property manager, if you have one, will want copies.

Once a tenant moves into your income property, he is entitled to a certain degree of privacy. Yes, you own the building, but unless there is an extenuating circumstance, you may not enter a rented unit without ample notice. In most states, you cannot show up at a tenant's door and demand to be let in or let yourself in. You must give the occupant twenty-four hours' notice before entering, and even then the reason for your entrance must be justified. Generally speaking, you cannot enter a rented unit just to see how things are going. You must be there because a repair is needed or because the current tenant is moving out and you need to show the property. Exceptions are made for emergencies.

If there is an immediate problem, such as an unexpected change in weather that could cause water pipes to freeze or burst or a disaster like a fire, landlords may usually enter the premises to prevent or address the emergency. Whenever possible, it is good practice to let the tenant know you need to come over right away, as it is always better to get his permission to enter the unit. Some states will also allow a landlord to enter the unit if an occupant has been missing or unavailable for several days. Always check with your local housing authority before assuming it is okay to go inside a rented unit.

If you employ a property manager, she is allowed to have a key to the property. The same rules of entry usually apply. Remember, since your property manager is your employee, you will be held responsible for her actions. Make sure you conduct a thorough interview and background check on all of your employees and review the housing laws in detail.

If you find that you have a difficult tenant and you are tempted to go over to the unit and have a few words with him or escort him out of the unit, we warn you against such behavior. If you need to terminate a rental agreement and evict a tenant, you must go through the proper channels. Never take the matter into your own hands. It is dangerous and illegal. Having keys and access to a rented unit is a responsibility that should not be handled carelessly. Know your rights and your tenant's rights.

What problems should I try to avoid as a landlord?

There are three major reasons landlords get themselves into trouble:

1. The landlord rushes the process and tries to skip steps.

2. The landlord makes emotional decisions instead of business decisions.

3. The landlord has lost sight of her big-picture business plan.

We have said that real-estate investing is a process that must be followed step by step. But between the time you close on a property and the time you start collecting rent, you may find yourself becoming increasingly panicked about finances. Perhaps you need to make renovations before you can offer the unit for occupancy, or maybe the closing itself is taking longer than you anticipated. At times like these, you may become so anxious that you accept the first tenant applicant who walks through the door, forgoing background or reference checks and rushing through rental agreements. Not surprisingly, it isn't long before this tenant starts making excuses for late rent or "forgets" the rules you had talked about.

Another common cause of problems is inexperience. If this is the first time that you have been in a management position, you may feel awkward if your tenant starts asking for favors. Wanting to help her out, you do so only to find yourself with a rented unit but no rent. We all want to be liked and we want to help others when we can, but in business this can be a very slippery slope.

Finally, if the day-to-day operations of your investment business are consuming all your time and energy, you may be losing sight of the bigger picture. During your first couple of income property deals, you may find yourself micromanaging the transactions, afraid that if you look away for a moment it will all fall apart. Neglecting to take things one step at a time, making decisions with your heart not your head, and becoming preoccupied with one project can lead to many problems.

What are common solutions to these problems?

The good thing about common problems is that they often have common solutions. Usually these solutions require that the business owner take a step back from the situation and look at things from an alternative perspective. As usual, this is where your financial team can help.

Your real-estate attorney, mortgage consultant, and Realtor can help you answer questions about the purchasing process so that you don't feel left out of the loop. Your financial planner may be able to help you feel more secure about your financial footing. And the professional investors you have met through networking can be a valuable sounding board, reminding you that a quick fix, like taking any tenant, can have expensive consequences.

Once your unit is rented, make sure that you protect yourself against a short-term problem becoming a long-term disaster. For instance, if rent is late, or short, and you decide to be accommodating, document the problem, detail how it will be resolved, and have all parties sign and receive copies of the note. If the problem is not resolved, you should seek legal advice. There is a fine line between helping someone and being taken advantage of. Talk with others in the business to make sure you are on the right side of this line.

The same help is available if you are becoming overly involved in a particular transaction. There is a process that must be followed, but you cannot control every aspect of the plan. Yes, you should always remain active in your business, but each deal is just a vehicle through which you achieve greater financial independence and security. Being detail oriented is not the same as being detail obsessed.

Many problems can be avoided if we rely on the experience and expertise of those who are seasoned veterans in the field. If you are feeling isolated, take a step to reconnect with your investment team and get yourself back on track. Your team helped you design your portfolio plan, and they can help remind you of your long-term goals.

What if the rent is late?

If your tenant has not turned in the rent on time, there are several alternatives within your legal rights, and there are several actions that could cause you more problems. It is important to know the difference.

Your knee-jerk reaction to not receiving your rent will most likely be anger, anxiety, and fear: anger that the rules are not being followed, anxiety over having to take time away from your busy schedule to fix this problem, and fear that this is going to turn into full-blown court battle. Do not act on these emotions. Do not storm over to your tenant's home and make threats, physically remove him from the grounds, or shut off the power. These are not legal options. Instead, keep your cool and reach out to your client. There is probably a simple reason that the rent is late, and one phone call can rectify the situation. Before you call your lawyer, call your tenant.

Document the incident, and keep this paperwork on file in case this incident is, in fact, the start of a bad habit. Documentation is key if and when problems become more serious. If your phone call does not motivate your tenant to pay the rent that is due, make an appointment to meet your tenant face to face. If your tenant refuses or does not show up, check to see if your state has a property mediator or arbitration services; your lawyer will know if these are available. A third party can often help settle disputes and get the renter/landlord relationship re-established. If these suggestions do not work, you may have to begin the eviction process.

Most rental disputes are handled in small claims court, and your lawyer can help you navigate these proceedings. Some states do not allow lawyers to argue cases in small claims court, but your legal team member can offer counsel before the proceedings and help you ensure all your paperwork is in order.

Evicting a tenant usually involves terminating the tenancy, serving notice, filing for and attending eviction proceedings, proving your case, winning your case, and being issued a warrant that permits a law official to remove your tenant. This is not an easy process, so you can see why trying to resolve a rental issue first makes the most sense.

Can I prohibit smoking?

The short answer is yes; legally you are allowed to prohibit smoking. As you are the landlord and owner of the property, you can decide whether you want your property to be nonsmoking. But as with many landlord decisions, because you have the legal right to do something does not mean you should do it. You want to make business decisions that will improve, not hinder, your business. To do this successfully, consider all sides of the issue.

If you are leaning toward a nonsmoking rental, you can take comfort in knowing that many bars and restaurants have gone nonsmoking and are still turning a handsome profit. Many renters may appreciate a smoke-free unit. But the name of the game in income properties is making a profit, so you need to consider if your renting pool is big enough to sustain this ban. If there are few renters and many vacancies, you could be alienating the few tenants available.

If you have chosen to buy in an area that is conducive to rentals, this may not be such a concern and you can write the ban into the lease. This is another reason why knowing your target area is so valuable. You want to buy in an area whose economic and social growth will lend itself to a healthy rental pool.

As the landlord of a single-family unit, you should let tenants know from the start that this is a smoke-free unit. However, if you are buying a multiunit property whose units are already rented to smoking tenants, you will probably have to wait until the lease expires to make changes to the agreement. If the lease does not explicitly state that smoking is allowed, with ample notice you may be able to enforce a nonsmoking policy. Giving your tenants plenty of notice about the change can help you make a smoother transition to the environment you want. Check with your local housing authority to see what the rules in your area are.

Should I prohibit smoking?

Most people acknowledge that smoking is an unhealthy habit that pollutes the body and environment. It can also ruin rental interiors by yellowing walls or burning carpets, so on the surface it would appear to make sense to ban smoking. However, as previously discussed, you must also consider your current rental market, your specific property type, and the effectiveness of such a ban.

Of course, you'll also have to think about how you will structure this rule. Do you plan to rent only to nonsmokers or smokers who say they will only smoke outside? Is the entire property nonsmoking or just inside the unit? Some landlords have found a happy medium by designating a specific smoking location, such as an outdoor bench with ashtrays, so as not to alienate otherwise potentially excellent tenants. How much thought and effort you want to put into managing your smoking tenants is up to you.

You should always consider the ramifications of any changes you make. If you have inherited a fully rented multiunit property that is running smoothly, you may not want to change the rules. The opinion of your local networking team will be extremely helpful in making this decision, as you may just find someone who has handled such a situation. It is always a good rule of thumb to proceed with diplomacy whenever you are handling tenant issues.

Enforcing your nonsmoking ban may lead you to evict certain tenants, which can be costly and time consuming. Smoking can damage your unit, but it may be the lesser of two evils. The best-case scenario for enforcing a nonsmoking policy is when the lease establishes this ban from the beginning of the tenancy. You can look for occupants who favor such a smoke-free environment. This way you will not be backpedaling or bargaining with your current tenants.

Should I prohibit pets?

The Humane Society of the United States estimates that nearly half of all renters in the United States have a pet. To exclude these people from your rental pool could make it harder to fill your vacancies. Yet concerns over damage to a unit and the legal ramifications of a dangerous animal prompt many landlords to simply say no to pets. What should you do? The Humane Society's Web site at *www.hsus.org* offers several articles on the subject.

If you choose to allow pets, screen the pet as you would the tenant. Meet the animal to see how it reacts to strangers, watch the dynamic between animal and owner, and ask several questions about the pet's history—whether it is declawed, spayed, or neutered, what type of training it has received, and its medical history, including vaccinations. The Humane Society Web site offers a pet application form, which can be filled out and kept with the tenant's other paperwork.

If you decide to allow pets, be very specific about your policy. Decide which types of pets you will allow, and be very clear about your expectations, just as you would with your tenant. Check with the local housing board to be sure that you can ask for a pet deposit in addition to the security deposit. This money can be used to treat animal-specific problems, such as having to clean the carpets due to strong animal odors. Also, check with the housing authority, your lawyer, and your insurance company to see if having a pet on your property would put you at risk should the animal cause damage to the unit or hurt someone else.

You will have to decide what your comfort level is. If you are an animal lover and owner, you may think that having tenants with pets is completely normal.

But don't assume that all animal owners are as responsible as you are. Take the time to screen all pets and protect yourself and your assets by familiarizing yourself with your legal rights. If you don't want to rent to tenants with pets, know that this decision could drastically limit your rental pool. Either decision has serious ramifications.

How can I enforce the rules?

Once you decide what the rules of your rented unit are going to be, you must know your rights as a landlord in enforcing them. Whether you are owed rent or suspect that your no-pet policy has been violated, there are certain rules of landlord and tenant relations that you must follow.

Most importantly, know the Fair Housing laws. You may not discriminate nor favor one tenant over another. This doesn't mean that a single mother from a minority class cannot be held responsible for paying the rent, but it does mean that the same accountability expectations must be applied to all of your tenants. The best way to do this is by being proactive.

Take time to think about what you will expect from your tenants. Never assume that a tenant has the same ideas as you about how your property should be treated, especially when it comes to cleanliness. Take pictures of the unit and do a walk-through, explaining that this is the way you want the unit returned. This is commonly called *end of term restoration*. Be very clear about when and how you expect the rent, at what point you will consider it late, and what penalties will be assessed.

In your lease or rental agreement, spell out all the rules in clear, easy to understand language. "Some pets allowed" is vague and can easily be misinterpreted. Be specific: "Only pet fish allowed." Review all the rules and regulations with your tenants. Do not merely send them home with the paperwork to read. Go through it together. Make sure all parties have copies of all paperwork.

From the moment you begin interviewing prospective tenants to the moment that they hand you back the keys and leave the unit, keep well-organized documentation. Most landlords assume that they should keep a copy of all payments, either cancelled checks or rent receipts. You should also add to a tenant's file any complaints made against him by other tenants and/or any warnings you have issued. Even if these occurrences were just conversations, be sure to make a written report of what was said between whom, about what, date it, and add it to the occupant's file. Having documentation will go a long way in helping you enforce the rules and proving that you have taken action because of misconduct, not because of prejudice. Keep all documentation forever, as tenants can decide later on, usually within six months to a year after the incident, that they want to file a complaint against you. If you are clear about your expectations in writing and keep notes about your occupant throughout the tenancy, renters are much more likely to follow your rules.

What if the tenants won't leave?

It can be unpleasant and disheartening to think, after all of your hard work securing your financial investment team, getting your rental agreement paperwork in order, and conducting thorough background checks, that your tenant/landlord relationship has gone sour and you must evict your tenant. Yes, this does happen, but keep in mind that you greatly reduce your risk of running into such trouble if you follow a business plan, make well-informed decisions, and surround yourself with experts. If an eviction is unavoidable, however, all of your hard work will not be wasted.

Having kept copious notes on your tenant, including a copy of the signed and dated rental agreement, notes on any violations including late rent payments, and documents on any tenant altercations, you can contact your attorney with this paperwork and provide evidence of wrongdoing. You will have to terminate the tenancy, wait for the tenant to refuse to remedy the situation—for instance, she will still not pay the rent—and wait for her to refuse to leave. You can then file an eviction lawsuit. Your attorney can counsel you on how to best proceed with an eviction, but we'll give you an overview of what to expect.

First you must serve an eviction notice to your tenant that states your reasons for eviction, and it must be served according to the statute of your state, which usually means hand delivering. The notice must also give a date that the tenant must vacate the premises, which can be anywhere from seventy-two hours to thirty days, depending on the circumstances. Make a copy of this notice for yourself, and keep it with your files. Since the occupant will probably not take this news well, consider a police escort when you present the eviction notice. Tenants can become angry that they are being evicted and ruin the property in retaliation. To protect yourself and your property, you may want to coordinate the police escort with a walk-through of your property to take pictures in anticipation of any problems that would require withholding security deposit money for damages. Remember to check your area's laws on entering a tenant's property. You must usually give at least twenty-four hours' notice. When your tenant is finally evicted, do another walk-through of the property to see if any damage has been done. Take more pictures, take more notes, and hold onto this file forever.

Keep in mind that the tenant has rights and can mount a countersuit. This can draw out the process for months and make a difficult situation even more exasperating. If you win your case, your local police department should deliver the court judgment to the tenant who will then have a specific number of days to leave or else be physically removed from the property.

Eviction proceedings are challenging and can sour you on real-estate investing. Taking the steps we have suggested can greatly reduce the likelihood that you will become entangled in one of real estate's messier problems.

What if the tenants ruin the property?

Tenants have many rights when it comes to renting a property, such as safety, security, access to heat and water, and privacy, but they also have responsibilities. Tenants must comply with the terms of the rental agreement, and they must care for the property and maintain it properly. Arguments can arise when there is a discrepancy between normal wear and tear and excessive damage.

Most state laws acknowledge that tenants have a responsibility to use the property for its intended use, keep the unit free from filth and discard garbage appropriately, not meddle with smoke detectors or carbon monoxide detectors, and not deliberately destroy or damage any part of the property. Knowing the difference between normal wear and tear and destruction is an important element of property management.

Usually landlords can deduct money from a tenant's security deposit and use those funds to return the property to its original condition when deliberate neglect or excessive damage has been done to the unit. Normal wear and tear, which does not warrant a deduction from the security deposit, includes:

- Upholstery
- Curtains or carpeting that show signs of sun fading
- Carpet wear in a high-traffic area
- Minor dents or nicks on walls from moving furniture or door knobs bumping the same spot
- Water stains in showers or sinks

In any home, colors fade and paint chips. This is why you should freshen up your unit between renters and keep on top of minor maintenance. On the other hand, holes in the wall, smashed windows, water/coffee/pet urine stains on wood floors or carpeting, or missing shelving or doors is not normal wear and tear. This damage happens because the property has been mistreated or neglected. Even if the tenant explains such damage was an accident, she is still responsible for the repairs.

You can add language in your rental agreement that explicitly spells out that a tenant is responsible for damages above ordinary wear and tear, again noting the condition of each aspect of your property in your walk-through checklist at the beginning of occupancy. If you are visiting the occupant during the tenancy and notice damages, address the situation right away by documenting the issue, sending a copy of the paperwork to the tenant, and following up to make sure the problem is taken care of. If you have taken the recommended steps to find an occupant for your property and remain a proactive and conscientious landlord, you will probably be working with tenants who want to resolve such problems. Be clear about your expectations, and you'll have a better chance of avoiding property damage.

If a tenant hurts himself on my property, can I be sued?

As the landlord, you are responsible for maintaining a safe property. You should make sure that all common areas, such as front porches, sidewalks, walkways, and staircases, are level and secure. If a tenant hurts himself on your property and can prove you have not addressed a problem or have neglected the area where the injury had occurred, you may be found liable.

For example, if housing codes dictate that you install a handrail on the front porch stairs and you neglect to do so, an accident occurring there could be your fault. The tenant could most likely prove that you knew a handrail was needed (it is a standard housing law that would have been addressed at your home inspection), that you chose to ignore the recommendation, the missing handrail made the steps dangerous, and your negligence caused an accident that seriously injured the occupant.

In essence, if you know there is a problem and you have refused to fix it, you can be held responsible for the injury. Ignorance is no excuse for breaking the law. If you waived your home inspection and did not know that a handrail was needed, you are not automatically excused from neglect. It is your responsibility to know what measures must be taken to make your property safe and secure. This is another reason we never advocate skipping steps: What you don't know could hurt you (and your tenant).

If, on the other hand, your tenant had removed the handrail and suffered an injury on account of his own dangerous behavior, you have a much better chance of not being found liable. Again, having pictures of the property included with your rental agreement can help protect you from problems such as these.

Another good reason to keep your property safe and secure involves liability protection from any person who happens to hurt herself or himself on your property. If the sidewalk in front of and adjacent to your property has a large crack or has settled unevenly, you could be held liable for any injuries that result from this. Unfortunately, instead of holding people accountable for watching where they walk, we often use the courts to blame someone else. Keeping on top of your property's maintenance needs can help you avoid expensive liability issues.

What if the tenant is breaking the law?

A tenant who breaks the law while occupying your property can become a very serious problem for you very quickly. One of the most disturbing of such issues occurs when a tenant becomes involved in drug dealing. It is critical that you do everything you can to avoid renting your property to such a tenant and immediately address the issue if a problem becomes apparent.

When you are interviewing tenants, make it clear that you will not tolerate any kind of illegal activity and that if you are made aware of such activity you will contact the police immediately. This clear statement, along with thorough background, references, and rental history checks, can help you deter law-breaking persons from pursuing tenancy with you.

If, despite your efforts, you think that you may have a tenant on your hands who is breaking the law, do not turn a blind eye toward the problem. If neighbors suspect illegal activity and are bothered or injured by it, your unit could be deemed a public nuisance. If a court determines that you were aware of such activity and did nothing to stop it, you could be heavily fined. Once you and your property are stigmatized as being involved with criminal activity, it can be very difficult to find upstanding future renters.

Should neighbors contact you with complaints or concerns, or if you are troubled by suspicious activity, such as late-night traffic or excessive, noisy partying, consult your local law enforcement officials for advice. Do not tolerate illegal activity on your property and do not try to work things out on your own. Enlist the help of experts who know how to deal with criminal behavior, contact your lawyer, and begin the eviction process.

When it comes to running a real-estate business, there is no gray area when dealing with illegal activity. Do everything you can to rent to law-abiding citizens, and work to remove any tenants who break the law.

What if I need to sell a rented property?

There may come a time when you need to sell an investment property in the middle of a rental agreement. Perhaps there is a new opportunity, and you need to let go of this unit to make yourself available for the next one. Maybe you are moving out of the area and do not want the responsibility of a long-distance income property. While every landlord has his own reasons, financial and emotional, for selling properties, always make sure that you consult with your financial team before moving forward with a sale. You may have options that you are not aware of, making it possible for you to keep your rented unit while addressing new opportunities. If selling is the right course of action, be aware that the tenants who currently reside in your property have rights.

Selling a rented property can become complicated quickly. To make the transition as smooth as possible, keep the lines of communication open. The first step is to tell your tenants that the unit is for sale. Some landlords may want to avoid this conversation, fearful that resentful tenants will damage the property or hinder the process, but it has been our experience that tenants become more upset when they are left out of the loop. Just because you are selling does not mean that your current rental contract is null and void. You must still respect the terms of entry, usually giving the tenants twenty-four hours' notice before showing the unit, unless other arrangements are made. Anyone who wants to show the property must abide by the agreement.

If you sell the property quickly, the tenants do not have to vacate until the end of their lease. It's possible that your tenants may begin looking for a new home as soon as you put the property up for sale and end the rental agreement prematurely. Discuss these options with your tenants.

If the buyers intend to continue renting the space, the new owners will take over the current tenants' leases until they end. If the new landlord wants to buy a vacant property and the occupants are on a month-to-month rental agreement, you can usually give your tenant between one and a half and two months' notice to vacate. Check with your local housing authority.

Selling a rented property is more complicated because there are more people involved. Treating your tenants with respect and knowing your legal obligations, and their rights, can help to facilitate a successful property sale.

Scenario: What if the renter wants to buy my property?

If a renter approaches you about buying your property, you should treat the potential transaction as you would any other real-estate deal. When we were approached by our tenants about buying one of our townhouses, they had a number and time frame in mind. Before we could even comment on the offer, we knew to check in with our team and weigh all of our options. You need to do the same.

Tenants can approach you about buying a property at any point during their tenancy. Being a savvy investor, you know that you need to have your finger on the pulse of the market. Before you jump on the opportunity to sell or too quickly dismiss the idea, ask yourself some important questions about the pros and cons of such a portfolio transaction.

- Is this a good time to sell?
- What is the tenant offering to pay?
- Is this in line with the market?

- Knowing the direction that the market is moving in, will selling this property put you in good standing for your next transaction?
- What is the tenant's time frame?
- What other projects do you have on the horizon and how will this transaction affect your taxes?

Check with your Realtor and ask for a market analysis of your property. Take time to examine your business calendar and consider when a sale would be most beneficial. In our case, the tenants loved the townhouse but wouldn't be able to begin the purchase process for another six months. We spoke to our financial team about this proposal and proceeded accordingly. We did not become greedy and insist on an immediate contract from our renters or put the property on the market at a higher listing price with hopes of having our tenants offer us more money. Instead, we considered their offer and time frame, countered, and came to a verbal agreement contingent on new credit checks and mortgage approval. Although we hadn't planned on selling, this profit-making opportunity presented itself. When we discussed the benefits of selling, minus the trouble of putting the home on the market, the idea made sense to everyone on our team. We could take our time knowing that another six months of rent was more secure, giving us time to prepare our next transaction.

If a tenant wants to purchase your unit, ask that she put a proposal together, including a preapproval from her bank and a time frame. Sometimes opportunities come knocking and you would be well advised to consider such unexpected deals with the help of your financial investment team. 🏠

What if a renter wants to sublet?

Depending on your location, you may find yourself the recipient of a request to sublet. While this idea may seem uncomfortable to you, considering how much time and effort you have put into screening your tenants, you may not have much choice in allowing such a setup unless you specifically state in the lease that the property is not to be sublet at any time, for any purpose, and all parties agree to this. A sublet is a temporary absence by the primary tenant for a specific time. The intention of the tenant is to return to the unit and resume occupancy once the specified term has ended. The new tenant must follow the proper protocol and remains accountable for all terms of the original lease.

A tenant who wishes to sublet must inform his landlord by mailing a notice of subletting intent by certified mail, return receipt requested, no later than thirty days before the proposed occupancy change is to begin. Included on the notice must be:

- Name of the subletting tenant
- Contact information for this new tenant
- Reason for subletting and the length of the term
- Original tenant's contact information during the sublet term
- Written consent of any other cotenants
- A copy of the signed sublease and a copy of the original lease

A landlord can ask for additional reasonable information, such as a letter of reference, but such requests must be made within ten days of the sublet notice receipt. A landlord must grant consent within thirty days of receiving notice unless an outstanding reason for denial is appropriate, which the notice of denial must cite.

A tenant may charge the occupant subletting an additional 10 percent of the rent since the property is furnished but may not charge any additional fees for use of the unit. The original tenant maintains that the unit is his primary residence, and he is the only one who can negotiate new terms when the rental agreement comes to an end.

Subletting is a very common practice in major cities. If you feel unsettled by this new arrangement, reach out to your local network of colleagues who may have experience with this scenario. They can help you get a handle on the new situation and offer suggestions for maintaining a productive and profitable income property.

What does lease with an option to buy mean?

When you and your tenants are ready to finalize a rental agreement, you may find that the new occupants have a few requests of their own, such as adding a lease with an option to buy clause into the paperwork. There are several different ways to word this language so that all parties feel secure in a possible future purchase. We'll take a look at the most common option.

In a nutshell, this clause means that the tenants are renting the property with an option to buy it at a future date. Tenants who are new to area, recently divorced, or contemplating a permanent career change may not be ready to buy right now, but they may like knowing that if they decide to stay in the area, they can continue living in the property they have come to know as their new home. Other tenants who have had credit issues in the past may be working toward rehabilitating their credit standing and feel that they will be in a position to purchase a home at a future date but cannot do so presently.

Usually the terms of this agreement are finalized upon the signing of the lease. At this time, the rental agreement will include the price of the property and the date it is to be sold. A landlord can charge a fee for including this option in the lease. This might take the form of an additional monthly fee that will be applied toward the down payment on the sale when the time is right. Here, a landlord has the security of knowing he has a serious buyer. The lease for such an arrangement often states that if the tenant decides not to buy the home, the additional funds are forfeited; after all, the landlord did not sell the property based on the notion that it would be bought by the tenant.

This scenario involves risk because the market could shift during the lease period, and the sale price you agreed upon earlier could end up being far below the market value at the time of sale. Therefore, it is important to work with your financial team to calculate a future sale price that will be profitable for you in any market.

This scenario can be used either in a seller's market, to prevent the landlord from selling the home before the tenant is ready to buy, or in a buyer's market, when there is not a high demand for homes. It is also a good idea to talk this clause over with your financial team. You can plan your next portfolio move based on the option-to-buy date.

What does right of first refusal *mean?*

Commonly referred to as a type of option-to-buy clause, a right of first refusal is a more informal means of planning for a future property sale with your current tenants. It is a less formal arrangement than an option to buy because you do not collect funds throughout the tenancy nor do you need to decide on a sale price when signing the lease.

If you have a property that you intend to sell but the market is making it difficult to do so, you may opt to rent the unit and wait for the market to shift in your favor. That way you can cover your mortgage and not compromise your asking price. If your tenants sign a one-year lease with you knowing that your intention is to try to sell the property at the end of the agreement, they may ask to have right of first refusal

This means that before you put the house on the market your tenants have the option of choosing to purchase at the listed price (a price worked out in advance by you and your financial advisor). The benefits are twofold: The landlord can forgo the process of selling the home on the market, and the tenants don't have to move. Time is your most precious asset, and you should always look into saving it.

Again, tenants who are new to the neighborhood or find themselves in a new family dynamic may like the idea of knowing they have the option to buy the home. As a landlord, it can be particularly nice to rent to tenants who are contemplating making your income property a permanent residence. Tenants with a sense of ownership may treat your unit with a higher degree of respect and responsibility. Even if they don't end up buying the unit, you will most likely have a clean and well-cared-for property returned to you. As with any wording in your rental agreement, be clear and specific, making certain that all parties appreciate the details of what is being negotiated.

Scenario: I'm uncomfortable talking about money and am avoiding raising the rent even though I have to. What can I do?

It can be very difficult to raise the rent, even in the best circumstances. Before you do, think about why you have to. Check the market and make sure that a rent increase will not drive out your tenant. Evaluate the benefits of the increase versus having to find a new occupant. While it is common to raise the rent periodically, it is not mandatory. You could be feeling hesitant because you are trying to make this decision on your own and your gut is telling you to ask for help. Turn to your trusted team and bounce your idea off of them before proceeding.

If you have the support of your team and know that the time is right and the additional increase is fair, raising the rent may still make you uncomfortable. We all want to be liked, and confrontation of any type can feel intimidating. But there are some things you can remind yourself of to help make the conversation more manageable.

You are a business owner. As a business owner you want to treat your clients—your tenants—well, but that does not mean that you should run your business into the ground. As a proactive landlord, you have attended to repairs, worked to make requested upgrades, and provided a safe and comfortable property. To continue to best service your tenants, a rent increase may be required. Stores, restaurants, and service industries must all raise their prices to stay competitive and grow. This is a necessary business decision.

Most tenants expect that the rent will increase at the time of renegotiations. If the market is favorable and the increase modest, most tenants will not think twice about paying the additional amount, especially if they have received an increase in income over the past year or so. You are not the first or only landlord to negotiate the rent. This is a common, expected practice.

You do not have to do this alone. If you feel paralyzed by the subject of money, talk to your more experienced landlording colleagues about their practices. How did they breach the subject? How was the information received? We tend to make things much more complicated in our minds and replay the worst-case scenarios even though things are hardly ever as bad as we expect them to be.

You have worked hard with your financial team to purchase a profitable property, interview and choose the best tenants, and maintain your income property. Your success depends on moving forward, not backward. The more experience you have as a property owner, the more secure you will be as a landlord. Until then, reassure yourself that you are taking care of business and ask for help in doing so.

Chapter Six Paperwork: Leases and Record-Keeping

Should I do a final inspection before tenants move in?

When you purchase a real-estate property you have the option of having a home inspection done before closing on the contract. Of course, we recommend that you take this opportunity to have an unbiased expert eye look at the ins and outs of the unit before you buy. But once you close and the property is yours, you will want to go over everything with your own critical eye.

Big and little problems should have been identified during the home inspection, but no matter how thorough an inspector is, things can get missed. This is especially common when people are living in the property during the transaction. You are entitled to a walk-through before closing on a property, but the excitement of the day, cramped scheduling, and an array of other circumstances can make this a less-than-ideal time to notice certain odds and ends. After your closing and before the tenants move in is a great time to check out your property undisturbed and unhurried.

Move through the unit as if you live there. Turn on all the faucets, flush the toilets, and run the showers. Check for ample water pressure, hot and cold water, and leaks. If there is a problem fixture, take care of it right away. Turning a blind eye to a minor problem can end up costing you a ton of money down the line. Changing fixtures is often a lot less costly than repairing damages.

Make sure doors, windows, cabinets, and drawers open and close smoothly. Closet rods, shower curtain rods, and towel racks should all be properly secured. Inspect the insides of closets and all cabinets, as they are prime hiding spots for mold and mildew. Look for any carpet stains that may have been hidden by the previous owner's furniture and determine if carpeting or flooring needs cleaning or replacement.

Return to the unit at night and enter the property as your tenant will. Is there ample lighting? Are the handrails secured? Are the staircases safe? Does the driveway, sidewalk, or walkway need attention? Part of renting a habitable unit is making sure that the property is safe. Motion-detecting lights can be easily installed to add security and safety. And, of course, you should have the locks changed.

If you are inheriting tenants, you don't need to wait until the lease expires to give a property your undivided attention. Make an appointment with the occupants to see if any maintenance repairs are needed. Making repairs and adding upgrades is a nice way to start your new landlord-tenant relationship.

Inspecting the unit thoroughly and making necessary repairs will prepare you to present the best possible home to prospective tenants, helping you earn the income you want. Once the unit is ready, take pictures and add them to your files to be used at your tenants' walk-throughs.

Should I have the renters sign a contract?

Yes. Yes. Yes. Under no circumstances should you rent your property without a contract or lease. Contracts protect all parties and can be written with everyone's best interests in mind, but, ultimately, you must guard yourself. This is your business, your money, your investment. Part of keeping your profit-making portfolio on track is having everything in writing.

Hopefully your tenancy will run smoothly and no disagreements will arise. After all, when things are going according to plan, there is no reason to consult the contract. But if a problem arises or an argument ensues, the first thing everyone does is reach for the contract. Legally speaking, the only way to resolve arguments between landlord and tenant is by reference to written rules and regulations.

In rental agreements, there are several key components that are too important to trust to a handshake and a good memory. In addition to these basic elements, add any additional points that relate specifically to your unit, such as which doors should be used by which tenants, parking spaces, changes to the interior and exterior of the unit, and security deposit returns.

Your rental agreement contract is a key piece of evidence should a dispute develop and should be kept in the tenant's file with her rental application, contact information, background checks, and unit photos. We hope that you will never have to rely on this paper trail, but if you do, you will be in much better standing with a clear, signed contract in hand.

Where can I find a rental agreement template?

Most large office-supply stores carry basic forms, and forms are also available for purchase online. Your team Realtor will have access to his company's standard form. For your convenience, we have included a sample lease in the appendix to show you what it looks like.

Just because you can easily get one does not mean that it is easy to understand. It is not easy to completely sidestep legal jargon in contracts because they are written by lawyers to protect legal rights. You should have a well-versed professional go through your boilerplate lease with you line by line to make sure that you comprehend what you are signing and what you are asking others to sign. Do not assume that all the legal mumbo jumbo is fine just the way it is. If a problem arises, you will be depending on that contract, and if you do not understand what you signed, you may be disappointed to find out you do not have the protection you thought you did.

Make sure that the rental contract that you choose is useful for your property. A residential lease differs greatly from a commercial lease, and the two forms should not be used interchangeably. Commercial leases are more specific than residential leases and often require much more negotiation between tenant and landlord to arrive at a manageable situation. These leases are usually for longer periods of time, command a higher rent, and outline the type of equipment or special features necessary to run a business on the premises. As far as the law is concerned, commercial renters do not have the same privacy rights as residential tenants, nor is there a limit to the amount of security deposit a landlord can require.

You may opt to create your own rental agreement using professional forms as a guideline. This way you know exactly what the contract says, having mapped out the rules and regulations in clear, clean language using short sentences and numbered paragraphs. Make sure you have your team attorney and Realtor review the contracts to make sure that you cover all necessary items and word the document in the manner which best fits your situation. Regardless of which format you choose, make sure you use a written contract.

Should I ask for cash or a check?

Approach real-estate investing as a business, not just a one-shot deal or get-rich-quick scheme, and maintain professional records. While some jobs and part-time or freelance situations run strictly on cash, real-estate investing does not, so we advocate collecting rents that will generate a paper trail. Checks, money orders, or cashier checks are your best bets for securing payment and covering all of your bases.

Before your tenant moves into your unit, you should collect a security deposit and first month's rent and make sure the checks clear to avoid having a delinquent tenant from the onset of the agreement. Insisting that the rent be paid by check is another way to weed out undesirables during the interview process, as you will prefer tenants who have sufficient bank accounts to draw from, not occupants who are living by the skin of their teeth and scraping rent together at the last minute.

If you are renting the same property to unrelated parties, as is common with units that have two or more bedrooms, insist that one check be sent for the entire amount of the rent. While accepting partial rents from individual tenants may sound harmless, it is more paperwork for you and can also lead to occupancy issues should a problem arise. If tenant A pays his half and tenant B does not pay his half, you are short half the rent. Tenant A can make a strong case for avoiding eviction since he paid and you accepted his share. If the rent is $1,000 a month, collect one check for $1,000. Make sure the check issued is from one of the tenants assigned the unit in the rental agreement. Do not accept a check written from a third party. Specify these points in the lease to avoid further occupancy issues.

If you are thinking about having your income property rent paid in cash to keep profits under the table or avoid paperwork, we caution against this as serious IRS penalties can occur. Also, if rent payments should stop or checks bounce, you need a paper trail in your tenant's file to use as tangible evidence to collect back rent or proceed with an eviction. Protect yourself and your investments by consulting with your accountant and insisting that rent not be paid in cash.

What is the difference between a rental agreement and a lease?

A rental agreement is typically used with short-term rentals whose tenancy exists on a month-to-month basis. This contract spells out the rights and responsibilities of each party and is considered valid and operational until terminated or amended. Usually, each party will have to give the other thirty days' notice before ending or changing the contract. Check with your local housing authority to confirm that this time period is acceptable. A rental agreement is a legal and binding agreement.

A lease is a contract whose term usually lasts at least a year. Like a rental agreement, a lease spells out the terms of the tenancy for a set period of time. Usually you cannot change the terms of the lease until the end of the contract. If you want to make a change, such as raising the rent or turning the property nonsmoking, you must get your tenant's approval in writing. Your tenant's willingness to oblige you will be her personal choice; a nonsmoking decision may not affect her lifestyle but a rent increase would. Be as specific and thorough as possible from the beginning. It may be harder to change things later on. Pay special attention to your rent requirements. You will want to balance the current market value with the trend of rising or falling rents in your area. While there is no way to predict the future, a booming rental market could mean lost profits for you if you do not adjust your rent regularly.

Unless your tenant fails to pay the rent or breaks another important item in the lease, you will not be able to evict her. Most of the problems we hear about real-estate investing have to do with tenant relationships. If you opt for a longer-term lease, take the time to properly screen all prospective occupants.

What items should be addressed in both rental agreements and leases?

As with all rental agreements, be they short or long term, there are several points that must be covered. We have included some of the most important points here, but be sure to check with your investment team and local housing authority to see if specific details apply to your rental market.

Tenants' names. If only one person is occupying the property, you need only one name. If two or more tenants reside in the unit, regardless of their relationship, all parties should be listed on the contract and sign their names. This makes clear that all residents are legally responsible for following the terms of the contract, including the rules and regulations and the rent.

Occupants. The persons who signed the lease are the only ones—plus any minors listed on the agreement—who may reside in the unit. This way you know that everyone living in the property has been properly screened by you. If a friend moves in or your tenant sublets without properly notifying you, you should be able to terminate the contract.

Tenancy. Specify whether this is a short-term rental agreement (month-to-month) or fixed-term lease (usually at least a year).

Rent. Specify the amount of rent due each month, when it is to be received (usually the first of the month), and acceptable forms of payment. It would be a good idea to specify fees for late payments or bounced checks.

Security deposit. Specify the amount of money due after checking to make sure you are complying with your local housing authority's guidelines, the purpose of the security deposit (to make repairs), and when it will be returned (upon completion of a final walk-through).

Notice of termination/notice of entry. Specify how much notice you require before terminating a month-to-month contract (typically thirty days) and point out that breaking a lease prematurely does not absolve the tenant for due rent. Specify how much notice, legally, you will give tenants before you or your property manager enters the property (typically twenty-four hours).

Illegal activity. Specify that under no circumstances will illegal activity, disturbing the peace, or becoming a public nuisance be tolerated.

Pets/smoking. Specify your policy on both.

Subletting. Specify whether you will permit subletting.

We cannot possibly cover every scenario that you will want to list in your rental contract. Use this list as a starting point and add the information that is necessary to protect both you and your tenant.

What are the pros and cons of a short-term rental?

Before advertising your property and interviewing prospective tenants, you must decide if you want to market your unit for short-term or long-term occupancy. When we speak of short-term rentals, we are talking about a month-to-month agreement. There are benefits and disadvantages to choosing this approach.

As always, you need to adjust your expectations to meet your market. You may find that in your area month-to-month contracts are preferred due to the type of client pool that is available. You do not want to limit or eliminate your options by proposing a year-long lease to renters who do not favor such a commitment. Many tenants like having a month-to-month contract, knowing that they can move out with thirty days' notice. This is especially helpful to people who are in the area on temporary business or who are new to renting.

For yourself, if the rental market is in high demand, you may like knowing that you can raise the rent accordingly and not have to wait a full year (the typical lease agreement) before cashing in on such a trend. Market direction aside, as a new landlord you may prefer to have a month-to-month contract. This way, if your tenants are not working out you can amicably terminate the contract quickly. Having learned from previous mistakes, your experience can make you more confident next time. Also, if you intend to sell the unit in a short period of time and are just renting while waiting for circumstances to make selling more favorable, a short-term rental is probably your best bet.

If you do opt for a short-term contract, keep in mind that you may end up doing more work to keep your units occupied. Because tenants are not committed to a lease, a high tenant turnover is not unlikely. Having done so much work to find financially stable and personally responsible tenants, you may become worn out if you have to perform this search over and over.

Changing locks, walk-throughs, background checks, and paperwork must be taken care of each time a new tenant moves in. Also, tenants who know they can leave at any time (after giving notice) may be less likely to take care of the property. If you have the time to do the necessary work and your market favors such conditions, short-term rentals could be a nice way to begin your landlording career.

What are the pros and cons of a long-term rental?

Long-term rentals usually have a tenancy period of at least one year. Like short-term rentals, you will have to know your local market and examine your comfort level before deciding if this is the route you want to pursue.

Long-term rentals can be very beneficial in areas where it is particularly difficult to find renters in the off season. Beach towns, for example, have an influx of renters in the summer months but can be hard to fill during the winter. In contrast, college-town properties can enjoy a prosperous school year but become deserted in the summers. You will have to determine if your seasonal rent can carry you through slower months or if you prefer to have a signed contract for an entire year so you will not have to worry about this down time.

If you are not in a seasonal location, you may favor a lease if there are several comparable vacancies in the area. As we discussed earlier, you should offer an amenity or condition that makes your unit exceptionally appealing. Having made those accommodations and drawn in tenants, you'll probably prefer to the security of a long-term rental agreement to prevent your tenants from moving into another vacant unit if the circumstances seem more favorable. Even if you are willing to do the work associated with high tenant turnover and month-to-month rentals, you may not have a tenant pool to work with.

Commercial property owners generally favor long-term rental agreements. Starting a business, relocating equipment, and building a company takes time and effort. A business owner is probably not going to want to commit to a unit if the rental agreement could be terminated with thirty days' warning. For this reason, it is not unusual for a commercial property to have a one-, two-, or three-year lease.

While having the security of a longer rental agreement is appealing, there are some drawbacks. Being new to contract negotiations and the real-estate market, you may find yourself with a less-than-ideal rental contract but no way to amend it. If, for example, you forget to specify no pets and your tenants bring home a new puppy, you will not be able to insist they give the animal away. You will have to wait until the contract comes to term before amending the language. If you opt for a long-term lease, make sure you have experienced colleagues and team members walk you through the written agreement to check that you have covered all your bases.

How legally binding is a rental agreement?

A written, signed rental contract, be it a fixed-term lease or a short-term rental agreement, is a legally binding document. It protects all parties involved and is one of your best sources of evidence should a problem arise. But as not everyone appreciates the legality of signing a contract, you should walk your new tenants through the contract and highlight the important points before giving them the document to read through on their own time. This way, you can be sure that you have reiterated its most important features.

Since your real-estate investments are intended to make a profit, call attention to the section pertaining to collecting rent and the penalties if rent is late. Clearly establish that the full amount of rent is due no later than the due date, usually the first of the month. If rent is twenty-four, forty-eight, or seventy-two hours late, you will expect a late fee in a particular dollar amount. Rent is not optional; it is required and expected. If rent is not received after this grace period, make it clear that you will start the eviction process.

Indicate clearly where the rent should be sent. We have encouraged you to insist on checks or money orders. As a beginning investor, chances are you will have the rent mailed to your primary residence. Save the tenant a step, and save yourself from excuses, by giving the tenant twelve stamped self-addressed envelopes. The easier you make it to pay the rent, the easier it will be to pay the rent on time. You can also require the tenant at lease signing to supply you with twelve checks dated for the first of every month for the following year and advise them you will be depositing that check promptly on the first to avoid delays in the mail or other inconveniences. You may also suggest that the tenant set up an automatic transfer of rent money from her account to your properties account for the first of every month. Add a notation to the rental agreement that these envelopes or checks were received or that you have agreed to a monthly auto-debit or transfer. You will also want to add a penalty fee for any bounced checks.

After reviewing each particular section, you and the tenant should initial next to the paragraph, indicating that it has been covered. Be sure and ask the tenant if he has any questions and respond to his concerns regarding any points in the contract. As important as it is that the tenant appreciates the contract, you must also hold up your end of the bargain. At the end of the contract, be sure to have a clear, simple statement such as, "I have read and understand the rules, regulations, and obligations of this contract and agree to abide by the terms of this contract."

Pointing out the particulars of your rental agreement, especially the rent, is not an overcautious or overzealous practice. It is a sound business idea that will help get you and your tenant off to a clear understanding of the tenancy responsibilities.

What is a maintenance agreement?

As a landlord you are obligated to provide and maintain a safe housing unit that meets basic habitability requirements as outlined by the local housing authority. These typically include access to heat, water, and electricity, as well as weatherproofing and a structurally sound building. Once a tenant moves in, it is your responsibility to maintain these things, making any necessary repairs along the way. The maintenance agreement is a part of the rental contract that spells out how repairs are to be handled.

One of the best ways to maintain a positive, profitable relationship with a tenant is by addressing any repairs in a timely fashion. Serious problems with plumbing or heating, such as burst pipes or lack of heat, should be handled immediately. In an emergency situation, you may be able to enter a tenant's property without notice, but it is best to cover your bases by outlining an appropriate protocol before repairs are needed.

Most states require twenty-four hours' notice before you enter a tenant's property, and this time frame usually accommodates all parties. Obviously, if the tenant is standing in a foot of water you will want to get over to the property sooner than later. But since emergencies can happen at any time, it is a good idea to state in the contract that if an emergency occurs you will do your best to reach the client, but to protect the unit and his belongings you may have to enter sooner than twenty-four hours. Be specific about what constitutes an emergency, for example, a fire or serious water leak.

Remember to include the name and contact information of your property manager if you are employing someone to handle maintenance. You should introduce this person to the tenant upon signing the contract. Remember that, as your employee, the property manager must abide by the rental contract.

If you do not handle requests for repairs in a timely manner or neglect to meet your legal responsibilities, the tenant may be entitled to withhold the rent until the problem is solved, hire a third party (plumber or electrician for example) to fix the problem and deduct her fee from the rent, or move out without financial penalty in the middle of a lease. Tenants may even go so far as to sue you for emotional stress and personal suffering. Avoid these problems by addressing repair issues in a timely and professional manner.

How can I minimize maintenance and repair fees?

A good defense is your best offense against wasting money, time, and energy. Being proactive starts with buying a solid building, continues through tenancy, and concludes only when you sell the unit.

For starters, always be accessible to your tenants. Your tenants should have all of your contact information, including work and cell numbers and e-mail address. You want to make it easy to reach you if a problem comes up. The sooner you know about an issue, the sooner it can be addressed. If a tenant can get in touch with you on the first try instead of having to leave a message, you can work out a convenient time to make a repair that day instead of having to wait the contracted twenty-four hours.

Always document any maintenance phone calls or communications. Document the problem as it was described to you, what steps were taken to fix it, and the time and date it was completed. If new parts were necessary or if a professional had to be called in, attach any receipts to the paperwork and have all parties sign that the problem has been fixed satisfactorily. Keep this paperwork in the tenant's file along with the rental contract, background checks, and other relevant paperwork.

Once a year, schedule a midlease walk-through with the tenants using the same maintenance checklist you utilized when the occupants first moved in. Go through the property with the tenants and check for leaky faucets, loose handrails, or misaligned steps. Note if any problems were found and address them immediately. Then have everyone sign the document stating that the unit is in satisfactory condition.

If you have a property manager, include him in this visit; do not merely send him out to perform the walk-through. You want to take advantage of being invited into the unit and keep your eyes open for any potential issues that go above normal wear and tear. If you arrive to find crayon markings covering a bedroom wall, let the tenants know the name of the hardware store where you prefer to buy your paint and remind them that such damage is their responsibility. Although you are there to address the property's maintenance condition, do not turn a blind eye to an obvious problem. Make a note of what you find, give the tenants a reasonable but specific amount of time to fix the problem, and check back to make sure the terms of the rental agreement are being adhered to.

When you look for ways to be part of the solution and take care of your property before, during, and after tenancies, you will have the potential to put more money in your pocket and less money into repairs.

Should I do all of the maintenance work myself?

Whenever we hear about landlords spending their weekends mowing lawns or trying to figure out how to rewire a faulty outlet, we are reminded of the saying penny-wise, pound-foolish. Your time is your most precious asset. If you are choosing to use that time pinching pennies, you could end up missing out on much more lucrative deals.

If you are a professional contractor, gardener, or electrician, you may have the ability to quickly and efficiently maintain your unit and repair damages. But for those investors who, like us, only have a basic understanding of such things, trying to find time to learn yet another profession can be costly and dangerous. In addition, your time could be better spent networking, working toward goals in your business plan, and canvassing the marketplace for changes and opportunities.

Since you are becoming involved in real-estate investing while balancing a full-time career and several other commitments, it is probably not realistic to think that you can do it all. Delegating responsibilities is one of the keys to success. Just like it is not necessary for you to become an expert in all areas of finance—that is why you are putting together a team of professionals—it is not wise to think that you need take care of every repair. Having a Rolodex of trusted service workers can help ensure that maintenance issues are addressed promptly and, most important, are dealt with appropriately.

We all want to keep costs down and capitalize on as much of our profits as possible. But this may sometimes cause us to become temporarily shortsighted. In the last chapter we talked about the benefits of tenant incentives and highlighted some of the ways that making your tenant part of the solution can save you both money. But keep in mind, shortcuts are not the same thing as incentive packages. When a problem comes up, you'll want it to be addressed by a professional.

Having a successful real-estate portfolio requires you to manage your business. You do not want to confuse being hands-on and knowing what to delegate to whom with being a micromanager. Use your time wisely and you are more likely to achieve greater success.

What if an issue comes up that is not addressed in the contract?

Despite your best efforts to set yourself up for success, you may find yourself having to handle unexpected issues. You have outlined the requirements of paying rent in a timely manner, made a decision about allowing pets, and taken copious notes about the condition of the unit. But three months into the lease your tenant rides into the development on a motorcycle and you have complaints about a noise ordinance violation on your hands. You did not specify no motorcycles, nor are they referenced in the development's bylaws, but this gray area is causing all parties involved frustration.

Since leases and rental agreements, and in this case, bylaws, are written by humans, it is impossible to remain flawless. Fortunately, having worked hard to set yourself, and your tenant relationship, up for success, you will most likely be able to work toward an accommodating solution together.

Regardless of the problem's details, overreacting and making threats is never a productive reaction. Instead of adopting an "I'm the one in charge around here" attitude, ask your tenant what the best course of action may be. In this example, it may turn out that he only enjoys his motorcycle on the weekends after 9 AM. Together you can speak with the housing co-op board and work toward a resolution that satisfies everyone. Once a resolution is reached, you can look to add an addendum to your contract to reflect the new issue.

If you see every problem as a reason for eviction or a personal threat, you will be much more likely to make mountains out of mole hills. The big issues—rent, illegal activities, background checks, and unit upkeep—will all be covered in a well-designed agreement. If a conflict arises over an issue outlined in the contract, you will most likely be well prepared to take action against the violation. Things are bound to come up along the way. If you look for a solution instead of an argument, you'll be more likely to continue a smooth relationship with your tenant.

Now that my property is rented, how can I keep track of paperwork?

In addition to taking on the new responsibilities of a landlord, you will also be in charge of bookkeeping. There are all types of bookkeeping software and manuals available, and as you decide which, if any, program you would like to use, make sure that it is doing what it should: keeping track of your paperwork and making profitability easier.

We strongly encourage you to work with your financial planner and accountant when determining how best to keep track of your business transactions. Having experts who are well versed in designing and implementing financial programs can help keep you organized from the start. Whether you choose to purchase a computer program—we like QuickBooks—or use a handwritten bound ledger will depend on your comfort level and your investment intentions. Since your intentions probably include growth, it is wise to start with a computer program that can grow with your investments so you do not have to spend valuable time updating your bookkeeping files down the line.

The purpose of bookkeeping is to keep accurate track of all the money going into and out of your real-estate business. Bookkeeping programs most commonly have columns labeled for easy use. The money that goes into your property is generated through rent. The money going out of your property includes mortgage payments, maintenance, taxes, and possibly utilities. In addition to the normal in-and-out flow of money, there will be other transactions you must keep a record of. If you employ a property manager, you should also add a line item for wages. Working with your investment team, set up your profit-tracking program with such appropriate headers as income (rent), outgo (mortgage), and expenses (maintenance).

The best way to check on the profitability of your investment is by keeping accurate track of paperwork. Take time to research the different types of bookkeeping materials as soon as possible and have your team experts help you design the program that is right for you so that when the time comes all you have to do is fill in the blanks.

How do I monitor expenses and profit?

When you put financial transactions down on paper you are forced to look at what is really happening. If the numbers don't add up or if you are failing to make a profit, an accurate bookkeeping system can help you figure out where you have gone wrong.

It's best to open a separate bank account for your rental properties so that your monthly statements include only your real-estate investments. Each month you can check your bookkeeping against your bank statements. If you accept cash, make sure that you keep your receipt book current as this will be your only record of rent paid. In addition to a ledger that notes mortgage payments, rent, and wages, you also want to leave room to detail expenses. Too often this is the area where landlords lose money.

If you replace a ceiling fan, hire a plumber to fix a faulty pipe, or have to replace a rotting piece of roof, do not pay these costs out of pocket and forget about them. Keep maintenance receipts with your paperwork, and make a detailed note of the expense in your ledger. Writing $65.50 is not enough; note the reason. While it is easy to convince yourself that $65.50 is not a lot of money and hardly warrants concern, leaving this expense off of the books is a poor business practice and an overlooked tax deduction. If in six months you pay for a ceiling fan, a plumber, and a roofer, the costs will make a considerable difference in your profit line. If you do not note these expenses, you are fooling yourself into thinking your property is more profitable than it is. Such financial omissions offer an unbalanced and inaccurate profit report.

Since you are counting on rent to make you money and keep your property profitable, it is worth noting again that accepting partial rent payments, doing your tenants a favor by letting them slide for a while, or not raising the rent when the time is right to avoid confrontation can all cost you money. Be honest in your business practices, with yourself and with others, be up front with your expectations, and stick to the terms of the lease. Bookkeeping does not cause problems, it reveals them.

How do I keep track of receipts?

Another bonus of collecting rent with a check, money order, or cashier's check is the assurance that the cashed check will act as a receipt for the tenant and yourself. A check that clears through a third-party banking institution automatically generates a time-stamped paper trail, giving you and your tenants the security you both want.

It is also a good idea to keep track of rental payments on a separate dated spreadsheet or another type of bookkeeping program. You will be able to compare your projected profits with your actual profit, make notations for maintenance repair costs, and note any late payments. If your tenant has signed a month-to-month contract, she should indicate the month she is paying for on the memo line of the check. Make certain that December's rent is credited toward December and not used to make up for a missed month or put toward a late payment. This kind of accurate bookkeeping is necessary if a problem should arise. If you charge a tenant a late fee, the check to remedy that issue should be separate and the memo line should indicate its purpose. Month-to-month rental agreements have a one-month term, and the payment should be accurately noted for that term. It is a good rule of thumb to follow this same practice with leasing tenants, but as their term is longer (usually at least one year), the memo line is not as critical as the debt period is spread out.

If you decide to collect rents in cash, be aware that many states mandate that you issue a rental receipt to tenants so that they have proof of having paid. Receipt books can be found at most large office-supply stores and are usually formatted with a tear-out sheet for the recipient and a bound carbon copy for the issuer. This way you will both have an identical copy of the rent receipt. It is critical that you maintain this receipt book accurately and do not lose it.

Even if your tenants pay by check, they may ask to have an additional signed receipt for their payment. Some states mandate that you must do this, but even if your state does not, there is no harm in obliging this request. If you should issue a receipt for a check that ends up bouncing, the bounced check will void the handwritten receipt. The receipt merely acknowledges receiving the check; it does not prove that the check was cashed. Be sure and keep a copy of the bounced check in your files. Always keep accurate track if rents are paid and add this information to your tenant file.

What if I lose my paperwork?

There is nothing more frustrating than being unable to find paperwork. It always seems that the one piece of paper you need is the one you cannot find. Whether you are preparing your receipts for taxes or having to prove that you did in fact tend to a tenant's maintenance request, misplacing paperwork can be a huge, costly headache.

Sometimes it's possible to retrieve files from secondary sources. If you misplace bank statements, you can request copies. Depending on your bank and its resources, you may even be able to view your account online.

If you lose a receipt for an item you bought for your property, such as replacement windows, use your credit-card statement as proof of purchase. File a copy to use for the tax deduction. Your tax attorney will have to instruct you on the best way to proceed. But as you want to take advantage of all the tax benefits available, it pays to keep all of your receipts in a neat, dated folder. Memories are unreliable; there is a much better chance that you will forget you bought the windows than there is that you will remember, search out the credit-card statement, and submit it for a successful deduction.

It is a good idea to make copies of important signed documents, such as leases, and keep the original in a safe location, such as a safe deposit box. If a tenant issue arises, verbal agreements do not hold much legal weight. Without proof of a contract, you will be left with nothing but your word.

If you should lose your tenant screening paperwork and a tenant files discrimination charges against you, there can be very serious consequences. You will find out how expensive such a mistake can be if you fail to prove that your decision to choose another tenant was based on legal, documented reasons.

Losing or even misplacing paperwork is a waste of your most important asset: time. The hours you spend scouring the home for a receipt, added to the time it takes to try to locate another source for the missing document, is time that you should be networking, researching, and developing your portfolio.

Do I need to provide my tenants with bank statements documenting their interest-bearing security deposit account?

We have talked a great deal about record-keeping for your own protection and benefit, but also remember to use your paperwork to meet tenant obligations. You will have to check with the laws of your state for specific rules regulating security deposit interest, but most housing laws require you to pay tenants the interest that accumulates on their security deposit account. Usually the interest must be paid annually on the anniversary of the rental contract. You may either give the money to the tenants directly or credit them the amount in the following month's rent. As security deposit money is not your money, it must be kept in a separate account. We advise what many banks have: a tenant-landlord account. These accounts protect you and keep your tenant informed. It is prudent to forward copies of this statement to your tenant. This way, you are not just telling your tenants how much interest has accrued, you are showing them in a statement for their own files that is cosigned in their name.

If your tenant has decided to move out, you must return the security deposit within thirty days (depending on the local housing laws) after he vacates. At this time you are also required to pay any interest owed to the tenant. Send the money certified mail with receipt or add a clause to the lease if you are handing over the money at a final walk-through that states the security deposit has been returned and the interest due has been paid. Of course, if there is a problem with the unit that needs financial attention, follow the steps outlined in the previous chapter before returning money.

Interest rates can vary over time, so you want to make sure that you credit or return the right amount of money to your tenants. The security deposit should be kept in an account that earns a regular rate of interest. If your tenant is on a month-to-month contract and moves out after eight months, you must pay the interest accrued during that time. The interest earned is the property of the tenant, and no money should be deducted for administrative fees or the like. Giving a copy of the bank statement for the interest-bearing security deposit account to your tenant and filing your copy with your financial paperwork helps to ensure that everyone gets the financial information and money they are entitled to.

What about hiring people to work "off the books"?

Whenever the conversation turns to taxes, there is no way to avoid the discussion about working off the books or paying someone under the table—where the employer does not claim the employee and no taxes are paid on wages. This practice is illegal and it is not worth the potential trouble it causes.

Hiring people to work off the books isn't a problem until there is a problem, and there is always a problem. As a new business owner, you want to conduct your practice legally and with integrity or you could end up with criminal penalties should you be audited. Paying everyone on the books is not always the cheapest choice, but it is the safest. While saving a few dollars may seem like a good idea, especially when you are trying to make every penny count, skipping steps is never the best route.

Since we are talking about record-keeping, let's look at the problem with hiring someone off the books. If your tenant calls to tell you that a water pipe has burst and the basement is flooded, damaging her washer and dryer, you have a serious problem on your hands that needs immediate attention. You call an acquaintance who does plumbing and electrical work on the side and he meets you at the unit. Knowing the importance of documentation, you write down the problem, have it fixed, and all parties sign off when the job is finished. You pay the plumber in cash, and everyone goes on their way. But twenty-four hours later the plumbing breaks down again, this time causing the toilets to back up. Now you have an uninhabitable unit. Angry that the job wasn't done right the first time, you call your acquaintance who is nowhere to be found. Your tenant is threatening to call her lawyer, and you have no case against the plumber because there is no proof of the work he completed, nor can you contact his supervisors because there are none. You call in a professional, pay more money to have this bigger problem solved, and begin fretting over how much money will have to be paid to salvage your tenant's belongings and fix the unit.

If the same situation happens with a licensed independent contractor, you have a receipt for the work he did, proof that the job wasn't completed correctly, and a means to sue him or his company for damages. If you do not have documentation, you do not have a case. With all of the hard work you have done to launch your new investment business, it pays to make the best choices and protect yourself and your portfolio.

Do I need a home office?

Ideally, you should have a home office with filing cabinets, a computer, storage space, and office supplies. Consult with your tax advisor concerning the tax benefits of a home office. If no such room exists, do not call an architect just yet. Before you decide to build an addition onto your home and call it an office, consider what a functional home office can accomplish and see if there is a ready-made location in your house that you can dedicate to your new venture.

Your space should have room for documents in file folders, a phone, calendar, business card organizer, and a hard top to write on. If you don't have a home office, you will most likely end up working from your kitchen table. If this is the case, dedicate a high cabinet to your paperwork. Use color-coded files to separate archived files that you want to keep but do not need to immediately access, accordion-style folders for tenant files, and accordion-style files for receipts. Three-ring binders can help you organize duplicate forms. Do not use shoe boxes to dump receipts into and hope that your accountant will be able to figure things out. Even if she can, it will cost you extra money. Have a place for everything, and keep everything in its place.

Decide when you are going to have office time. Looking over financial statements and comparing bank statements to profit margins takes concentration. Do not try to get dinner started, watch TV, and record maintenance spending on your computer program all at once. Allot a specific time every day for business, and take this time seriously. When you are finished with your business, put everything back where it belongs until you are ready to use it again. Having several to-do piles around the house usually means that not much is getting done. It is not enough to say you are going to go over the books soon; you must actually do it.

A home office is an ideal location from which to run your business because we expect that only business will be conducted there. But for many of us, this area can become a dumping ground for bills, magazines, and projects. Regardless of your house plans, you need to organize yourself to use office space, be it at the kitchen table or in a separate room. Take time to look at potential work areas, invest in organizing materials that are useful, and dedicate time to go to work. Give yourself a three-month deadline, and check your progress. If your organizing system is not working, enlist the help of a professional. It may be time to bring this expert on board with the rest of your investment team.

What are the tax benefits associated with rental properties?

Owning real estate has several tax benefits, which is one of the reasons many investors are drawn to property ownership in the first place. Tax law is complicated, and we do not advocate going it alone. You want to work with your accountant to make sure that you are taking advantage of the many tax deductions you are entitled to. If you miss out on these opportunities, you are missing out on additional income-property profits. Any time you can put more money in your pockets, you want to do so.

The whys and hows of tax deduction are best left to an accounting expert. But we'll list five of the most common deductions that most landlords can benefit from:

- Interest payments—Interest paid on mortgage loans to purchase or improve your property may be deductible.
- Repairs—As it is your responsibility to maintain the property, you can deduct the cost of repairs, provided they are necessary (like addressing a plumbing problem) and you have receipts for the parts and labor.
- Travel expenses—Driving to a tenant's unit to evaluate a problem or driving back and forth from the supply store to the unit to make a repair can be deducted. A simple way to do this is by keeping track of your mileage and taking the standard deductionof 44.5 cents per mile (2006) of business travel. The rules for this are spelled out on the IRS Web site, *www.irs.gov*.
- Wages—If you employ a property manager, you can deduct his wages.
- Investment team—Fees paid to your investment team may be deductible as these experts are integral to your business operations.

Other deductions may include long-distance travel, insurance premiums, and a home office. But as there are many gray areas when determining what constitutes a legal deduction, we urge you to proceed with caution and heed the advice of your team experts. The IRS will take a closer look at your tax forms should you insist that your family trip to Disney World with the kids was a business trip. While it may be true, you will have to have the proper documentation to prove your case. With all the possible deductions available, it is foolhardy to start inventing reasons for deductions. Keep accurate records and follow the law and you will reap the tax advantages available.

What are capital gains taxes?

Capital gains taxes are taxes that you must pay on profits realized from the purchase and sale of property. The tax amounts vary depending on the property type, amount of profit realized, and amount of time you owned the property. It is important to keep in mind when buying and selling your investment property that profits are taxed, and payment is mandatory. Buy and sell properties with the help of your financial team to limit your tax obligations.

A capital gain is the amount of money remaining once you take the sale price and subtract the carrying costs and the purchase price of the property. Your accountant will help you determine what is profit and what is not. If the property you sell produced a profit—and we hope it does—you would want your team of advisors to review the sale and advise you on how much capital gains tax you can anticipate.

Consult your tax advisors for specific guidance, but generally speaking, if you are selling a property you have lived in for at least two years, any profits realized up to $250,000 for an individual and $500,000 for a married couple are not taxed. Any profits beyond that are taxed. Knowing this, you may be able to take advantage of some excellent upgrading opportunities. Homeowners can move every few years and gain tax-free money with the help of the government.

Investment properties, however, are treated differently by the IRS and are taxed at higher rates than owner-occupied property. In most cases, if you buy and sell an investment property within one year of purchase you will be taxed at the rate you normally pay. If your taxable income is in the 33 percent tax bracket, your capital gains tax will be at 33 percent. This could end up cutting into your profit, something you want to avoid if at all possible. Your financial team can counsel you on how to defray costs with the help of a 1031 exchange (see the next question). If you buy a property and hold onto it for one year or more, the tax rate changes considerably. The capital gains tax rate lowers to 15 percent of the profit.

When planning your next investment portfolio move, you will need to assess the pros and cons of selling before and after one year's time. Consulting with your financial team can help you make a more profitable decision.

What is a 1031 exchange?

It is likely that if you hear veteran real-estate investors talking about capital gains taxes, it won't be long before they start throwing around the term *1031 exchange*. Many investors, including ourselves, are interested in building a lucrative income-generating portfolio over time. A 1031 exchange can be a financially sound way to help make that happen.

A 1031 exchange, also called a *like kind exchange*, is a government-allowed tax deferment of capital gains taxes. This can happen if the investor is to make a purchase of another investment property immediately after the sale of his previous investment property. The new purchase must be similar to the last one. To facilitate the like kind exchange, you need to identify the new property, and the new closing must happen within a specific period of time from the date of sale of the old property. All profits from the sale of the old property must be rolled into the purchase of the new property. In essence, you are replacing one investment property with another.

This tax deferment makes sense because you are not actually walking away with any profits; you are rolling them over into a new investment. Since you are not required to pay taxes on the previously sold property, which would cut into your profits, you have more money to use toward your next purchase.

The "like kind" stipulation means that if you sell a single-family residential property, your next purchase should be another, higher-priced, single-family home. Likewise, if you were to sell an apartment building, you would replace it with a larger apartment building. Since this is a deferment of taxes, not forgiveness, the taxes will be due at some point in the future when you sell a property and don't purchase a new one.

These 1031 exchanges are usually handled by specific 1031 tax attorneys. Your team of experts should be able to refer you to a qualified individual to assist in this complicated but important feature of tax law. This tool can allow you more leverage on a yearly basis by postponing taxes to a year when cash is more readily available. Because tax law is so specific, with requirements and regulations often changing, it is important to seek advice from an experienced 1031 tax attorney so that you can take advantage of this tax deferment.

Scenario: I've had a really nice relationship with one of my tenants, who has been offered a job transfer and needs to get out of his lease early. What should I do?

This is a tough situation. Usually when we talk about having to enforce the rules and regulations of a lease, we need to do so because a troublesome tenant is not abiding by the contract. But when you have a tenant who has been timely with rents, low maintenance, and agreeable, it can make enforcing the rules feel mean spirited. In these circumstances, consider possible solutions that can satisfy everyone.

Make your tenant an active member in remedying this problem. Remind him that he signed a contract for a set time and is responsible to see out his obligation. If he can find another tenant to take over the lease, you will oblige, once the proper background checks and references are found to be in order. Yes, you could demand that the tenant pay you what is due on the lease, then re-rent the unit, having made some extra cash along the way. But just because you can do this doesn't mean you should. Income properties are about making money, not taking advantage of other's people circumstances. You could take out new ads for your soon-to-be-vacant unit and ask the current tenant pay for this expense. Running several ads will still be cheaper than coming up with six months' rent, and either way you need a new tenant. Helping each other satisfy a potential problem is an amicable way to part company and stay financially solvent.

If he hasn't already done so, the tenant can inquire about having his new company pay off his lease. Major corporations that aggressively recruit new employees know this can often lead to financial conflicts. Having a company pick up the remainder of the rent owed on the lease is not an uncommon request or practice. You may also consider subletting the unit for the remainder of the lease. Many corporations lodge new recruits in furnished homes for training, and your tenant would not immediately need his furniture, making subletting a possibility.

How flexible, or firm, you want to be with letting a tenant out of his lease is completely up to you, but remember, six months from now you will probably have no relationship with this tenant but you will have expenses. Business is business and should be treated as such. Don't confuse being flexible with being foolish. 🏠

Scenario: I have never been good at keeping track of receipts or reading financial statements. How can I get organized?

This is not a problem limited to real-estate investors but is a problem many businesspeople wrestle with. Not being able to stay organized plagues everyone from corporate executives to stay-at-home mothers. Putting together a system that works for you is critical to the success of your investment business.

A great place to look for valuable advice comes from people who already have a system in place. Reach out to your investment team and your business colleagues and ask what works for them. Networking is not just about getting an edge on the real-estate market but also about learning how to structure your business practices. For many of us who are beginning this venture with full-time careers and commitments, balance must be a new skill we acquire among others.

If you know that you are not inclined toward organization, do not assume that you will magically rise to the occasion once you take on a new commitment. In fact, if your current filing situation is already in jeopardy, meaning your birth certificate and social security card are in a shoebox somewhere, taking on more paperwork might cause a complete catastrophe. Use this time to get your current situation well in hand and you'll have a much better chance of breaking old chaotic habits and building new, more organized systems.

You did not get into your current state of disarray overnight, and you won't solve your problems in a day either. Instead of spending a ton of money on expensive filing systems and vowing to get everything into its rightful place once and for all, tackle the project as you would real-estate investing: one step at a time. Use a daily planner to make a reasonable plan for getting on track. Review our comments regarding home offices and implement some of the strategies mentioned there.

A business does not stay organized merely because it starts that way either; it takes constant maintenance to remain on top of paperwork and filing systems. Allot a specific amount of time to straightening up your work space. This may mean thirty minutes each Saturday morning or five minutes each evening before dinner. This is not a time for shuffling papers but a time to discard dated material like old real-estate magazines, file a new business contact, or transfer receipts into folders.

Staying organized is as critical to your success as starting organized. Take time to make this happen with a realistic maintenance routine. 🏠

I have always done my taxes on my own. Is it really necessary to have them professionally done?

Perhaps you have always felt comfortable doing your own taxes because your needs have been straightforward: You only file for yourself, and you have a limited financial portfolio. Having learned from past years' experiences what to do, you feel confident that you have done a good job filing on your own. But beginning a new business venture means your tax situation has changed. No longer can you rely on what has worked in the past, because you haven't yet developed experiences to pull from. Now would be an excellent time to enlist the professional services of a tax accountant.

Despite advances in computer software that make filing online easier and more efficient, these programs cannot replace the experienced counsel of a tax accountant. Tax laws, particularly real-estate tax laws, frequently change. There is no guarantee that the prepackaged program you are depending on will have the latest versions. Even more importantly, there is no way that a computer program can discuss your needs with you.

Having your taxes filed by a professional is also an excellent time to discuss the direction of your portfolio. This is a time to look at what is really going on with your investments. How much profit are you actually making? What is the ideal time, from the standpoint of taxes, to make your next portfolio move? Are there tax breaks you are not aware of that you could be working toward? While preparing your own return may look like an easy way to keep on top of your business and perhaps save some money, having a well-trained, expert eye look at your financial standings without becoming emotionally engaged can be a valuable checkpoint to make sure you are on track.

You have worked hard to get your business off the ground and deserve a professional who will take care of you. Working with a tax accountant who specializes in real-estate portfolios is another way to better serve your business.

Chapter Seven Expanding Your Empire

How important is it to build equity in an investment property?
Regardless of whether you are talking about your primary residence or an investment property, a goal of all homeownership is building equity. Simply stated, equity refers to the difference between the current market value of a property and what you owe on your mortgage.

When we talk about the current market value of a property we are not referring to a fanciful number that we think our home is worth. We are relying on a credible comparative market analysis performed by our reputable team Realtor or calculated by having a home appraisal done by a certified professional. Once we know what our property would likely sell for in today's market, we subtract our remaining mortgage balance from that number. For example, if the property is valued at $250,000 and there is $195,000 remaining on the mortgage, the home equity is $55,000.

The longer you own a property, the more mortgage payments you will make and the more likely the market value will increase. This makes building home equity a relatively natural part of homeownership for level-headed real-estate owners. Since making timely mortgage payments is a key component of real-estate ownership, building equity is a byproduct of taking care of your financial responsibilities.

The equity that you build into your home is available for use through home-equity loans or lines of credit and can be a valuable resource with which to make further real-estate purchases, complete home improvements, or even pay down credit-card debt. But beware: Using your home's equity to indulge in a lifestyle that is beyond your financial capacity is foolish and risky. In recent years the booming real-estate market, coupled with low interest rates on mortgages, has enticed many homeowners to pull money out of their homes for immediate gratification purposes instead of using it to further develop their financial stability. Equity in your house is valuable and should be used for important reasons.

For the real-estate investor, home-equity lines of credit can be used to finance your next property or make improvements on your current real estate (thus building further equity in the property). As a smart business investor, continue to keep an eye toward future profits and look for the best means by which to use your home equity.

How do I build equity in my investment property?

Building a home's equity happens over time as you pay down your mortgage and own your property. As the value of your home increases with the market and your mortgage obligation decreases, the difference between these two numbers, the home's equity, grows. In addition to letting your real estate prosper over time, there are strategies to build additional equity in your home.

For starters, you can immediately lower your mortgage obligations by making a substantial down payment when you first buy your property. Your down payment is the initial equity in your home. Since home equity grows as the number of mortgage payments you have to make decreases (because more money goes toward the principal later in the loan's life), setting yourself up with fewer mortgage payments to begin with can move you further down the equity line.

As we talked about in Chapter 3 on mortgages, property owners are not limited to long-term, thirty-year fixed-rate mortgages. For income property owners who are looking to make property purchases for business reasons and therefore may not be looking to hold onto a unit for an extended period, shorter loan programs can necessitate that the principal be paid down faster. This strategy can increase home equity more quickly.

When deciding which mortgage program will work best for your portfolio plan, it is well worth investigating whether additional mortgage payments are allowed by your mortgage carrier. Talk with your lender about making additional monthly principal payments when possible. The faster you pay down your mortgage and reduce your debt, the faster your home equity grows. It's important to also note that the more principal you pay down, the less overall interest payments you will have to pay, which is an additional savings.

Finally, making home improvements can increase your property's market value. When deciding which projects to take on, review our suggestions from the previous chapter. You want to invest your money in advantageous upgrades and repairs that will make a significant difference in your home's worth. For instance, while a perennial garden is lovely, a refurbished bathroom is a more profitable investment project. Working with your mortgage consultant and financial team, you can discuss the possibilities of using an equity line to finance the projects that will bring in greater market value and increase your home's equity. This strategy could be a true win-win situation.

There has been much talk about the possibilities available with home-equity lines of credit or loans and the benefit of building additional equity into your property. Discuss these suggestions with your financial team to determine if your portfolio could benefit from such strategies.

When should I refinance my investment properties?

Refinancing is always a hot topic of discussion in real estate. Since we have encouraged you to look for opportunities to make money in any market, it makes sense that you would be interested in refinancing properties to maximize your profit. While there are no hard and fast rules for choosing the right time, there are several considerations that can help you determine the best course of action.

When it comes to ideal timing, your mortgage representative can be instrumental in helping you take advantage of the market. Proactive mortgage consultants will keep you up to date on market trends with e-mail alerts and mailers, but you can also contact your consultant whenever you are interested in discussing a new plan of action. You'll want to talk about the current market value of your investment property, which can be found by contacting your team Realtor and doing a comparative market analysis. Be ready to discuss your refinancing goals by knowing your current rate and payment, whether you plan to shorten the term of the loan, increase the term, or want to take cash out of the property. Your mortgage consultant can correlate your intentions with the current market and advise you about whether it is in fact a good time to refinance and realize these goals.

Some people insist that you should not refinance unless the current interest rate is 1 percent lower than your current mortgage rate, but this is not always good advice. If, for instance, you have a high loan amount, say $400,000, and it is possible to shave off 0.75 percent from your rate, saving you $200 per month, you may want to take advantage of this opportunity. On the other hand, if you already have a low rate and a 1 percent decrease would only save you $35 a month, it may not be worth it. In some cases, a rate drop could allow you to take out $50,000 of the home's equity for investing, without having to raise your payment at all. Taking advantage of this route, you could consider purchasing another property with that "found" money and increasing your portfolio's inventory while keeping your payment and rate the same.

Refinancing is more than just paying a lower rate. It can also be a way to use your money in a different capacity. For this reason, it is important to keep an open dialogue with your mortgage consultant and financial team members.

What is a limited liability company?

A limited liability company, typically referred to as an LLC, is a legally binding business organization that is separate from its owners, meaning personal finances are separate from business finances. As the name implies, the company provides limited legal responsibility, making it ideal for small business owners such as real-estate investors. There are several advantages, and a few disadvantages, for organizing an LLC.

On the upside, since LLCs are privately run companies, there may be no board of directors or shareholders to check in with, a lot more financial and professional flexibility, and a great deal less paperwork than a typical corporation. Instead of being locked into a fifty-fifty profit split in a partnership, members of an LLC can negotiate more flexible profit plans. Because financial responsibility is limited, LLC members cannot usually be held personally responsible for company debt. The amount of people who comprise the LLC will determine the tax structure, but all LLCs can usually take advantage of tax benefits with the help of an experienced and knowledgeable accountant. While there is necessary state-mandated paperwork and procedures to follow to establish an LLC, discussed in further detail in the next question, the personal protection and business advantages often make the process worthwhile.

On the downside, since there is no board or boss, an LLC can potentially become very disorganized. Many of us are used to following someone else's protocol and have never had to design a business agreement before. And since no meetings are mandatory and minutes do not have to be kept, you could find yourself in a heated he-said-she-said dispute. While you may form an LLC in your own name—known as a sole proprietorship—it is much harder to get a group of partners to agree on the direction of the company.

Since most people are unaware of the responsibilities or the protection offered by an LLC, it is wise to work with a knowledgeable attorney who can help you structure your business to maximize advantages and limit disadvantages. We have multiple limited liability companies to protect our personal assets and help organize our business intentions. As your portfolio grows, it would be worth investigating whether forming an LLC would be advantageous to your financial future.

How do I form an LLC?

While forming an LLC is not a particularly difficult or laborious task, this is a very state-specific question and is best handled with the advice of an experienced attorney. However, we can give you a general overview of what to expect if you and your team decide to move forward with an LLC.

First, you'll want to choose a name for your limited liability company. In order to comply with your state's rules, make sure the name is not already taken, that certain prohibited terms are not used, and, of course, it must end with the *LLC* designation. While you may be tempted to come up with a flashy name, since this is a business keep it professional.

In all fifty states you will need to file articles of organization. These are relatively short, self-explanatory documents. The basic requirements are member's names and the LLC name and address. The parties involved in an LLC are referred to as members, not shareholders or partners.

Once your paperwork is accepted and registered, file your LLC paperwork with your secretary of state, along with the required fees that can range anywhere from $100 to $800. While you can file the paperwork by yourself, we strongly recommend that you get help from your attorney to make sure that you are completing the forms properly.

Once you complete this process, you should create an operating agreement. While these are not required by many states and do not have to be filed with the secretary of state, it is highly advisable to outline the terms of ownership and business operations. Make sure to define each member's vested interest in the company, each member's responsibility, the profit-sharing distribution, and rules for management, including provisions for death, divorce, and selling out. While no one likes to go into a new business venture thinking about failure or fallout, it is important to outline what will happen to the business before a crisis, not after it. Since this is not a corporate structure, which can live indefinitely with different business affiliates joining and leaving the company, an LLC's existence is dependent on its members, and specific provisions must be made to ensure its continuation.

Finally, you will need to abide by any state laws that mandate the necessity of licenses, permits, and tax ID numbers. Again, since each state has specific rules and regulations, be sure to work with your attorney and tax accountant to set your LLC up for success.

What is the difference between an LLC and a partnership?

If your portfolio grows and you are interested in better protecting your assets and/or possibly partnering with another investor, you should take some time to compare an LLC to a partnership. We have several different LLC businesses and found that the structure fits our needs, allowing us the freedom to run our investment business our way and the comfort of knowing that we have taken formal steps to protect our interests. But as the terms *LLC* and *partnership* are often (mis)used interchangeably, it is a good idea to look at both options.

A limited liability company is a formal, registered business that protects members from creditors coming after personal assets should the venture fall into debt. Partnerships are much less formalized, and the participants and the business are considered one and the same, meaning if the business cannot cover its debt, debtors can seek the personal assets of the partners. In some cases, it may be possible to designate a partnership as limited. Unfortunately, since many partnership agreements are informal, participants often overlook this option.

While it may seem a time-consuming hassle to register your business as an LLC or draw up a partnership agreement, without such a legal agreement you will run into problems quickly. The idea that things will work themselves out in business is a mistake. You should always enter into a new business relationship with written rules that cover profit sharing, expansion, dissolution, and decision making.

After the initial paperwork is filed for an LLC, you can enjoy the flexibility of a partnership relationship and the protection of a corporation. We encourage you to talk to your financial team about the benefits of formulating an LLC.

What type of protection do I have with an LLC?

When we talked about homeowner's insurance earlier, we outlined some of the protection available through different policies. Now that your portfolio is growing and you are beginning to reap the benefits of your hard work, it is a good time to take a look at better protecting what you have worked so hard for.

One of the most popular reasons to form an LLC is personal protection against lawsuits or business debt. As a property owner, whether residential or commercial, you will constantly be dealing with the public. While homeowner's insurance and liability insurance are prudent, necessary steps that provide protective coverage, a limited liability company takes this protection a step further.

While you will approach your business with every intention of paying all bills on time, it can be comforting to know that if a problem arises and creditors come calling your primary residence and private possessions will not be taken. You may want to believe that people are upstanding citizens, but you cannot overlook the very real threat of a miscellaneous lawsuit filed by an unscrupulous tenant. The LLC's assets will be used to address these problems.

There are circumstances, however, in which a member of an LLC can be held liable. If you personally injure an individual, fail to comply with employees' wage tax regulations, or use the LLC's assets and profits for personal use, you can forfeit your liability protection. Many new LLC owners overlook the importance of keeping business and personal transactions separate and carelessly commingle money. When you set up your LLC, do not neglect to open a separate checking account and possibly a credit card for the exclusive use of your business. This account should have enough finds to run your business. Without this separate account, it may be difficult to prove that you actually have an LLC. A limited liability company can afford you additional protection, but you must comply with the rules governing such a company and not misuse or abuse your business if you want to avoid problems down the line.

Should my spouse be listed as a member in my LLC?

If you are considering forming a limited liability company, one of your biggest reasons to do so is protection. Having worked hard in your business and personal life, you do not want to see your assets called into question or threatened should a problem arise. For this reason, adding your spouse to your LLC makes a great deal of sense.

Practically speaking, you want as many people advocating for your investment portfolio as possible. If your husband, for instance, is an active member of the PTA or works in a large corporate firm in your target market, he has access to a host of potential resources. The more connections you can make the better. Investing really is a family business. Even if your spouse does not see himself as an investor, he has a personal stake in the family's finances and therefore in your real-estate ventures.

If the general public views your spouse as your business partner, he could be held to the same standards as you. If he is not part of the LLC and actions are brought against him by your debtors, your assets may be vulnerable. If you add your spouse to the LLC, he will be protected in the same way that you are. Since this is a private business, members may work as much or as little as they like. Whether your spouse only mentions your new acquisitions in passing or aggressively campaigns to find new leads isn't the point. All members of an LLC are protected regardless of their contribution.

Do not assume that your spouse is automatically considered a member of your LLC, despite your joint tax returns. You must follow the regulations of your state to make sure that each member of your LLC is properly listed. Your team's attorney can help make sure you are complying with the rules and regulations. Having your spouse listed as a member of your LLC helps protect your entire family from liability and can also encourage him or her to take a more active role in your new investing venture.

How can I grow my real-estate investment portfolio?

Although at times it may seem that you will never get started, with adequate planning, solid professional advice, and a well-executed business plan, you will be poised for your next portfolio move sooner than you think. Once you have completed your first transaction you will have a much clearer appreciation of the direction you want to move in. While we cannot predict which real-estate projects will be the most lucrative or know where your preferences will lead you, we can suggest a route that may prove beneficial.

One of the best things you can do if you want to enjoy continued real-estate success is to become an expert in your field. You won't reach this status after renting one income property, but taking the time to reflect on the decisions that led you through your first investment purchase can give you clarity about where to go next. If you find yourself drawn to vacation properties, learn everything you can about the type of people who vacation in a particular spot: what their motivations for travel are and how you can better serve their needs. The more time you dedicate to becoming an expert in a field, the better prepared you will be to anticipate a new need and develop your own niche.

If you tap into a seasonal vacation community that caters to upper-middle-class families who are looking for great dining, spa treatments, and kid-friendly activities but the current amenities seem to leave guests feeling unsatisfied, you have discovered a niche market. Should this community decide to expand or renovate to better suit the needs of the community, you can consider getting on board in the preliminary stages of planning and development knowing that this plan will fill a need. Instead of just being a vacation property investor, you can become an expert vacation property investor who caters to a high-end niche market. In real-estate investing, it can be profitable to know the ins and outs of a particular market.

The learning curve for your first purchase is enormous. You may now realize that commercial properties are not within your comfort zone, seasonal rentals are considerably more high maintenance than you had anticipated, or studio apartments are not desirable in the area in which you're investing. Knowing where not to go and what not to do is just as vital to your success as celebrating the right decisions you have made. By studying current market trends, networking, and always looking ahead, you can better develop a professional investing portfolio that is focused and rewarding.

Should I sell smaller properties for one bigger unit?

When real-estate investors get started, they can hardly imagine having one successfully rented property, let alone multiple income units. For this reason, we often hear newer investors talking about trading up or flipping a property. But it may not be necessary to give up a new property to capitalize on another opportunity.

Instead of getting into an income property with one foot already out the door, or setting an arbitrary date by which you want to flip, think about the benefits of building on your portfolio. While we do not want to miss out on the next right deal because we have become overly attached to or emotionally fixated on a unit, there can be advantages to managing multiple properties, even as a beginner investor.

Since you have spent so much time and energy finding, purchasing, and renting your unit, it would be a shame to scrap that work. You may want to look at a portfolio plan that is geared toward owning and operating several smaller properties and using the profits to buy a larger unit. You can learn the business and make money on smaller properties, and when the time is right use these profits and this knowledge toward bigger projects.

Once you have a property that is enjoying a steady profit, you can talk to your financial team about how to best use this money to move forward. We always want our money to be working for us. When we take profits from one unit and apply it to the purchase of another unit, we extend the life of that money and benefit from its multiple uses. Instead of thinking we have to sell right away in order to increase our profitability, we can make our next purchase and increase our inventory without having to sacrifice a money-making medium that is already working.

Of course, there may come a time when selling smaller properties will be the right choice, but you do not have to approach your blossoming business thinking that it is the only choice. Work with your investment team to develop a lucrative plan of action.

When should I take a calculated risk?

Risk is a part of every financial venture. Whether you choose to invest in stocks, antiques, or real estate, no transaction is ever guaranteed to make money. Once we accept that risk is a part of every transaction, we know we need no longer wait for a perfect scenario for investment because it doesn't exist. All financial ventures should be approached as calculated risks.

This does not mean you should throw caution to the wind and dive headfirst into every available opportunity. It is important to look for ways and means to lower your risk. Experience will certainly open your eyes to the difference between sound advice and exaggerated boasting. Sound advice will rely on having systems in place and following well-outlined steps to achieve a goal. Boastful exaggerating will sound too good to be true.

When we talk about "calculated" we mean well-researched, team-supported, and manageable. As you build your portfolio, continue to involve your team in decision making. Even though you may no longer need to reach for the phone every time a question pops into your head, do not assume that there is nothing left to learn from experts who have dedicated their professional lives to finance. We can convince ourselves that we have the situation well in hand because we do not want to hear contrary advice, regardless of how beneficial it could be. It is your portfolio, and ultimately the decisions are yours to make, but independent does not mean isolated.

Gradually you will begin to network with a community of investors who share your interests. Use these connections to further develop your expertise and pursue your market. Collaboration can be an exciting way to learn more about the real-estate investing field and stay current and committed to market trends. The more you work with winners, the greater chance you have of learning from other people's mistakes and reducing your own chances of risk. By communicating with your team, remaining teachable, and taking notice of successful investment patterns, you can approach future transactions aware of the risk factors without being paralyzed by them.

How do I stay ahead of the curve?

All investors wish they had a magic crystal ball to see what the future will bring. But until one exists, it is important for the real-estate investor to stay current and take notice of changing markets, consumer habits, and seasonal highs and lows. While there are always deals to be made, when you come in at the tail end of an area's potential you will have to work harder for less. The object of the game is to have the foresight to take advantage of changing trends without taking unnecessary chances. There are a few strategies that may help you walk this fine line.

It is always a good idea to surround yourself with people who are smarter and more experienced than you. While it can feel good to be the room's go-to guy and have people hang on your every word, we can only get better at investing when we seek out businesspeople who are at the top of their real-estate game. To effectively do this, we must remain humble, continue to ask questions, and seek out investors who have the portfolios we aspire to. Often the best place to be when trying to stay ahead of the curve is in the middle where we can learn from the experts and reach out to the novice. That way, we are learning with foresight and hindsight.

It bears repeating that education is an enormous advantage in the business world. Read a variety of financial books until you find a philosophy that strikes a chord, then use the suggestions in your own practices. Attend reputable professional seminars that cater to your business, and subscribe to relevant periodicals. Read success stories to find out how other people did it. Keep an open dialogue with your team and take time to review and adjust your business plan. Stick with what works and implement new strategies where necessary.

Keep networking with successful investors who are excited about your business plan because a similar plan has worked for them. While those who have struck it rich may have exciting anecdotes, they may not have a lot of substance to offer. Seek out those who subscribe to a proven plan of action, have a sensible and profitable business plan, and enjoy what they do. By continuing to focus on the process, not the product, you will gain knowledge of how others met their goals. Remember, a top-of-the-line golf club may be a great product, but unless you practice your swing the ball is never going to make it to the hole. While no crystal balls exist, you can put yourself in a position to better forecast real-estate trends and take advantage of what you've learned.

How do I get in on the next big thing?

There are usually two ways to get in on the next big thing. You must create it, or you must be invited to join it. Since you are likely to be pursuing real-estate investing on a part-time basis, you're unlikely to create the next must-have trend. Therefore, you want to put yourself in a position to be invited to join a potentially profitable new deal.

Professionalism is instrumental in making this happen. Having business cards, attending seminars, and speaking knowledgeably about your portfolio plan and your past investing experiences can help you project yourself as a serious investor, not just someone who is looking to ride on the coattails of others. Being invited to join a new venture does not mean that you sit around waiting for opportunity to knock. You must put yourself in a readily available position and show you have something to contribute.

To do this you must be aware of financial and cultural trends. The only certainty in life is that things change. You want to evolve with the process and move in new directions. For example, technology has completely changed the professional work day. Telecommuting has made it possible for businesspeople to live farther away from major cities. Areas in the Poconos in Pennsylvania that were once exclusively vacation homes are now havens to people employed in New York City. This is happening in communities throughout the United States. We began to take notice of new housing developments sprouting up in these once-seasonal towns. We reached out to area professionals in our network for advice and learned of an up-and-coming townhouse development being built to meet this growing need. Our awareness and networking led us to purchase a profitable townhouse, which has been one of our more lucrative investments.

Keep apprised of local trends in your area and reach out to investors in your network to hear what their thoughts are. There are plenty of deals to be made for everyone. In fact, by coming up with a great idea and sharing it with others, you are more likely to be on the receiving end of the next big thing sometime down the line.

What happens if I fall off track?

As you build your portfolio, gaining insight and experience in real-estate investing, you should assess what you have and decide on the best direction. Take a step back to consider what you have and what you want and determine if you should continue down this track or make adjustments to your portfolio. If your plan seems to have taken a detour, it may be time for a change.

When you first sat down to organize your business plan, we suggested that you add measurable checkpoints to help determine if your portfolio was indeed making progress. Take a look at these checkpoints and compare your goals to your actual inventory. Are the properties you are currently holding making those goals happen? If you are meeting your goals, congratulations; if not, it's time to look at what is preventing you from the success you had planned for.

Perhaps you have met many of your preliminary goals, but now you find that your portfolio is growing stagnant and no new developments are on the horizon. This often happens when we have exhausted ourselves starting up a new business and find we have little energy left to make the business grow. After one or two deals, we intend to take a break from purchasing. But a short break turns into a long hiatus, and we realize that we are no longer taking an active role in our investing future. At this point, it is time for a change in business practices.

Catch up on the trends by hitting one or two of your favorite real-estate Web sites to examine the condition of the current market. If nothing new is happening with your portfolio, it may be because you are approaching it as a buyer when it is more conducive to selling. The buy-and-hold method may work, but because the real-estate market tends to be cyclical, you could get a much higher return on your investment by playing both sides of the field. Reacquainting yourself with what is going on today can help shed light on your plan.

Check in with your financial team and inquire about new developments they are seeing in today's market. Check through any newsletters or mailers they've sent you. Use these as a jumping-off point for a conversation that takes a closer look at your own needs. It is not unusual to lose momentum once your business is up and running, but because a great deal of the hard work is already done, you would be doing yourself a great disservice by putting your portfolio on autopilot.

When should I update my business plan?

As we just mentioned, getting off track is often a result of letting your portfolio run itself. One way to get back in the game if you seem to be stagnating or losing ground is by keeping your business plan current. A business plan is an excellent tool, but unless you use it, it loses its effectiveness.

If it has been more than six months since you have taken a look at your plan, review all of the key sections, noting new sales or purchases, new competition, and the state of the market. Make notes as you move along; this will help you organize market research.

Take a look at your mission statement and see if you are meeting your goals. Since you are in charge of your business, it is up to you to make sure your statement clearly defines the direction you want your real-estate investing to move in. With some experience under your belt, you may now realize that your mission statement was overzealous or fell short of the mark. Tweak this statement to best suit your portfolio plan.

Next look at your action plan. Are you doing everything you intended to do? Have you targeted a demographic that is yielding profitable income properties, or has your focus shifted to another area? If it was your intention to work with residential properties but you have networked with commercial building owners and are drawn to this market, update your plan to reflect these changes.

Lastly, give yourself a good reality check. Measure your goals against profits and losses, noting your rental income, maintenance fees, and additional expenses. If you have fallen behind, set short-term manageable goals to get back on track and readjust your long-term goals. An obstacle that may have seemed insurmountable to a beginner, like maintaining accurate tenant files, may be part of your regular routine now that you're an experienced landlord. Set new goals where applicable and you may find new motivation. A business plan that is continuously updated and used on a regular basis can help you better manage your business, stay on track, and remain excited about your real-estate investing future.

How can I best manage my assets?

The best way to manage your assets is by remaining an active participant in your portfolio's progress. It can be tempting to turn the deal making over to your financial team, wait for opportunities to come to you, or follow along with the real-estate investing crowd, but this backseat position could jeopardize your financial future.

A well-educated, enthusiastic financial team can be a critical part of your growth, but these professionals are not responsible for your success. With a variety of different clients with different needs, they cannot be expected to find you great money-making deals and hand them over for a small commission. A good team is interested in working with you, will keep you informed about what new ideas and products they can offer, and looks forward to hearing what your plans and intentions are. Yes, members of your team may call if a property deal becomes available that you may be interested in, but you should not rely only on these calls. Stay current on your market and contact your team with ideas and projects. Everyone prefers to work with motivated individuals. Take your business seriously and your assets will benefit from your hard work.

Keep networking with reputable, successful investors who are engaged in their business and you'll remain engaged with your assets. One of the reasons that so many adults make time for book clubs, continuing education classes, or volunteer their time is the chance to be with others who share their interests. Business is not a hobby, but the most successful businesspeople enjoy what they do. Spending time with other area professionals who treasure their assets, are excited about market trends, and are enthusiastic about new developments can inspire you to remain an active manager of your portfolio.

Managing your assets also means doing what is best for you, and this may sometimes go against conventional wisdom. Trends should always be considered, but they are not law. If everyone is selling their rental properties but you have a reliable, low-maintenance tenant in a solid building, it may not be the right time for you to jump on board the selling ship. Keep current and informed and stay in touch with your financial team, and you can make the best choices for your assets, regardless of what direction popular opinion takes. An active role in your portfolio's growth is always an important part of financial success.

How can I stay informed about the real-estate market?

Staying active means staying informed. By now you have probably sought out different news sources, subscribed to a financial magazine, or added favorite links to your computer and tune into news reports that you have come to trust for accurate and timely information. All these resources are useful in getting a picture of the real-estate market.

If you have not already done so, subscribe to a local newspaper. It is a convenient way to keep on top of local developments, not only in the real-estate market but in your community. If you hear new schools are being built, you know the community is growing. If there are coupons and solicitations to try a new restaurant, you know that new businesses are moving into the area. Knowing if taxes are going up, community activities are being planned, or libraries are struggling to stay open gives you the insight you need to help plan your next portfolio move.

We recommend creating a customized homepage that delivers current real-estate information to you. If you visit *www.google.com* and select the "personalized home" icon you will be prompted to a new screen from which you can customize the types of news delivered to you daily. An "add stuff" icon allows you to browse material, including finance news, economic updates, and weather links. Using the "search homepage content" icon, you can narrow your selections and customize your page to suit your needs. Instead of receiving general real-estate information you can focus on your local area and access detailed articles, blogs, and reliable news sources. Each day, pull up your customized page and read the news you need to know. This free service is easy to set up and maintain.

With so many news sources to choose from, there is no reason not to be an informed consumer and entrepreneur. Organize your sources to bring you relevant, reliable information and you will have a much better handle on your local market.

How can I make the most of my networking?

Networking is more than handing out your business cards and hoping for the best. It is about building relationships. Now that you have a more focused idea of the direction you want to take, you can focus your networking efforts to make the most of your contacts.

When building your network, remember that quality is more important than quantity. It may look good to have a shoebox filled with business cards and phone numbers, but if your network is a mile long and only an inch deep, you don't have much to work with. Before you can expect to receive, you must give. Target a handful of contacts who seem to have the same type of business philosophy and portfolio plans as you, and look for opportunities to strengthen these relationships. Recall key moments in your conversation and follow up with that restaurant name you recommended, an interesting article that may be of service, or an invitation to an upcoming event. Projecting yourself as someone who listens and takes initiative is a good way to separate yourself from the crowd. Just remember: Be available, not overbearing.

Many people make the mistake of only networking when they need something. If you call someone you have met once or twice and propose that the two of you combine funds in a new joint venture, you can be pretty certain that this contact will quickly get off the phone (then change his number). Slow and steady wins the relationship race. Cultivate relationships now so that when an interesting opportunity becomes available you know the right people to contact for the right reasons. Instead of smelling desperation, they will be more likely to spot a smart prospect.

Like exercising, you can't give it all you've got one day and expect lasting results. If you want to get something out of a network relationship, you have to put in time and effort. Many well-organized networking groups have committees that are run by volunteer members. Offer your services. Handing out nametags at the registration booth may not seem glamorous, but it is the perfect opportunity to introduce yourself and shake hands while showing that you are committed to the organization. Become an active member, not just a passerby. Building networking relationships can be an important and enjoyable way to stay informed and energized about your real-estate investing portfolio.

Will my team change as my business grows?

With growth it is safe to assume that change is inevitable. What works for us in the beginning is not guaranteed to work forever. Approximately every six months you should take time to evaluate your financial team.

It usually takes at least one or two completed transactions to really get a feel for who is capable of what, so until then work on building the relationship instead of critiquing it. Once you have experienced what your professionals have to offer, consider if you have the best players for your team. Use the following questions to help you evaluate each expert:

- Am I satisfied with the level of knowledge and skill this person brings to the table?
- Are my questions and concerns welcomed?

- Are my questions answered clearly and coherently?
- Am I satisfied with this professional's attention to detail, turnaround time, and ability to meet deadlines?
- Is this person cooperative and enthusiastic? Does she work well with other players on the team?
- Does this person take the initiative and reach out to me with new products or ideas?
- Does this professional look for ways to help me grow my business, or are her ideas stagnant?
- Has this professional's input and advice yielded positive or negative results?
- Is this person well regarded by colleagues in her field?
- Is this person organized and efficient?
- Does this professional solve or exacerbate problems?
- What is my gut feeling about this person's ethics and abilities?

Most likely these questions will not yield simple yes or no answers. Since no one is perfect, there are bound to be areas for improvement. You want to work with people who get the job done and because of their level of expertise, demeanor, and commitment to success.

You will find that your needs will grow regardless of how effective and competent your original team is. When the time comes to add new members, use your interview questions as a guide. Working with a property manager, builder, contractor, or lawyer are all possibilities. You have the tools to build the team you want and can choose how to best proceed. A well-thought-out evaluation of team performance can help keep you moving in the right direction.

What if I no longer want a particular person on my financial team?

If after using the previous questions as evaluation guidelines you realize that one of the professionals on your team is no longer your best choice, you should make a change with confidence and care. Knowing that a well-orchestrated team is essential to get the job done, you'll want to make the best choices for your portfolio.

Ideally, you should not be scrambling around for a new mortgage consultant two weeks before you are supposed to close or desperately searching for a tax accountant on April 1. Evaluating your team between projects gives you the peace of mind to make a change on your timetable. If you have to, complete the transaction you are involved in then make a change. You are much more likely to make a well-thought-out decision when you are not engaged in a stressful situation.

Since your financial team members are not employees, working with someone new will usually require little fanfare or confrontation. If, for example, a new real-estate agent has been seeking you out and has contacted you about some potential income properties he thinks you could be interested in, you should investigate these prospects. Your former agent may catch wind of this new relationship and contact you, but it is completely up to you if you want to explain your decision or not.

On the other hand, ending a relationship with a financial advisor may require a few formal but simple steps. If you are unsatisfied with your current advisor it is well advised to have your new advisor lined up so the transition is a smooth one. Businesspeople often change advisors, and the process of moving policies or accounts from one institution to another usually requires little more than your signature on some paperwork. What is important is not losing track of your finances or convincing yourself that you now know enough to go it alone. One or two transactions does not an expert make. Change from one financial advisor to another, not from one advisor to no advisors.

As your portfolio grows, your needs and preferences will grow along with it. Continue to protect yourself and your assets by working toward having the best people on your team.

How can I best set myself up for retirement?

Retirement is your icing on the cake. You can spend your time enjoying travel, pursuing hobbies, or visiting with friends and family. A well-planned retirement can offer you freedom—personal and financial.

A solid business plan is a key component in retirement success. In this book we have talked about using real-estate investing as a vehicle to help you obtain your short- and long-term financial goals. Having benchmarks built into your business plan will help you stay on track. If you are not meeting your short-term goals, it is unlikely your long-term retirement goals will come to fruition. Checking your progress along the way can give you time to readjust your spending, whether that means subscribing to a new budget, downsizing, or taking a more aggressive approach to saving. While there will continue to be demands on your income that may make short-term goals more difficult to realize than you anticipated, having a business plan can help you keep your eye on long-term goals.

For many people, our consumer-inspired society makes it difficult to live without the latest and greatest must-have product. While there is nothing wrong with enjoying your daily life, there is no denying that planning for retirement takes restraint. Since it is easy to convince ourselves that things are more financially sound than they really are, we tend to overspend and underplan. Having a written plan of action that is discussed and utilized with a team of financial experts can be just the dose of reality we need to remember our responsibilities to ourselves and our families.

If you decide to make real-estate investing part of your investment plan, you will soon realize that it takes a great deal of hard work and perseverance to make an income property work. Building wealth and enjoying a successful retirement are not simple goals. If they were, everyone would be living much more comfortably in their golden years. But by taking your financial future seriously and making necessary adjustments in your current lifestyle, such successes are possible.

Long-term goals are realized by meeting short-term objectives. Work with your financial team to make sure you are taking the necessary steps to enjoy retirement.

How will I know that I've succeeded in real-estate investing?

This is an extremely difficult question, and the details of the answer will differ for everyone. However, there are some common denominators of success to review.

When talking about success, we are not solely focused on whether our investments are making money. Measuring success is really a quality-of-life question. You can amass a huge empire of profit-making income properties, but if you have schemed and connived to get what you have, are you really successful? On the other hand, you may find that by taking all the right steps and moving through your business plan with honesty and integrity you have only a few properties in your portfolio that are yielding modest returns. Does that make you less of a success?

The most successful people we know do not look at their accomplishments as a checklist to be completed and discarded. Instead, each new project is a steppingstone to something else. Making money is an important accomplishment because it affords them the lifestyle they want—not only luxury items but time with their family, freedom, and contentment.

Since this is a book on real-estate investing, you are probably concerned with financial success. You want to dedicate your time to a business that will provide you with monetary security. But ask yourself: What do you want security to buy? Most likely your answer will include personal comforts. If that is indeed the case, check to see that you are meeting these objectives. Are you balancing career and family? Do you have time to enjoy hobbies and interests? Are you turning off the cell phone and computer at night to enjoy rest and relaxation? Are you looking after your health? While getting a new venture off the ground certainly takes a great deal of sacrifice and commitment, alienating relationships, becoming ill, or trying to keep up a breakneck speed is both dangerous and often disastrous.

Only you can judge if you have succeeded in real-estate investing. The better question to ask yourself is if you have used real-estate investing to create the lifestyle that makes you happy.

Should I concentrate on having a diversified portfolio or concentrate my energies and money in real-estate investing?

When businesspeople speak about having diversified portfolios, they are often concerned with lowering their risk. If one investment were to plummet, be it in stocks, bonds, or real estate, the other investments would help counterbalance the loss. This is a common approach to investing and one that makes sense. Fortunately, when we are talking about real-estate investing, we can consider diversifying within one medium.

When you diversify your risk, you also diversify your possible returns. Simply put, the more you put in, the more you get out. If you spread yourself too thin, you may be doing more harm than good, especially since it is hardly likely that you will become an expert in the stock market, antiques, collectibles, and real estate. But since real estate has many different opportunities to pursue, you can diversify while still specializing in one field.

Real estate works on a local economy. Let's say you have two successful vacation destination properties at a ski lodge near your home. You enjoy catering to this particular clientele, prefer newer models (less maintenance) to older models, and have educated yourself about the vacation preferences of baby boomers (your target demographic). Thanks to your strong networking relationships, you are invited to participate in an income investment opportunity on a beachfront property. You familiarize yourself with the area, bring yourself up to speed with the details, and present the idea to your financial team who give you the green light. Since the beachfront properties are in a totally different location—and therefore a different economy—from the ski resort, you have just diversified your portfolio. But instead of spreading yourself too thin or taking on an entirely new money-making vehicle, you have used your expertise to grow your real-estate portfolio.

Using your initial investment as a way to grow your portfolio in different directions gives you a solid foundation from which to branch out. Over time, your portfolio could include properties in several different areas yielding several different rates of return. All these projects work in unison to give you more experience. When it comes to financial success, knowledge is an excellent source of power.

What is the best real-estate investing advice you've ever received?

Throughout this book we have worked hard to convey our experience and recommendations in a friendly and practical manner. We know how overwhelming it can be to begin a new financial venture. Because we have suffered setbacks and celebrated accomplishments, probably the best parting advice we can give is this: Real-estate investing is about progress, not perfection.

We have done well in real estate because we decided to commit to a plan. Instead of being extremists—waiting for ideal circumstances before making a move or jumping in head first—we set ourselves up for success with a financial plan that relied on small steps. Knowing that when we started we were far from being real-estate investing experts, we surrounded ourselves with the best in the business. It is estimated that about 80 percent of financial business, real estate and otherwise, is done by about 20 percent of the people. We sought out these 20 percent and learned from them, wanting what they had: a profitable action plan for building a lucrative investment portfolio. We have used our own action plan to help you devise yours.

It has been our intention to provide you with a user-friendly book for beginning your own real-estate investing career. Our recommendations are only the tip of the iceberg, a mere first step. Seeking out personalized financial advice is critical to success, as your investment team will help you devise a portfolio plan based on your needs, goals, and expectations. Real-estate investing is not a passing trend, nor is it a guaranteed method of making you a millionaire. But for us it has been an exciting and profitable vehicle for achieving our financial goals. We hope it becomes the same for you. We are pleased to have helped you begin this exciting new business venture and wish you luck, and much continued progress, on your new financial endeavors.

Scenario: Now that I have finished reading this book, what is the best way to continue making use of it?

When we set out to write this book, our intention was to provide you with a resource you could turn to time and time again. Now that you have finished reading it, you can add this title to your list of resources and use it as a ready reference.

Many times when we are reading we like to go through all the information first to get a big-picture feel. Having done that, you can now go back to the beginning chapter and approach our methods and suggestions with a critical eye. Do not feel obligated to treat this book like a borrowed library book; make it your own. If you have not already done so, highlight pages or questions that are pertinent to your situation. Use the inside cover to keep a running list of contacts and phone numbers. Clip a pen and additional blank index cards to the back cover so that when you need to make a longer notation or you get a great idea you have a means of recording your thoughts.

There is no right way to use this book, but there is a wrong way. Reading through cover to cover and taking action on only the points you remember is not a good plan. We have tried to give you a step-by-step guide to take you through the real-estate investing process. There are too many details and decisions to make to leave them up to your memory. Wherever you are in your process, be it organizing your team, researching your market, or interviewing tenants, open this book to the correlating chapter. This is not a venture you should undertake alone. Having resources can help you stay on track and prevent you from feeling overwhelmed or isolated.

There are further reading suggestions in Appendix D to help you organize your plans and continue moving forward. This book, like pertinent articles, additional titles, and Web site newsletters, should not just take up space. Make each your own and you will end up with an extensive knowledge base that can grow and change with your portfolio's performance.

Appendix A Sample Lease

LEASE

THIS IS A LEGALLY BINDING LEASE THAT WILL BECOME FINAL WITHIN THREE BUSINESS DAYS. DURING THIS PERIOD YOU MAY CHOOSE TO CONSULT AN ATTORNEY WHO CAN REVIEW AND CANCEL THE LEASE. SEE SECTION ON ATTORNEY REVIEW FOR DETAILS.

This Lease is made on _____ 20 _____

between the Tenant(s):_____

whose address is _____

_____

referred to as the "Tenant."

and the Landlord_____

whose address is _____

_____

referred to as the "Landlord."

The word "Tenant" means each Tenant named above.

1. Property. The Tenant agrees to rent from the Landlord and the Landlord agrees to lease to the Tenant the property known as: _____ , referred to as the "Property."

2. Term. The term of this Lease is for _____ months starting on _____ , 20 _____ and ending _____ , 20 _____ . The Landlord is not responsible if the Landlord cannot give the Tenant possession of the Property at the start of this Lease. However, rent will only be charged from the date on which possession of the Property is made available to the Tenant. If the Landlord cannot give possession within 30 days after the starting date, the Tenant may cancel this Lease.

3. Rent. The Tenant agrees to pay $ _____ as rent, to be paid as follows: $ _____ per month, due on the _____ day of each month. The first payment shall be a security deposit of $ _____ and is due upon the signing of this Lease by the Tenant. The Tenant must pay a late charge of $ _____ for each payment that is more than 5 days late. This late charge is due with the monthly rent payment. First month rent shall be paid prior to occupancy.

4. Use of Property. The Tenant may use the Property only for the following purpose(s):

_____

_____

_____

_____

5. Eviction. If the Tenant does not pay the rent within _____ days after it is due, the Tenant may be evicted.

The Landlord may also evict the Tenant if the Tenant does not comply with all of the terms of this Lease and for all other causes allowed by law. If evicted, the Tenant must continue to pay the rent for the rest of the term. The Tenant must also pay all costs, including reasonable attorney fees, related to the eviction and the collection of any moneys owed the Landlord, along with the cost of reentering, rerenting, cleaning, and repairing the Property. Rent received from any new tenant will reduce the amount owed the Landlord.

6. Payments by the Landlord. If the Tenant fails to comply with the terms of this Lease, the Landlord may take any required action and charge the cost, including reasonable attorney fees, to the Tenant as additional rent. Failure to pay such additional rent upon demand is a violation of this Lease.

7. Care of the Property. The Tenant has examined the Property, including all facilities, furniture, and appliances, and is satisfied with its present condition. The Tenant agrees to maintain the property in as good condition as it is at the start of this Lease except for ordinary wear and tear. The Tenant must pay for all repairs, replacements, and damages caused by the act or neglect of the Tenant or the Tenant's visitors. The Tenant will remove all of the Tenant's property at the end of this Lease. Any property that is left becomes the property of the Landlord and may be thrown out; the cost of which to be charged to the tenant.

8. Quiet Enjoyment. The Tenant may remain in and use the Property without interference subject to the provisions of this Lease.

9. Validity of Lease. If a clause or provision of this Lease is legally invalid, the rest of this lease remains in effect.

Other Provisions: Tenant may not alter or paint premises without written agreement of the landlord.

If Lease is not to be renewed, Tenant or Landlord must notify the other ___ months in advance of nonrenewal. Lock Box will be installed ___ month prior to end of Lease, and premises must be shown between the hours of 9 AM and 8 PM.

Parties: The Landlord and each of the Tenants are bound by this Lease. All parties who lawfully succeed to their rights and responsibilities are also bound.

Attorney Review: The Tenant or the Landlord may choose to have an attorney study this Lease. If an attorney is consulted, the attorney must complete his or her review of the Lease within a three-day period. This Lease will be legally binding at the end of this three-day period unless an attorney for the Tenant or the Landlord reviews and disapproves of the Lease. You count the three days from the date of delivery of the signed Lease to the Tenant and the Landlord. You do not count Saturdays, Sundays, or legal holidays. The Tenant and the Landlord may agree in writing to extend the three-day period for attorney review.

If an attorney for the Tenant or the Landlord reviews and disapproves of this Lease, the attorney must notify the REALTOR(S) and the other party named in the Lease within the three-day period. Otherwise this Lease will be legally binding as written. The attorney must send the notice of disapproval to the REALTOR(S) office. The attorney may also, but need not, inform the REALTOR(S) of any suggested revision(s) in the Lease that would make it satisfactory.

Agency Relationships: By signing below the Landlord and Tenants acknowledge they received the Consumer Information Statement on New Jersey Real Estate Relationships from the brokerage firms involved in this transaction prior to the first showing of the property.

Realtor Recognition. It is understood that Wyndemere Real Estate Co., Inc. has procured the Tenant(s) and will be paid $_____ by Landlord.

This commission will be due and payable at the receipt of security deposit and payment of one month's rent.

Entire Lease. All promises the Landlord has made are contained in this written Lease. This Lease can only be changed by an agreement in writing by both the Tenant and the Landlord.

Signatures. The Landlord and the Tenant agree to the terms of this Lease. If this Lease is made by a corporation, its proper corporate officers sign and its corporate seal is affixed.

Additional Provisions:

_____

_____

_____

_____

_____

_____

Witnessed or Attested by: _____Landlord

_____ Tenant

ADDENDUM B

DISCLOSURE OF INFORMATION AND ACKNOWLEDGMENT ABOUT LEAD-BASED PAINT AND/OR LEAD-BASED PAINT HAZARDS LEASES

I.   LEAD PAINT WARNING

Housing built before 1978 may contain lead-based paint. Lead from paint, paint chips, and dust can pose health hazards if not managed properly. Lead exposure is especially harmful to young children and pregnant women. Before renting pre-1978 housing, lessors must disclose the presence of known lead-based paint and/or lead-based paint hazards in the dwelling. Lessees must also receive a federally approved pamphlet on lead poisoning prevention.

II.   PROPERTY ADDRESS: _____

III. LESSOR'S DISCLOSURE (initial) (To be completed and signed at time of listing)

(a) Presence of lead-based paint and/or lead-based paint hazards (check one below):

Known lead-based paint and/or paint hazards are present in the housing (explain):

Lessor has no knowledge of lead-based paint or lead-based paint hazards in the housing.

(b) Records and reports available to the lessor (check one below):

Lessor has no reports or records pertaining to lead-based paint and/or lead-based hazards in the housing.

Lessor has the following reports or records pertaining to lead-based paint and/or lead-based paint hazards in the housing, all of which lessor has provided to its listing agent, and has directed its listing agent to provide lessee or lessee's agent with these records and reports prior to lessor accepting any offer to lease (list documents below):

(c) If there is any change in the above information prior to lessor accepting an offer from the lessee to lease, lessor will disclose all changes to the lessee prior to accepting the offer.

IV. LESSOR'S CERTIFICATION OF ACCURACY
Lessor(s) have reviewed the Lessor's Disclosure in Section III and certify, to the best of his/her/their knowledge, that the information they have provided is true and accurate.

Lessor _____ Date _____

Lessor _____ Date _____

V. LISTING AGENT'S CERTIFICATION OF ACCURACY
Listing Agent certifies that he/she has informed the lessor of the lessor's obligations under 42 U.S.C. 485d and is aware of his/her responsibility to ensure compliance.

Listing Agent _____ Date _____

VI. LESSEE'S ACKNOWLEDGMENT (initial) (The Lessor's Disclosure in Section III and Certification in Section IV and the Listing Agent's Certification in Section V to be completed and signed prior to lessee signing this Addendum B.)

(a) Lessee has received copies of all information listed in Section III above.

(b) Lessee has received the pamphlet "Protect Your Family From Lead in Your Home."

(c) Lessee has (check one below):

Received a 10-day opportunity (or mutually agreed upon period) to conduct a risk assessment or inspection for the presence of lead-based paint and/or lead-based paint hazards; or

Waived the opportunity (or mutually agreed upon period) to conduct a risk assessment or inspection for the presence of lead-based paint and/or lead-based paint hazards.

VII.　LESSEE'S CERTIFICATION OF ACCURACY

Lessee(s) have reviewed the Lessee's Acknowledgment in Section VI and certify, to the best of his/her/their knowledge, that the information they have provided is true and accurate.

Lessor _____ Date _____

Lessor _____ Date _____

VIII.　LEASING/LESSEE'S　AGENT'S　CERTIFICATION　OF ACCURACY

Leasing/Lessee's Agent certifies that the lessee has received the information in section VI (a) and (b).

Leasing/Lessee's Agent _____ Date _____

Appendix B Sample Forms and Worksheets

Tenant's Checklist (Move-in Form)

INVENTORY AND CONDITION OF LEASED PREMISES: PRE-LEASE

Lessor/Landlord: _____

Lessee/Tenant: _____

Address of leased premises: _____

_____

_____

Term of Lease: _____

Begin: [date] _____

End: [date] _____

The purpose of this form is to catalogue all furniture, furnishings, fixtures, appliances, and personal property upon/in the leased premises that Tenant is responsible for returning in as clean and good condition as on the day of commencement of the Lease, normal wear and tear excepted. In addition, the condition of the premises should be noted when appropriate, including newness and/or condition of carpet, paint, etc.

Landlord should catalogue the presence of, and check and note the condition/working condition of each item in the leased premises. Tenant shall then review and check all listed items, immediately after Tenant moves in, indicating agreement or disagreement with Landlord's assessment, and adding comments as necessary. Tenant shall then sign this document in acknowledgment of the terms hereof and of the presence and condition of the catalogued items, including the following:

Landlord assessment   **Tenant assessment (check, or give reason)**

[item]   [condition]   [agree]   [disagree & reason/comment]

_____

_____

_____

_____

_____

_____

_____

_____

_____

_____

Inadvertent exclusion of any item from this catalogue does not relieve Tenant of the duty to use the item reasonably and return it in same condition as at inception of this lease, normal wear and tear excepted.

Tenant has reviewed this document and agrees that in consideration of the use and possession of the catalogued items during the term of this Lease, Tenant has checked all items and found them to be present and in the same condition as indicated by Landlord, or else has noted any discrepancy. Tenant further agrees to return said items at the expiration/termination of this lease as discussed above. Tenants, if more than one, agree that signature by one Tenant suffices for agreement by all Tenants.

Signature of Tenant: _____ Date: _____

Tenant [print name]: _____

Signature of Landlord: _____ Date: _____

Landlord [print name]: _____

©2004 USLegalforms.com

Tenant's Checklist (Move-out Form)

INVENTORY AND CONDITION OF LEASED PREMISES: POST-LEASE

Lessor/Landlord: _____

Lessee/Tenant: _____

Address of leased premises: _____

_____

_____

Term of Lease: _____

Begin: [date] _____

End:[date] _____

This catalogue should be compared to the Pre-Lease catalogue at the expiration or termination of the Lease. Each item in the Pre-Lease catalogue should be noted below, and its present, post-lease condition noted. If the post-lease condition differs from the pre-lease condition for reasons other than depreciation by reasonable wear and tear, this should be noted. Tenant should then state agreement or disagreement with the new assessment.

Landlord assessment   **Tenant assessment (check, or give reason)**

[item]   [condition]   [agree]   [disagree & reason/comment]

_____

_____

_____

_____

_____

_____

Landlord assessment		Tenant assessment (check, or give reason)	
[item]	[condition]	[agree]	[disagree & reason/comment]

_____

_____

_____

_____

_____

_____

TENANT SIGNATURE

Tenant has reviewed the premises and the above notations made by the Landlord. By signing below, Tenant warrants the accuracy of the above assessments, or disagrees with those assessments as noted by Tenant in the above spaces.

Tenants, if more than one, agree that signature by one Tenant suffices for signature by all Tenants.

Signature of Tenant: _____ Date: _____

Tenant [print name]: _____

Signature of Landlord: _____ Date:_____

Landlord [print name]: _____

Background Check Consent Form

CONSENT TO BACKGROUND AND REFERENCE CHECK

In consideration of solicitation of my application for employment, or application for lease of premises, I, [print name] _____, do hereby give my consent to [potential employer or landlord]: _____, and the authorized agents thereof, to check the references listed on my application, and to check my background in any way, including but not limited to contacting any and all persons and business entities in order to inquire regarding any and all information relating to myself, provided that said inquiries be limited solely to the purpose of consideration of myself for possible employment or tenancy.

Signed _____ Date: _____

Print: _____

(print name)

©2004 USLegalforms.com

Pay Rent or Quit Notice

7-DAY NOTICE TO PAY RENT OR LEASE TERMINATES:
RESIDENTIAL

TO: Tenant(s):   FROM: Landlord

_____   _____

_____   _____

_____   _____

_____   _____

Address of Leased Premises: _____

NOTICE IS HEREBY GIVEN that you are in breach of the Lease Agreement
on the above described lease premises due to failure to timely pay rent. Except
as provided below, within **seven (7) days** after service of this notice upon you,
you must pay in full to Landlord the rent and other charges now due and
unpaid, as follows:

$ _____ Rent for _____

$ _____ Late Charges _____

$ _____ Other _____

$ _____ Other _____

$ _____ Total (exclusive of further accruing costs)

Payment will be accepted only by:
☐ cash   ☐ money order   ☐ cashier's or certified check
☐ personal check

IF YOU FAIL TO TENDER FULL PAYMENT, **your Lease will be
terminated** and you must surrender possession of the premises to Landlord. If
you fail, within the **seven (7) days** notice period, either to pay the total charges
in full, or to surrender possession of the premises, legal proceedings will be

commenced against you to recover possession and to recover a judgment for the rent and damages for your unlawful detention of the premises, and all costs of court including attorneys' fees to the extent allowed by applicable law and/or the lease agreement. Surrender of the premises does not relieve you of liability for the outstanding balance.

The **seven (7) days** notice period described herein shall expire at:

_____o'clock [am/pm], on the _____ day of _____, 20 _____

LANDLORD RESERVES ALL RIGHTS AND REMEDIES UNDER THE LEASE AGREEMENT AND UNDER APPLICABLE LAW, INCLUDING BUT NOT LIMITED TO CONTRACTUAL DAMAGES FOR UNPAID RENT, AND NOTHING IN THIS NOTICE SHOULD BE CONSTRUED AS A WAIVER OR RELINQUISHMENT OF SAME.

Signed, _____ this the _____ day of _____, 20_____.

Signed: _____
Landlord/Lessor, or authorized agent

©2004 USLegalforms.com

Cure or Quit Notice

NOTICE OF BREACH OF SPECIFIC PROVISIONS OF
WRITTEN LEASE WITH RIGHT TO CURE: RESIDENTIAL

TO: Tenant(s):   FROM: Landlord

_____   _____

_____   _____

_____   _____

_____   _____

Address of Leased Premises: _____

You are advised that you are in violation of the following provision(s) of the lease:

[identify lease provision]

The reason you are in breach of the provision(s) above is the following:
Pursuant to the lease, you are provided with this written notice of the breach.
You are given _____ ( ) days from the date of your receipt of this notice to cure the breach, or the lease shall stand terminated and I will pursue eviction remedies.
Signed, this the_____ day of _____ , 20 _____ .

Signed: _____
                    Landlord/Lessor, or authorized agent

©2004 USLegalforms.com

Unconditional Quit Notice

NOTICE OF BREACH OF SPECIFIC PROVISIONS OF
WRITTEN LEASE WITH NO RIGHT TO CURE: RESIDENTIAL

TO: Tenant(s):   FROM: Landlord

_____   _____

_____   _____

_____   _____

_____   _____

Address of Leased Premises: _____

You are advised that you are in violation of the following provision(s) of the lease:

[identify lease provision]

The reason you are in breach of the provision(s) above is the following:

Pursuant to the lease, you are provided with this written notice of the breach and termination of the lease due to the breach. Due to the nature of the breach and in accordance with the lease provisions, there is no right to cure this default. The lease is therefore terminated effective _____ ( ) days from the date of your receipt of this notice. Please vacate the premises and provide the keys to me by the termination date.

Signed, this the_____ day of _____ , 20 _____ .

Signed: _____
                        Landlord/Lessor, or authorized agent

©2004 USLegalforms.com

Notice of Outstanding Charges

Date: _____

To: _____

_____

_____

Your payment for outstanding charges has not been received as of the above date. Please send a separate check or money order (do not combine it with the rent payment) upon receipt of this letter to avoid further charges. Your payments will be applied as follows: First to late charges, second to other charges due, and third to rent.

Description of Outstanding Charges:

Additional Information

Late Charges: _____

Utilities: _____

Other: _____

Rent: _____

Total Due: _____

Your payment should be sent to:

Owner/Management

Phone:

Cash Flow Analysis

Gross Income:

Estimated Annual Gross Income   _____

Other Income   _____

Total Gross Income   _____

Less Vacancy Allowance   _____

Effective Gross Income   _____

Expenses:

Taxes   _____

Insurance   _____

Water/Sewer   _____

Garbage   _____

Electricity   _____

Licenses   _____

Advertising   _____

Supplies   _____

Maintenance   _____

Lawn   _____

Snow Removal   _____

Pest Control   _____

Management—Offsite   _____

Management—Onsite   _____

Accounting/Legal   _____

Miscellaneous   _____

Gas   _____

Telephone   _____

Budget for Replacements   _____

Total Expenses   _____

Net Operating Income   _____

Debt Service:

1st Mortgage   _____

2nd Mortgage   _____

3rd Mortgage   _____

Total Debt Service   _____

Cash Flow: _____

Appendix C Real Estate Investing Questions

Chapter One

1. Why is everyone talking about investing in real estate?
2. Is real-estate investing a passing trend?
3. What are the myths of real-estate investing?
4. Am I too young to start this?
5. Am I too old to start this?
6. What does a real-estate investor look like?
7. How do I determine my financial literacy?
8. How can I become more financially literate?
9. Can I be a successful real-estate investor?
10. Should I do this full time?
11. Are there big beginner mistakes I should avoid?
12. How do I know I'm financially ready to invest in real estate?
13. How do I know I'm emotionally ready to invest in real estate?
14. How do I get started?
15. Is there a formula I should follow?
16. Can you walk me through a sample business plan?
17. Who can help me put this plan into action?
18. Why can't I do this all on my own?

19. Who is qualified to give investment advice?
20. Is there financial advice I should be wary of?
21. When will I know it's the right deal?
22. Is it true you need money to make money?
23. What is earned income?
24. What is portfolio income?
25. What is passive income?
26. What are assets and liabilities?
27. How can I build profitable assets while limiting liabilities?
28. How safe is this type of investing?
29. Am I guaranteed a profit?
30. Will this make me rich?
31. Will this make me poor?
32. How long will this take?
33. How can I better educate myself about real-estate investing?
34. I am committed to seeing this investment opportunity through. How can I best devise realistic goals and benchmarks to make sure I am on the right path?

Chapter Two

35. What are the benefits to assembling a team?
36. Who are the right people for my team?
37. Can I trust a professional recommendation from a business associate?
38. Can I trust a professional recommendation from friends and family?
39. Is it important to like the players on my investment team?
40. What if I make a bad first impression?
41. Should my financial team be associated with each other?
42. What paperwork should I have on hand before assembling my team?
43. What can I expect to find on my credit report?
44. Where can I get a copy of my credit report?
45. How important will my credit score be?
46. Should I improve my credit score before I begin assembling my team?

47. Why do I need a financial planner?

48. How can I prepare for my interview with a financial advisor?

49. What interview questions should I ask my financial planner?

50. Are there questions my potential financial advisor should ask me?

51. Which financial advisors work best with beginner investors?

52. How are financial advisors paid?

53. Is there a common financial formula all advisors use?

54. What are my options when choosing a mortgage broker?

55. Which lenders work best with beginner investors?

56. Which interview questions should I ask my mortgage consultant?

57. Are there questions my potential mortgage consultant should ask?

58. Will my credit be affected by consulting different mortgage consultants?

59. How do I choose the right real-estate agent?

60. Which interview questions should I ask a real-estate agent?

61. Are there questions my potential Realtor should ask me?

62. How can I find a reliable Realtor out of state?

63. Should I opt for a real-estate attorney?

64. Do I need a tax accountant?

65. Are there tax accountants who specialize in investing?

66. Do I need additional insurance policies to protect my new interests?

67. How long should it take to assemble my team?

68. I don't have time to interview dozens of different people. How can I find the best people in the shortest amount of time?

69. I now have all the right people in place. How hands-on do I need to be?

Chapter Three

70. How do I begin the process of financing my investment?

71. What is a mortgage?

72. Why should I contact a mortgage representative before searching out properties?

73. How do I apply for a mortgage?
74. What paperwork do I need to apply for a loan?
75. What is a preferred lender?
76. How can I most efficiently compare lenders?
77. Can I trust Web quotes and e-programs?
78. Is there a difference between preapproved and prequalified?
79. How do interest rates affect my cash-flow potential?
80. How much money should I be prepared to put down?
81. How much cash should I have on hand?
82. Are there specific loan programs that can save investors money?
83. How risky are nontraditional approaches to investment financing?
84. How can I learn the language of lenders?
85. What kind of loan should I apply for?
86. What is a fixed-rate mortgage?
87. What is an ARM?
88. What is an option ARM?
89. What is an interest-only loan?
90. What is HUD?
91. Can I qualify for an FHA loan?
92. What is an FHA 203k loan?
93. How do I buy with no money down?
94. Do these investor loans have hidden fees?
95. What if my investment property doesn't appraise?
96. What is a good-faith estimate?
97. Do I need private mortgage insurance (PMI)?
98. What is an 80/20 loan?
99. Can I use the equity in my primary residence to purchase an investment?
100. Can I purchase an investment property before I buy my own primary residence?
101. What does *owner occupied* mean, and how will it affect my loan?
102. Is it a good idea to buy and rent new construction?
103. Is it a good idea to buy a fixer-upper?
104. Should I look for properties that are in foreclosure?

105. Can I take a renovation loan on an investment property?
106. What is Section 8 housing?
107. What if I default on my investment's mortgage?
108. I have the opportunity to buy an investment property, but I'm planning on buying my own home. Can I do both, and is it a good idea?
109. I've just come into some substantial money. Should I pay cash for my investment property or take out a mortgage?

Chapter Four

110. How does buying an investment property differ from buying other real estate?
111. How much money should I spend on an investment property?
112. Which types of real-estate properties are available for investment purposes?
113. How do I decide which type of investment property is best for me?
114. Which type of property tends to be more profitable: residential or commercial?
115. What is a net, net, net lease, and could I benefit from it?
116. What does *mixed use* mean?
117. What is a spec house?
118. Is land a good investment?
119. Should I buy a large piece of land with a house and subdivide some of the land?
120. Should I buy a property in a vacation destination?
121. Should I buy real estate in a town I just visited on vacation?
122. What do I need to know about buying in unfamiliar territory?
123. What, if any, are the advantages of buying a time share?
124. Can any type of property be rented?
125. Doesn't all real estate appreciate over time?
126. Are certain rental properties more lucrative than others?
127. How can I calculate my income potential?
128. How can I find out what other area properties are renting for?
129. How much rent should I charge?
130. How do I find a qualified Realtor in my area?

131. What questions should I ask my Realtor about his expertise?
132. What questions should I ask when looking at properties?
133. How does my wish list change since I'm not living there?
134. How important is the neighborhood?
135. How important are the schools?
136. What is a seller's market?
137. What is a buyer's market?
138. Which market is more challenging to make money in?
139. Can I hold onto a property too long?
140. Can I give up on a property too soon?
141. How can I spot a great opportunity?
142. When is something too good to be true?
143. How can I increase my chances of being at the right place at the right time?
144. Do I need a home inspection?
145. Do I need homeowner's insurance?
146. What can I do to avoid becoming too emotionally attached to my investment?
147. Since I don't plan on living in this property, do I really need to spend so much money on inspections and insurance?

Chapter Five

148. Why are the Fair Housing laws so important to a landlord?
149. What accommodations must be made for disabled tenants?
150. How can I make sure I'm following the Fair Housing laws?
151. Where can I find renters?
152. What are effective ways to advertise for tenants?
153. Should I rent to friends?
154. Should I do a criminal background check on renters?
155. How can I check a renter's credit history?
156. Would current landlords and employers give false information?
157. Are there red flags I should look for when interviewing potential tenants?
158. How can I reduce tenant turnover?
159. Is there anything that must be done to the property between renters?

160. Can I offer tenants incentives?
161. Should I put in appliance upgrades?
162. Should I invest in remodeling projects?
163. Should I furnish the property?
164. What if tenants want to make repairs themselves?
165. What if tenants want to make upgrades themselves?
166. When should I raise the rent?
167. Should I insist on renter's insurance?
168. Why should I collect a security deposit?
169. What are a move-in checklist and an exit checklist?
170. When do I return the security deposit?
171. How hands-on should I be?
172. Do I need a property manager?
173. How do I find and employ a property manager?
174. Who should have a key to the property?
175. What problems should I try to avoid as a landlord?
176. What are common solutions to these problems?
177. What if the rent is late?
178. Can I prohibit smoking?
179. Should I prohibit smoking?
180. Should I prohibit pets?
181. How can I enforce the rules?
182. What if the tenants won't leave?
183. What if the tenants ruin the property?
184. If a tenant hurts himself on my property, can I be sued?
185. What if the tenant is breaking the law?
186. What if I need to sell a rented property?
187. What if a renter wants to sublet?
188. What does *lease with an option to buy* mean?
189. What does *right of first refusal* mean?

Chapter Six

190. Should I do a final inspection before tenants move in?
191. Should I have the renters sign a contract?
192. Where can I find a rental agreement template?
193. Should I ask for cash or a check?

Chapter Seven

223. Should I sell smaller properties for one bigger unit?
224. When should I take a calculated risk?
225. How do I stay ahead of the curve?
226. How do I get in on the next big thing?
227. What happens if I fall off track?
228. When should I update my business plan?
229. How can I best manage my assets?
230. How can I stay informed about the real-estate market?
231. How can I make the most of my networking?
232. Will my team change as my business grows?
233. What if I no longer want a particular person on my financial team?
234. How can I best set myself up for retirement?
235. How will I know that I've succeeded in real-estate investing?
236. Should I concentrate on having a diversified portfolio or concentrate my energies and money in real-estate investing?
237. What is the best real-estate investing advice you've ever received?

Appendix D Further Information

Business Tools

- Business plans—Offers a variety of sample business plans, tools, blogs, and links for organizing your new business's vision and direction.
  www.bplans.com
- Business plans—Browse through detailed business plans, visit consultant links, and compare business software products.
  www.businessplans.org
- Financial software—This is the site for QuickBooks, the user-friendly accounting software that is geared toward building an organized business.
  www.quickbooks.com
- Small business administration—Offers services, tools, and local resources for starting and maintaining your own small business.
  http://www.sba.gov/starting_business/planning/basic.html

Credit Checks

- The three major credit repositories to check your credit report and score:
  www.transunion.com, www.equifax.com, www.experian.com

Realty

- National Association of Realtors—A site geared toward professional Realtors. You can find links to local Realtors and read about what is happening in this field.
  www.Realtor.com
- U.S. Department of Housing and Urban Development—Check this site for a complete list of the Fair Housing laws, home ownership questions and answers, and government housing programs.
  www.hud.gov

Suggested Reading

- Entrepreneur.com—A wide range of business tools are available, as well as an online newsletter and timely feature articles.
  www.entrepreneur.com
- FinishRich Media—David Bach's FinishRich Media Web site has links to his free newsletter, radio show, and best-selling books, all of which are geared toward helping people make an action plan to achieve wealth.
  www.finishrich.com
- CNNMoney.com—Internet home to *Fortune* magazine, *Money* magazine, *Business 2.0* magazine, and *Fortune Small Business* magazine. Contemporary, level-headed articles and advice about a wide variety of personal finance interests.
  http://money.cnn.com
- Rich Dad—The home site of acclaimed author, speaker, and financial guru Robert Kiyosaki has links to his best-selling books, online articles, and community links.
  www.richdad.com

Professional Referrals

- Thomas E. Coronato—Coauthor of this book and a Retail Mortgage Sales Supervisor specializing in new construction and renovation. I've written mortgages all over the country for first-time home buyers and investors alike. Please contact me at:

www.thomascoronato.com

thomas.coronato@wellsfargo.com

info@thomascoronato.com

Office: 973-615-4279

- Helen Coronato—Coauthor of this book and a licensed Realtor. I'm also an author and program facilitator who hosts a monthly radio talk show. For more information about this book and other projects, please visit:

www.helencoronato.com

- Mark Sessanta—Our financial advisor since the beginning, Mark has been instrumental in facilitating our financial portfolio plans and welcomes your questions.

Independence Planning Group

Office: 610-440-0458

Fax: 610-440-0632

Cell: 908-319-2274

Mark_A_Sessanta@ipgroup.com

www.ipgroup.info

www.leapsystems.com

- Alex Fleischer, CPA

P.O. Box 97

Netcong, NJ 07857

Office: 973-714-8966

Fax: 908-444-8178

alexpf6@yahoo.com

- Bruce Speier—A CPA, Bruce holds a master's degree and a bachelor's degree from Rutgers University and also has unique industry experience in manufacturing, retail, and professional service businesses.

Office: 973-334-1500

www.coronatoandspeier.com

Foreclosure Information

- Foreclosures.com—A company that offers tools to help you locate and buy foreclosed properties throughout the United States. You'll also find advice to help you learn the differences between legitimate foreclosure deals and offerings that might be questionable.
  800-310-7730
  www.foreclosures.com

For Sale By Owner Resources

- Forsalebyowner.com—FSBO sellers can advertise their properties here and find marketing advice and general information to help them get a contract and complete the sale.
  888-933-8900
  www.forsalebyowner.com
- Owners.com—A Web site where you can advertise your properties to buyers worldwide. Resources include general information to help you sell your real estate.
  866-797-5025
  www.owners.com

Hazardous Substances

- U.S. Centers for Disease Control—The CDC is a government agency that provides information to help you learn about radon gas, toxic molds, asbestos, and other similar topics that affect your health and your real-estate transactions.
  800-311-3435
  www.cdc.gov
- Environmental Protection Agency—The EPA is a U.S. government agency that monitors environmental hazards such as asbestos, radon gas, molds, buried storage tanks, and other toxic materials important to anyone who plans to buy or sell real estate.
  202-272-0167
  wwww.epa.gov

- National Flood Insurance Program—FEMA offers details about the National Flood Insurance Program.
  202-566-1600
  www.fema.gov/nfip

Home Repair and Home Warranty

- About Home Repair—A Web site devoted to providing repair and update how-to information for homeowners.
  212-204-2710
  www.homerepair.about.com
- American Home Shield Warranties—A company that provides home warranty coverage to home-buyers, home-sellers, and current owners who plan to keep their homes.
  800-827-4636
  www.americanhomeshield.com
- HMS Home Warranties—HMS sells home warranty policies throughout the United States.
  800-941-9000
  www.hmsnet.com

Advice on Being a Landlord

- Apartment Living/Rental—A user-friendly Web site that offers insights into the world of rental living. Get help with leases and general tenant-landlord relations.
  212-204-2710
  www.apartments.about.com

Appendix E Glossary of Terms

1031 Exchange:
An Internal Revenue Service–endorsed transaction that allows a person to sell investment property and replace it with another property while deferring payment of capital gains taxes. IRS rules must be followed carefully to achieve an allowed transaction.

acceleration clause:
A clause in most home-loan contracts that allows the lender to demand full payment of your outstanding loan balance if you default on the loan or if you transfer title to another individual without lender approval.

adjustable-rate mortgage:
A loan with an interest rate that can go up or down. Rates are usually tied to an economic index.

amortized loan:
A loan where the periodic payments include both principal and interest.

appraisal:
In real estate, a report that estimates the value of a property or the

inspection process that takes place before the report is compiled.

balloon mortgage:
A loan that requires the full remaining principal balance to be paid at a specific time.

biweekly mortgage payment:
A repayment plan in which you make a half payment every two weeks rather than a full payment each month and resulting in thirteen payments per year instead of twelve. Biweekly payments reduce the total interest paid and the time it takes to pay a mortgage.

buyer's agent:
A real-estate agent who has signed a contract to work for a buyer. The agent's loyalty and fiduciary responsibilities are to the buyer.

comparative market analysis:
Also called a CMA, an opinion of a property's value based on past sales of similar properties. CMAs are often calculated by real-estate agents prior to listing a property for sale.

condominium:
Also called condo. A unit in a multiunit building where the owner holds full title to the unit and its air space, but not the land beneath it or above it. The owner has an interest in common elements of the development that are held jointly with other unit owners.

contingency:
A contact provision that requires a specific event to occur before the contract becomes binding.

contract for deed:
A type of seller financing in which the seller retains title to a property until the buyer has made payment in full.

cooperative:
A unit in a multiunit building where each owner occupant owns stock in a corporation rather than possessing a deed to real property.

deed of trust:
A security instrument that's used to transfer partial title to a trustee until an associated lien is paid in full. The trustee is a neutral party who has the power to foreclose if loan payments are not made as stated in the contract.

deed restrictions:
Limits placed on the use of a property. Recorded on the deed.

discount points:
Fees paid to a lender to lower the interest rate. The cost of one point equals 1 percent of the loan amount.

dual agent:
A real-estate buyer's agent working with a client who views or buys a listing held by the agent's firm.

due-on-sale clause:
A clause in a mortgage contract that allows the lender to demand the loan be paid in full if the borrower transfers ownership of the property that secures the lien.

easement:
The right to use another party's land for a specific purpose.

encroachment:
A building, fence, or other structure that touches or crosses the boundary line of an adjacent property.

equity:
An owner's financial interests in a piece of real estate, calculated by subtracting the dollar amount of liens against the property from its fair market value.

escrow:
Valuable items that are held by a neutral third party until provisions of the contract controlling them are met. In real estate, it often applies to your earnest money, also called a good faith deposit.

escrow account:
An account that holds funds for another for a specific purpose. For instance, a lender collects monthly tax and insurance payments, placing them in an escrow fund and paying the borrower's related bills when they are due.

exclusive agency listing agreement:
A real-estate listing contract in which the seller gives a specific real-estate agency the right to sell the property, but retains the right to sell it herself without paying a commission if she finds a buyer who has not been introduced to the property by the agency.

exclusive right-to-sell listing agreement:
A real-estate listing contract in which the seller agrees to pay the

agency a commission no matter who finds a buyer for the listed property.

facilitator:
A term used to describe real-estate agents who do not have a legal obligation to represent either a buyer or seller. The agent's job is to act as a neutral assistant to help the parties close a transaction. Not applicable in every state.

Fair Housing Act:
A federal law that prohibits housing discrimination on the basis of race, color, religion, sex, national origin, familial status, or disability.

fair market value:
The highest price a property would sell for in a reasonable length of time, provided both buyer and seller are knowledgeable and not under duress to buy or sell.

Fannie Mae:
Formerly a government agency called Federal National Mortgage Association, this corporation purchases mortgage loans on the secondary market, which helps keep funds available for real-estate loans.

first mortgage:
The mortgage-related lien that will be paid first when a piece of real-estate is sold or foreclosed.

fixed-rate loan:
A loan where the interest rates stays the same during the entire length of the loan.

foreclosure:
A legal procedure in which property used to secure a debt is recovered and sold by the lienholder in order to satisfy the debt. Also used to describe a home that's been through the foreclosure process.

Freddie Mac:
Formerly a government agency designed to provide secondary market services for low-income loans. Freddie Mac is now involved with all types of loans on the secondary market.

Ginnie Mae:
Ginnie Mae was created when Fannie Mae became a private corporation. It provides a secondary market for low-income and other special-assistance loans, and guarantees principal and interest

payments to investors who buy mortgage-backed securities.

grantee:
The person who receives real estate from a grantor.

grantor:
The person who transfers real-estate title or to a grantee.

gross rent multiplier (GRM):
A method used to estimate value for income-producing properties by looking at the amount of rents collected versus sales prices of similar properties.

hazard insurance:
A policy that protects a property owner against loss from listed hazards such as fire, wind damage, and vandalism.

homeowner's association:
An association that manages the common areas of a condominium, planned unit development, or townhouse complex; an association made up and managed by owners who live in a specific housing development, overseeing issues such as road upkeep, deed restriction compliance, and other issues important to all owners.

HUD:
The Department of Housing and Urban Development, a government agency that oversees fair housing issues and numerous other mortgage and rent-related programs.

HUD-1 settlement statement:
The standard settlement statement that must be used for federally related mortgage loans.

HUD code:
A uniform code developed and overseen by the federal government that stipulates building codes that must be used for manufactured housing sold in the United States.

income capitalization:
A type of appraisal that uses income and expenses to estimate the value of an income-producing property.

lease:
A written contract between a property owner and a tenant that outlines the time period, required payments, and all other conditions under which the tenant has legal possession of the real estate.

lease option:
A type of lease in which a portion of each month's payment includes

an additional amount that is applied toward a down payment if the tenant chooses to purchase the property during the specified time period.

lessee:
The tenant named in a lease document.

lessor:
The landlord named in a lease document.

lien:
A document granting a creditor the right to sell property that secures a debt if the borrower defaults on the loan.

life estate:
An interest in real estate that is limited in duration to the lifetime of the person designated on the deed.

manufactured home:
Housing that is built to conform to a federal code and transported to a building site on its own wheels.

material fact:
Factual details about a property, such as the age of its roof and details about the age and condition of its components.

mitigation:
An action that's taken to permanently eliminate or reduce a potential hazard; commonly heard in the home-buying community to describe the installation of radon reduction systems.

modular home:
Housing that is built in modules at a factory to conform to building codes at its ultimate designation. Transported to the building site on flatbed trucks and assembled.

mortgage:
A document that pledges real estate as security for a debt.

mortgage broker:
A businessperson who earns a fee by bringing together a borrower and a lender. Mortgage brokers typically work as agents for numerous lenders.

open listing:
A type of real-estate listing contract in which the seller agrees to pay a commission to an agency that finds a buyer for a property, but

retains the right to sell the property without owing a commission. Unlike exclusive agency listings, open listings can be signed with multiple agencies.

PITI:
The term used to describe the combination of principal, interest, taxes, and insurance due for a loan.

pre-foreclosure:
A property that is on the verge of foreclosure; formal foreclosure may not have taken place, but warnings may have been issued by lenders.

primary mortgage market:
The market in which mortgage loans are originated by banks, savings and loans, and other similar lenders.

private mortgage insurance:
Insurance coverage that most lenders require when making a real-estate loan for which the buyer makes less than a 20-percent down payment.

quitclaim deed:
A deed that allows the grantor to convey whatever interest he or she has in a property without guaranteeing that others have relinquished title.

REIT:
An investment company that owns and operates income-producing real estate and sometimes finances real-estate transactions. REITs sell shares of stock to individual investors.

REO:
Real-estate owned properties are foreclosed properties that have been acquired by the lender at auction.

RESPA:
The Real Estate Settlement Procedures Act is a law that attempts to ensure that buyers are given disclosures and estimates of closing costs by their lenders. It standardizes some of the forms used during real-estate closings.

restrictive covenants:
Restrictions to land use that usually apply to all properties within a specific development.

right-of-way:
A type of easement that conveys the right to pass over a tract of land.

second mortgage:
A mortgage that includes a recorded lien against a property, but in line to be paid after the first mortgage. Second mortgages are usually paid in order by the date they were recorded—first recorded, first paid. Also called a junior mortgage.

secondary mortgage market:
A market where existing mortgages are purchased from originators and resold to investors. The secondary mortgage market was created to keep funds flowing back to originating lenders so that they can continue to make new home loans.

seller's agent:
A real-estate agent whose loyalty and duty is to the seller of a property.

site-built home:
A house built entirely on-site, with no sections preassembled in a factory.

survey, boundary survey:
A measurement of a tract of land that shows its size, its boundaries, and the presence of all buildings associated with it. Surveys are performed by licensed surveyors.

time-share:
A vacation unit that can be owned by many individuals. For a traditional time-share, each owner holds title to the unit for a specific time each year.

title examination:
The process of examining public records associated with a property in order to determine facts about its ownership during a specific period of time.

title insurance:
An insurance policy that insures against loss due to defects in a real-estate title. Excluded losses are explained in each policy.

townhouse:
A unit in a multiunit complex that's normally attached to its neighbors along side walls. Each owner holds title to the unit and the land beneath the unit, and shares ownership of common areas with other owners. Also called a town home.

Index